College Reading and Study Skills

College Reading and Study Skills

A Guide to Improving Academic Communication

THIRD EDITION

Nancy V. Wood

Director, Study Skills and Tutorial Services
University of Texas at El Paso

Holt, Rinehart and Winston
New York   Chicago   San Francisco   Philadelphia
Montreal   Toronto   London   Sydney
Tokyo   Mexico City   Rio de Janeiro   Madrid

For Sam, David, and Joe

Acquisitions Editor: Charlyce Jones Owen
Developmental Editor: Charlotte Smith
Senior Project Editor: Lester A. Sheinis
Production Manager: Annette Mayeski
Design Supervisor: Gloria Gentile

Library of Congress Cataloging in Publication Data

Wood, Nancy V.
  College reading and study skills.

  Includes index.
  1. Study, Method of.   2. Reading (Higher education)
I. Title.
LB2395.W63   1986   378'.1702812   85–13927
ISBN 0-03-001574-X

CBS COLLEGE PUBLISHING
Holt, Rinehart and Winston
The Dryden Press
Saunders College Publishing

Preface to the Third Edition

The purpose of this edition, as of the first and second, is to provide students with the skills necessary for success in college classes. Especially emphasized are the basic communication skills as they are used in an academic setting. There are chapters to help students learn to *read* textbooks and library materials, to *listen* to lectures, to *write* papers and examinations, and to *speak* in class discussions and give oral reports. When students can do a good job of communicating, they possess the skills most essential for academic success.

The material in this book follows the sequence of tasks that students are expected to perform when they enroll in college. This sequence remains the same as that of the second edition. In Part 1 of the book, students are encouraged to consider their reasons for coming to college and to decide how to organize and approach their studies. They are also taught ways to improve their concentration and motivation, subjects of major concern to most students.

In Parts 2 and 3, they are taught how to learn during class time and how to read their textbooks. Part 4 teaches students to take examinations successfully, and Part 5 teaches students a process for doing written assignments. Part 6 summarizes the skills taught in the book and invites students to make a final evaluation of their own skills via a checklist of study techniques.

Numerous examples, many newly selected for this edition, are used to illustrate procedures and theory: Examples of lecture notes illustrate note-taking skills; passages from current textbooks serve to develop reading skills; sample notes and written passages illustrate the various stages of writing papers; and study sheets and exam answers, written by students, demonstrate how to study for and take exams. Practice exercises appear at the end of each chapter. These exercises take several forms: checklists that invite self-evaluation, objective questions to ensure that students comprehend the essential points, suggested activities that require application of the new skills in the students' other classes, new topics for Learning Journals that encourage reflective self-assessment and further application of skills, and a new campus resources sheet to encourage students to seek outside help. New and varied "Application of Skills" exercises have been added to every chapter in an attempt to encourage students even more persuasively than in past editions to use what they have learned.

The first edition of this book, before it was published, was classroom tested with two groups of students. The first was a group of early-admission students, and the second was the group of provisionally admitted students referred to in To the Student. Both groups read the preliminary text and responded to a questionnaire. Specifically, they were asked to identify difficult vocabulary, confusing passages, and chapters that were too difficult or too long, and to evaluate the exercises at the end of each chapter. These students' readings of the manuscript resulted in some significant changes. If enough students indicated they would not follow a particular suggestion, it was eliminated. Exercises were included only when there was nearly unanimous agreement that they were worth doing. Chapters identified as too difficult were simplified, and chapters identified as too long were shortened. The resulting chapters can be read by most students, with ease, in less than thirty minutes.

Since publication of the first edition, I have continued to test the theory and exercises in this book with at least a thousand additional students each year at this university. A team of colleagues who taught the course in which this book was used have met with me weekly during the past eight years to discuss and experiment with better ways of teaching these materials. Our students have also evaluated this book each semester. The new ideas and exercises that emerged from our weekly planning sessions and from student questionnaires were then tested in our classrooms. Those that worked best are included in this third edition. Other ideas that emerged from these meetings and this teaching are now included in the Instructor's Manual. Included in it are answer keys to the exercises in the text, class designs, examinations and answers, ideas for additional class activities, materials, and exercises, and a final evaluation instrument. To obtain a complimentary copy of the Instructor's Manual, write to the English Editor, College Department, Holt, Rinehart and Winston, 383 Madison Avenue, New York, NY 10017.

The ten reading labs appear once again in the Appendix. Their purpose is to extend students' ranges of reading speed, to encourage students to develop the habit of selecting and reading books for pleasure, and to teach students how to skim when special situations call for this skill. These labs can be done consecutively in ten days, or they can be spread out over a semester. Each lab takes thirty to forty-five minutes to complete, is self-instructional, and can be done in class. Experience with the students who tested these materials shows, however, that these labs are also effective when assigned as outside work. The students time themselves and write summaries of the material they have read to be evaluated later either by the instructor or by another student. An advantage of students evaluating each other's summaries is that they become familiar with more than one book, their own and their classmate's.

Besides the changes already mentioned, this third edition includes other additions and changes: (1) The number of chapters has been reduced from twenty to sixteen to make the book easier to use in short courses and terms as well as in semesters; (2) Boxed minimal study skills have been added to Chapters 1–15 to emphasize what students should do "at the very least" if they cannot always use all of the skills taught; (3) New material, which reflects current research in learning, has been added in the areas of personal learning styles, time management, class discussion techniques, thinking and reasoning skills, and management of the testing environment, particularly by using positive self-talk and learning to handle distractions; (4) Part 3, *Reading the Textbook,* contains a new chapter on surveying that emphasizes perceiving organization and chunking material, and a new chapter entitled "Reading the Chapter" that places relatively less emphasis on reading paragraphs and more on reading longer sections of material; (5) Part 4, *Taking Exams,* includes new examples of types of exam questions and new ways to help students prepare for them. Also added is a new section on how to take essay exams; (6) Part 5, *Writing the Paper,* has a new chapter on writing college papers that emphasizes process, purpose, prewriting activities, and rewriting and revision. Also new are the latest recommendations for doing in-text citations. The chapter on the library includes new information on using computer indexes and doing computer searches. (7) Part 6, *Summary,* places new emphasis on the skills and attitudes needed for success both in college and in the workplace. A Likert scale has been added to the checklist of study techniques to provide new opportunities to study and evaluate students' use of the skills taught. Finally, (8) the reading list in the Appendix has been extended and brought up to date. Its purpose is not only to provide suggested books for reading-lab practice, but also to encourage students to do more leisure reading.

In preparing the manuscript for this third edition, I have had valuable help from the tutors and the instructors who make up the staff of the Study Skills and Tutorial Services department at the University of Texas at El Paso. I would like to thank them and the students we teach. Both groups have contributed much to this edition. In particular I would like to thank Evelyn Posey, Maryann Burlingham, Sandra Sweeney, and Gladys Shaw for devising some new and creative exercises for this edition. I am also grateful to Ruth Pepin, Suzanne Stearns, Anita Hanke, Susan Fowler, Melissa Wiseman, Lisa Peticolas, and Jean Patterson for their contributions, their patience, and their care in testing the new ideas and exercises for this edition in their classes. James A. Wood has helped me generate and develop many ideas for all editions of this book. Helen Bell helped update the material on doing library research. Exam questions in Chapter 12 were drawn from actual examinations given by the faculty at the University of Texas at El Paso. Melissa Spresser has been exceptionally capable and supportive in helping with the preparation of the final manuscript. I also want to thank those who have read and commented on the manuscript: Greg Alexander, Portland Community College; James L. Brother, Hartford State Technical College; Gladdys W. Church, SUNY at Brockport; John H. Corcoran, Glassboro State College; Timothy E. Dykstra, Franklin University; LeAnne Higgs, Franklin University, Harold N. Hild, Northeastern Illinois University; Vance Rhoades, Brewton-Parker College; Norma V. Spalding, San Jose State University; Carlene Walker, University of Texas at El Paso. I also wish to thank the following reviewers for this edition: Colleen Fairbanks, University of Michigan; John Howe, Community College of Philadelphia; Linda Knight, York Technical College; Becky Patterson, Anchorage Community College; W. Donald Smith, Lane Community College; Rory Stephens, Northeastern Illinois University. When they see that I have followed much of their advice, they will realize how much I have valued their comments.

I extend my sincere thanks to the Holt staff: Charlotte Smith, Charlyce Jones Owen, Lester A. Sheinis, Annette Mayeski, and Gloria Gentile. These individuals have provided me with the editorial guidance, encouragement, and professional expertise that was indispensable for completing this project.

N.V.W.
El Paso, Texas

To the Student

When you pick up a study skills textbook, you have the right to ask two questions. The first is, "Are there really study skills I can learn that will make me more successful in college?" The second is, "Will this book help me learn these skills?"

In the first edition of this book, to answer these questions, I told about a group of freshman students who had not met ordinary admissions requirements at the University of Texas at El Paso. They were admitted with the provision that they make C's or better their first semester or they would have to drop out. Some of these students took the study skills course I was teaching and used this book. This group of students learned and practiced the material in this book for one semester. More than three-fourths of them made the grades required for regular academic status. Less than one-fourth of the other provisionally admitted students, who had no study skills training, were able to achieve the same status.

Since that time I have tested the material in this book with at least 7,000 additional students, 5,000 of whom were provisionally admitted. Nearly all of the provisional students who made the grades to continue at the university also completed the course in which this book was used as the textbook.

All of these students were successful because they learned and used certain skills that the other students did not have. These skills often make the difference between staying in school successfully or getting poor grades and becoming discouraged.

To do well in college you will need to learn to concentrate, listen, read and write well, join in class discussion, adapt to different types of classes and professors, and make efficient use of your time. This book will provide you with the information and practice exercises to help you learn these skills.

You will have to use what is in this book rather than just read it, if it is to work for you. The students who gave this text its trial run were willing to use it, apply it, and experiment with it in all of their classes. Some students went even further — they changed and adapted some of the skills to meet their own individual preferences or particular needs in other courses they were taking. The information in this book will help you, too, if you use it as these students did.

Contents

College Reading and Study Skills

PART ONE
Getting Started

1

Improving Your Concentration and Motivation

When you have finished reading this chapter, you will know the following:

1. How to concentrate on reading this and other textbooks.
2. How to maintain a high level of motivation.
3. How to deal with problems that can interfere with concentration.
4. How effective study skills can improve concentration.

The Link between Concentration and Motivation

Concentration and motivation are closely related. Good concentration results from keeping your mind on what you are doing, keeping a high level of interest, and ignoring all distractions. Good motivation results from having clear reasons for being in college and having a strong desire to learn and do your best.

Strong motivation will help you concentrate and good concentration will help you stay motivated. The purpose of this chapter is to suggest ways to

3

improve both your concentration and motivation so that you will achieve the greatest possible success in college.

Improve Your Concentration as You Read

Even though you have read only a few lines so far in this chapter, your mind may already be starting to wander. Here is a system for reading, then, that will help you immediately to concentrate. (Find more details on this system in Chapter 9.)

1. Underline the words and phrases in a paragraph that state the central thought.
2. Jot the main idea of the paragraph in the margin.
3. At the end of each section, in your own words, write a brief summary of the main points.

The following section of material has been marked for you. Study it as an example, and then continue to mark this book, and your other textbooks, in this way. You will find that you have to concentrate to jot down main ideas and summary points.

Motivation, a Key to Concentration

It is easier to keep a high level of concentration when you want to do the work you have set for yourself. The following suggestions will help you stay motivated.   *stay motivated*

1. Have a boxed(reason) for going to college and   *① have reason for college*
keep that reason in mind Figure 1.1 summarizes the responses that 572 freshman students recently gave in response to a questionnaire asking them to check off their reasons for being in college. As you read through the list, check your own reasons for coming.

Most students checked three or four different reasons. Look at what you checked. Do you agree with the majority? The reasons checked most frequently were "because I want to become an educated person" and "because I want to prepare myself for a specific job or profession." You need to remember your own good reasons for coming to college in order to stay motivated.

I Am Going to College . . .	% of 572 Students Polled	Which Ones Would You Check?
a. because I don't want to get a job right now.	4%	_____
b. because I'm afraid I won't be able to get a job without a college education.	41%	_____
c. because I want to prepare myself for a specific job or profession.	97%	_____
d. because my parents want me to and I want to please them.	19%	_____
e. because I want to find a husband/wife.	2%	_____
f. because my best friends decided to go and I wanted to stay with them.	2%	_____
g. because I want to become an educated person.	86%	_____
h. because I had heard about college social life, and it sounded fun.	5%	_____
i. because I want to occupy a particular place in society (e.g., middle or upper class).	37%	_____
j. because I want to change careers.	2%	_____
k. because I was bored and needed new interests, friends, and ideas in my life.	5%	_____
l. because I need more education in order to advance in my present career.	22%	_____
m. because I want to use my V.A. benefits.	2%	_____
n. other	10%	_____

Figure 1.1   The age range of these students was 16–55. Sixty percent were members of ethnic minority groups, and 52 percent were female.

2. Set specific ⏐goals⏐ — long-term, short-term, and alternate   Psychologists tell us that we lead happier and more productive lives when we are working toward goals. Goals can be both long-term and short-term. Choose a tentative major and begin to work toward a long-term vocational or professional goal as soon as you can. Visualize the life this goal will allow you to lead five years from now whenever you have trouble concentrating. Set short-term goals daily. Make a mental plan of each day's activities the night before or when you wake up. Then set deadlines and work to

[margin notes:] ② set goals

long-term: job

short-term:
mental plans
- deadlines

reach your daily goals. When you finish, <u>reward yourself</u> for your accomplishments. At times you may find that the goals you have set are either impossible to reach or in some way a mistake. In such cases, develop <u>alternate goals</u> that will involve and motivate you as much as your original ones did.

- rewards

alternate goals

3. Work to guarantee **early success** Start immediately in each class to do your best work. This way you will <u>give yourself the best opportunity for some immediate success.</u> Early success earned by work well-done will motivate you and make concentration on future projects easier.

③ do first assignment well

success = success

4. Reward yourself for reaching your goal Especially, plan regular rewards for meeting your daily short-term goals so that you will finish your work and also have something to look forward to at the end of the day.

④ Rewards [shoot pool, play video games]

5. Think of the consequences of not meeting your goals On days when concentration is particularly difficult, <u>visualize the life you are likely to lead if you do not meet your educational goals.</u> Most students quickly rekindle an interest in school assignments when they contemplate a lifetime of working at the jobs they hold in the summer or after school.

⑤ think: what if I don't?

Sum. stay motivated to aid concen. Remem. reasons for coming, set goals (long, short, alternate). 1st assign. done well. Remem. consequences of not doing.

CONTINUE TO READ AND MARK THIS BOOK IN THIS WAY.

This method not only helps you to concentrate on your reading, it helps you to remember what you have read by employing some of the psychological factors that influence learning. (1) It enables you to perceive the author's *organization* of ideas, aiding both comprehension and memory. (2) It encourages you to *react* to the author's ideas (note the reader's comment in square brackets in the margin). And (3) it forces you to *repeat key ideas* in your mind as you write them in the margin and rewrite them in your own summary.

It will also help you to concentrate on your reading if you stop now and survey this book in order to get an understanding of what it contains and how it is organized. Turn to page 78 and follow the steps for surveying a book. You will learn more about surveying when you read Chapter 7.

Learn How to Handle Internal Distractions

You can further improve your concentration and motivation by coping with the thoughts and emotions that cause your mind to wander while you are studying. Some of the most common distractions can be dealt with as follows.

1. Take care of the small jobs you suddenly remember You have two choices of action when you suddenly think of something you need to do: either stop and do it immediately, or write it down, along with a time for doing it, so that it will not continue to distract you.

2. Avoid worrying about problems that have no immediate solutions Vague, unstated problems cause worry that can interfere with both motivation and concentration. Isolate and understand a problem by writing or talking about it. Then, think of solutions, even though they may not be perfect ones. Discuss the solutions with a friend or counselor or write them down. Finally, work to solve your problem. When you have done everything you can, put the problem out of your mind and resume work on the goals that are most important to you.

3. Daydream productively An extremely successful businessman once told an interviewer that he daydreamed all the time, always about future business ventures. His success came from translating his daydreams into reality. You can learn to daydream about completed assignments and then work to make your daydreams real. Avoid other nonproductive daydreaming while you are studying.

4. Keep interested Search for material in a class or assignment that is interesting and important to you. Try to relate such material to the goals that brought you to college in the first place. Refresh these goals in your mind when your interest lags.

Think of yourself five years from now. What would you like to know in addition to what you do in your job? College is the best chance to explore various fields and to find out about subjects new to you. Seek classes that will both improve your employability and enrich your leisure time. Such variety will help you stay interested.

Finally, if you get tired of studying one subject, switch to another, and if you get tired of studying after a couple of hours, take a break. You do not have to switch or take a break, however, if your concentration and motivation remain at a high level. Some students can maintain a high level of interest while studying for several hours at a time.

5. *Work to improve your confidence* Build confidence by doing difficult things that are important to you. Getting started on a difficult job is often the hardest part. It gets easier as you get closer to the end. When the job is completed, you will have gained some confidence, and confidence from various successes will accumulate and will improve your ability to concentrate.

6. *Learn to deal with nervousness or tension* Anyone who spends his or her life doing challenging and difficult things has not totally banished nervousness. Its cause is excess physical energy that is generated by your body to help you do something that is important to you. The best way to deal with nervousness is to try to figure out what is pressing you and then get to work on it. Your nervousness will gradually go away as you concentrate on completing your project. If you still feel nervous when you have finished, work off your excess energy through physical activity. When you have worn yourself out, take a long hot bath or shower, get to bed early. You'll feel better the next day.

7. *Cope with depression* Its cause can be loneliness, homesickness, anger, or disappointment with yourself. Family, illness, and money problems can also cause depression. If you are subject to depression, you should know that you can make things worse by not eating regularly, by not sleeping enough, by getting a bad hangover, and by not getting regular exercise. Fight depression by regulating your living habits and by trying to figure out what is depressing you. Talk to a friend or a counselor in your college's counseling office. Such help is usually free. If you're having a bad day, try to find something to salvage it. Do a job that you have been putting off for a long time. Your depression will usually lift faster if you give yourself the satisfaction of completing something that has been bothering you.

8. *Work yourself out of mental dead ends* When you are blocked by a difficult assignment and feel that you cannot concentrate, break it down into parts and calculate the order in which you will do them. Next, physically isolate yourself from all distractions. If you can't find seclusion in the library or your room, find an empty classroom or even an empty car. Then start on the first step. As soon as you can, set a deadline so that you can see the end of what has bothered you for so long. Give yourself a big reward when you finish. You will deserve it.

9. *Use positive self-talk* Turn negative statements that filter through your mind into positive statements. Instead of thinking, "I'm tired, I'm bored, I can't do this," consciously think instead, "This is the best part of my day, I feel energetic, this is interesting, I can do this." Include positive self-images with your positive self-talk. Stop imagining yourself as poor in math or poor in English or unable to concentrate, and relabel yourself as a success. Visualize yourself receiving your diploma, successfully interviewing for a job, working at something you really like to do. Frequently remind yourself of the value of the work you do now and later both to yourself and to others.

Learn to Avoid External Distractions

Make a list of the external distractions that interfere with your efforts to concentrate. For most students this includes televisions, radios, telephones, refrigerators, magazines, friends, and family members. Shut off, shut out, and shun all of these during those periods of time you have set aside for study.

no play

Learn to Avoid the Common Work Dodges of Students

Getting an education is hard and sometimes painful work. When this is the case, it is human nature to find ways to avoid it. And when you successfully avoid your work, you never give yourself a chance to develop your powers of concentration. The internal and external distractions just described can interfere with concentration, as can the following very common work dodges. Learn to recognize and avoid them.

no excuses

1. Avoid idle conversation   It's fine to talk to your friends if you really have nothing that has to be done or if you are rewarding yourself for something you have just finished. Most students, however, must learn to say, "I have to study—I'll see you later," or they may talk their way right out of college.

2. Know when you are rationalizing   Common rationalizations or excuses you hear students use are, "The professor is no good"; "The textbook is boring"; "This place doesn't really care about students"; "That professor's test questions sure don't come out of the book or his lectures"; "I studied everything for ten hours and I still got an F"; "I don't have to read the textbook in this class because it isn't important"; "I don't have to go to class because I read the textbook"; "Everyone in the whole class flunked the test, so it must have been a bad test"; and "I've studied two hours. That's enough for one day."

It's all right to say these things if they make you feel better temporarily. After you finish rationalizing, however, you should take a good look at the *real* reasons why you said what you said and then do what you can to make the situation better. There will be a lot of suggestions in this book to help you solve your *real* problems in school.

3. Avoid drugs and alcohol when you are studying   Don't tell yourself that you can think and remember while you are drinking or high. If you like to drink beer, study first. Open a beer when you've finished.

4. Stay healthy   Some students get mild illnesses frequently. If this is one of the ways you dodge work, start studying in bed. You'll get well faster.

Exercise, walk, run, or play sports several times a week. Students who never move become lethargic and have difficulty concentrating. Regular exer-

STAY ACTIVE

cise, worked into your schedule at appropriate times, will make you more alert, more energetic, and will improve your ability to concentrate.

5. *Stay awake when it is time to study* When you sleep a lot in the daytime and play most of the night, you are dodging your schoolwork. If you get so tired you can't think, set the alarm for short, fifteen-minute naps. They are more refreshing than a three-hour nap. Then get back to work.

6. *Go to class and do all assignments* Of all the advice given so far to improve both your concentration and your motivation, this may be the most important. No one can stay motivated to concentrate on material that contains great gaps caused by missed classes and assignments.

Develop Effective Study Skills

Schedule the responsibilities

You can, finally, work to improve your concentration and motivation by developing more effective ways to study and learn. It may help to think of the study skills that you will be learning and practicing as falling into three categories. The first category includes good advice, such as finding a time and place to study, filling out time schedules, analyzing class responsibilities, organizing study materials, and even finding materials in the library. A second category of study skills includes new behaviors that you will want to practice at every opportunity until they become habitual, including, for example, new ways of improving your memory, concentration, and motivation; managing your time by doing regular, planned study; attending class regularly; doing all assignments accurately and on time; being responsible for books and materials; coping with stress; and using positive self-talk. The third, and last category of study skills, which are given special emphasis in this book, are the academic communication skills, which include both receiving and sending skills. You *receive* communication at college by *reading* textbooks, library books, and examination questions and *listening* to lectures, assignments, and discussions. You *send* communication at college by writing papers and answers to exams and by *speaking* in class discussions and giving oral reports.

In order to become proficient in all three study skills categories you may have to recondition yourself by experimenting with new methods until they suit you and by replacing your old habits with new ones that will produce better results. Your old habits won't change, however, unless you *use* new methods of study every chance you get. As you read this book, remember that study skills aren't to be studied, they are to be *used*.

Once they have one good semester behind them, most students go on to make a success of college. Select classes and a class load you think you can handle. If you've made a mistake by signing up for too much, cut back. Then use what you can from the following chapters to make each semester a successful one.

At the Very Least . . .

This chapter has dealt with the ideal way of improving your concentration and motivation. If you can't follow all of the suggestions every day, *at the very least* do this much:

1. Set some goals — even if they are tentative.
2. Start underlining and writing notes in all of your textbooks.
3. Try some positive self-talk.

SUMMARY

Improving your ability to concentrate and remain motivated can make you more successful in college. Marking your textbooks as you read is one way to guarantee good concentration. Having a reason for being in college, setting goals and deadlines, and rewarding yourself can help you stay motivated. You can improve both concentration and motivation by avoiding internal and external distractions and avoiding the work dodges common to students. Improved study skills can also help you achieve a consistently higher level of concentration and motivation. If you can successfully complete one semester, other successful semesters will usually follow.

Self-Test

Do you know what will be demanded of you as a college student? Not knowing what to do or how to do it can be a major distraction that can interfere with your concentration and your education. Test yourself on what you know and don't know right now. Answer each question by checking Yes or No.

Look at your No answers. If you have answered No to 75 or 80 percent of the questions — that is, all but three or four — you are a pretty typical beginning college student. Notice that to the right of each of your answers is the chapter number where you can start reading to change your No answers to Yes. When you can answer all of these questions Yes, this book will have done for you what it was intended to do.

	Yes	No	Find Out How in Chapters:
1. Do you know what kind of notebooks best keep your class materials organized?	____	____	2
2. Do you know how to figure out what each professor expects of you so you will get a good grade in each class you take?	____	____	3

	Yes	No	*Find Out How in Chapters:*
3. Do you know how to take notes on a fifty-minute lecture and how to study them later?	____	____	4
4. Do you have a method for spotting and learning the specialized vocabulary and concepts in a college class?	____	____	5
5. Do you know how to make worthwhile contributions to class discussion?	____	____	6
6. Do you know how to read and take notes on a textbook and three or four supplementary paperback books for one course without the constant supervision of the teacher?	____	____	7–9
7. Do you know a quick and efficient way of taking notes on your reading?	____	____	9
8. Do you know how to improve your memory of what is said in class and what you read?	____	____	10
9. Do you know how to think about and reflect on what you are learning?	____	____	10
10. Do you know how to study for and take exams?	____	____	11 & 12
11. Do you know how to analyze a failed exam in order to keep from failing the next one?	____	____	12
12. Do you know how to plan, research, write, and revise a term paper?	____	____	13
13. Are you able to find a book and a magazine article on a particular subject in a large university library?	____	____	14
14. Do you know how to find specific information for research purposes without reading the entire book?	____	____	14
15. Do you know how to adapt your written paper for oral presentation to the class?	____	____	15

Exercise

Topics for Your Learning Journal

1. Either by yourself or as a class project, make a list of everything that interferes with your concentration. Now make another list of everything that improves your concentration. Finally, write a brief concentration plan for your unique lifestyle that includes all the concentration enhancers that work for you.

2. Either by yourself or as a class project, make a list of some causes of worry, stress, and depression. Now make a second list of ways to cope with these negative feelings. Finally, write a brief stress plan for yourself that includes

all of the ways you can best manage your stress and other negative feelings.
3. Briefly write short-term goals for the following:
   a. *For this week.* Include what you want to accomplish.
   b. *For each course in which you are enrolled.* Include why you are taking it, what you want to learn, and what grade you would like to achieve.
   c. *For this year as a whole.* Include specific knowledge, changes, and competencies you would like to achieve, and why they are important to you.
4. Now do some tentative planning for a long-term goal.
   a. Make a list of your special interests and abilities.
   b. List two or three college majors that would be compatible with your special interests and abilities.
   c. Imagine yourself ten years from now. Write specific details about what you would like to be doing. Include specific activities, your location, your lifestyle, and your type of work.
   d. Set a tentative, long-term goal for a job or profession that would, as much as possible, satisfy your interests, abilities, and preferred lifestyle.
   e. List everything you will have to do to achieve this long-term goal in the next ten years.
5. Set alternate long-term goals: List two or three alternate goals for jobs or professions in case you are unable to achieve your first long-term goal.

2

Organizing Your Study Materials, Study Place, and Time

When you have finished this chapter, you will have decided the following:

1. What kind of notebooks to buy.
2. Where you will keep your study materials.
3. Where you will study.
4. How you will manage your time.

Free Your Creative Energies

You will free your creative energies and improve your ability to concentrate if you make some initial decisions about routine at the beginning of the semester and then turn those decisions into daily habits. Think what a waste of time it would be to have to decide each day whether or not to brush your teeth. You will also waste time by deciding more than once about the matters discussed in this chapter. Turn as many of your daily activities as possible into routine habits so that you can use your creative energies to concentrate on new material and ideas you are learning in your classes.

Organize Study Materials in Notebooks

When final exam time comes, you must be able to put your hands on the material to study. All lecture notes, reading notes, class handouts, returned exams and papers, and mimeographed information need to be in some order so that you can find them easily. The important thing is that you have some kind of system.

Be ready to start taking lecture notes at your very first classes. Buy your notebooks and have them full of plenty of standard size paper (8½ by 11 inches). Don't buy smaller paper. It is easy for professors to lose, and it's hard for you to study small pieces of paper. Take two pens with you to your first classes.

There are at least three basic ways to organize your study materials in notebooks. One of them or a combination of them will work for you. Whatever system you choose, remember that the cardinal principle for organizing class materials is to keep all materials for each course separate from each other.

Spiral Notebooks

Advantages

All lecture notes for each course are bound together separately and permanently.

At the end of a semester class notes can be filed and easily found months or years later.

Disadvantages

No convenient place to put handouts and other loose papers such as missed notes (unless you buy notebooks with pockets already bound into them). Easy to take the wrong notebook to class by mistake. (Write subject of each notebook on front in big black letters.)

Loose-Leaf Notebooks with Dividers

Advantages

All materials for all courses can be kept together.

Loose materials can be punched and inserted next to the material they are meant to accompany.

Easy to xerox borrowed notes and insert them where they belong.

Disadvantages

If you fold and stuff loose materials into notebook because it's too much trouble to punch holes, you end up with a mess.

Some papers tear loose and need to be repaired.

Folders with Double Pockets

Advantages

Lecture notes may be kept separately in right-hand pocket along with blank paper for future note taking.

Disadvantages

If you drop a folder, the papers fall out. Can be disastrous on a windy day. (Best to carry all folders in a zipper bag or

Advantages	*Disadvantages*
Other materials, such as mimeographed pages, assignment sheets, and returned papers, may be kept in left-hand pocket.	briefcase at all times.) Folders are somewhat fragile. They may begin to fall apart before semester is over and have to be replaced.
You can loan notes without loaning entire notebook.	
No need to punch holes.	
Ready to file permanently at end of semester.	
Folders are cheap.	

Decide Where to Keep Assignments

Make assignment sheets for each class before the first day (see Figure 2.1). Put them where you can find them easily in your notebook. Record all assignments on this sheet in as much detail as possible. Cross them off as you complete them. Always write the due date for each assignment so that you'll get your work in on time.

You may prefer to buy an assignment book or a week-at-a-glance appointment book. Whichever system you use, make certain to always write down every assignment along with the date it is due.

Establish a Headquarters and a Place to Study

You will need a "headquarters" where you can keep not only lecture notes and other materials you accumulate in class, but also textbooks, library books, supplementary paperback books, xeroxed copies of articles from periodicals, paper, and pens. Ideally, your headquarters will have a desk where you can study in seclusion and shelves where you can stack all of the materials for each of your classes separately. When everything is stacked according to classes, you will be less likely to lose track of various books and papers. The stacks don't have to be neat.

You may want to keep materials for your M-W-F classes separate from your T-Th class material. This makes it easier to find what you need each morning.

If you live with other people and can't set up a desk and bookshelves at home, "headquarters" may have to be a corner of a room or even some boxes under your bed. You will keep your books and materials together there, but you will actually study in a number of other places.

If you *want* to work, you will find that you can do so almost anywhere. You need enough seclusion so that you can concentrate and feel psychologi-

Assignment _History_	Date Due
Read pp. 21-75 of text	Mon., Sept. 21
Quiz on first 75 pp. of text	Fri., Sept. 25
Read 1ˢᵗ half of _Uncle Tom's Cabin_	Thur., Oct. 1
Finish _Uncle Tom's Cabin_ and turn in 500-word paper on its social and political influences when first published.	Fri., Oct. 15

Figure 2.1 An example of an assignment sheet

cally and physically comfortable. You don't have to sit in an uncomfortable, hard chair to make yourself work.

Here is a list of possible study places. The list is deliberately varied. Check those that might be good for you.

1. A big chair in an out-of-the way room   yes ＿＿   no ＿＿
2. On your bed   yes ＿＿   no ＿＿
3. The kitchen table   yes ＿＿   no ＿＿
4. The dining room table   yes ＿＿   no ＿＿
5. A card table set up in the least-used room of the house   yes ＿＿   no ＿＿
6. Your car parked on a side street or in a parking lot   yes ＿＿   no ＿＿
7. An out-of-the-way stairway at school   yes ＿＿   no ＿＿
8. A cafeteria or a restaurant while you are eating   yes ＿＿   no ＿＿
9. Out-of-the-way corners of the library   yes ＿＿   no ＿＿
10. Empty classrooms (often available in the late afternoon)   yes ＿＿   no ＿＿

You need to have alternate places to study so that if you start to work in one place, are interrupted, and can't concentrate, you can pick up and move before an uncomfortable amount of frustration sets in. Just be sure that wherever you study, you take along the books, notes, pens, and paper you need to get the particular job done.

There will be days when you have to study, but you don't feel like it. On such days you need a special place, completely free from diversions, where you go *only* to study and which, because of habit, always signals "study" to you. Seek out such a place and use it regularly as your retreat when you can't concentrate. Try to find a place completely free from diversion—no refrigerator, no telephone, no magazines, no television.

When you get to your place, think through the work you have to do. If there's a lot, jot down the jobs on a list and then number them in order of priority. Pick the *most pressing* item on the list and then get to work on it immediately.

[margin handwritten note: work on item first]

Learn to Manage Your Time

Effective time management is a result of both conscious effort and experience. If you have time problems while you are at college, they will probably be caused by one of the following: First, compared to high school, where you were in class more hours, it seems that you now have time to burn. You get a false sense of security, and you let time slip away without getting enough work done. Or, second, you are taking classes and labs, working part-time, and you may also have family responsibilities. It seems that there is no way to find enough time to do it all. Whichever category you fall into, your problems are real ones. Use the following suggestions to help you manage your time effectively.

[margin handwritten note: solve your problems concerning Time]

1. Make a Time Analysis Worksheet Figure 2.2 is an example of a completed Time Analysis Worksheet. Fill out one of these at the beginning of each semester to help you analyze your *fixed time commitments*, which are written on the analysis sheet, and your *available study times*, which are boxed in with heavy pencil. This sheet has two purposes: (1) to help you focus on your daily time commitments and learn them, and (2) to help you find the hours when study would be possible. A blank Time Analysis Worksheet is provided in Figure 2.3. When you have written in or crossed off your fixed time commitments, count to make sure that you have twice as many hours of flexible study time as you have time in class. If you do not have enough study time, cut back on some of your other commitments or make some trade-offs so that you will create ample time for study. For example, if you have home responsibilities, ask family members to help with some of them so that you can find the time you need to study.

[margin handwritten note: worksheet]

2. Make a Time Management Worksheet One of the most difficult aspects of time management is learning to estimate the amount of time it takes you to do different tasks. Most inexperienced college students underestimate the time they will need to complete college assignments. During your first days at college notice how many pages you can read in an hour in each of your textbooks, how long it takes to write a two-page paper, find materials in the library, or work a set of math problems. Armed with this information about your own time requirements, make a Time Management Worksheet like the one in Figure 2.4:

a. Divide a piece of notebook paper into five columns and label them.
b. Write major, time-consuming tasks in column 1. It is not time efficient to use

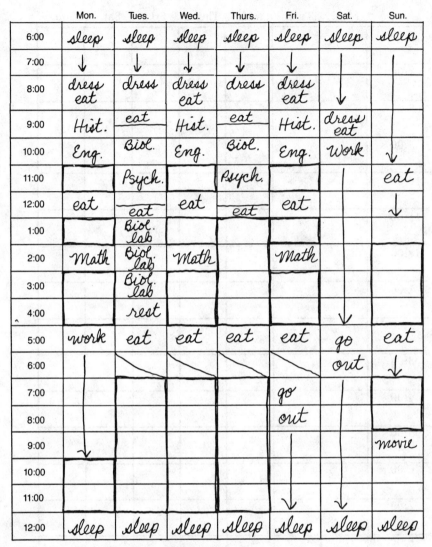

	Mon.	Tues.	Wed.	Thurs.	Fri.	Sat.	Sun.
6:00	sleep	sleep	sleep	sleep	sleep	sleep	sleep
7:00	↓	↓	↓	↓	↓		
8:00	dress eat	dress	dress eat	dress	dress eat	↓	
9:00	Hist.	eat	Hist.	eat	Hist.	dress eat	
10:00	Eng.	Biol.	Eng.	Biol.	Eng.	Work	↓
11:00		Psych.		Psych.			eat
12:00	eat	eat	eat	eat	eat		↓
1:00		Biol. lab					
2:00	Math	Biol. lab	Math		Math		
3:00		Biol. lab					
4:00		rest				↓	
5:00	work	eat	eat	eat	eat	go	eat
6:00						out	↓
7:00					go		
8:00					out		
9:00	↓						movie
10:00							
11:00					↓	↓	
12:00	sleep	sleep	sleep	sleep	sleep	sleep	sleep

Figure 2.2   A Time Analysis Worksheet

this worksheet for reminders, for appointments, or other tasks that do not take several hours of time.

c. Write due dates in column 2.

d. Estimate the time you think it will take you to complete the entire task and write it in column 3. If you are unsure of the time required, overestimate. This allows time for occasional interruptions.

Remember that library research always takes more time than you think it will. Estimate how long you think it will take, and add two hours.

	Mon.	Tues.	Wed.	Thurs.	Fri.	Sat.	Sun.
6:00							
7:00							
8:00							
9:00							
10:00							
11:00							
12:00							
1:00							
2:00							
3:00							
4:00							
5:00							
6:00							
7:00							
8:00							
9:00							
10:00							
11:00							
12:00							

Figure 2.3 A blank Time Analysis Worksheet

Task	Date Due	Time Required	Start by	Completed
Read *Grapes of Wrath*.	April 25	15 hours	April 10 — Read an hour a day 10-11 p.m.	
Write paper on *Grapes of Wrath* - 500 words typed.	April 30	outline - 2 hrs. draft - 2 hrs. revise - 2 hrs. type - 2 hrs. total - 8 hrs.	April 26 (2 hrs/day for 4 days) 1-3 p.m.	
Do math problems pp. 46-48.	May 1	3 hours	April 30 7-10 p.m.	
Read *Intro to Engineering* 30 pages.	May 3	4 hours	May 2 7-11 p.m.	

Figure 2.4   A Time Management Worksheet

e. Consult your Time Analysis Worksheet for available study time. Then commit the time you will need in order to meet the due date to do the task.
f. Now use the time you have found to complete the assignment. If something interferes, find another time and commit it by writing it down.

You do not have to become a slave to Time Analysis and Time Management worksheets. Use them when you need them: at the beginning of semesters to get off to a good start, or when you feel pressured by a lot of work and need to feel reassured that you really do have time to get everything done.

3. Get off to a fast start   When you start to study, get right to work. Have your study area ready: cleared space, sharp pencils, plenty of paper and supplies. Leave it that way each time you finish studying so that you won't waste time getting ready to study. If you are in the middle of a project, leave it out so that you can get right back into it. When you start, you need to have decided exactly what you want to accomplish and how much time it should take you. Use some positive self-talk to remind yourself what you want to do, how long it will take, what the benefits will be, and that you *can* do it. Some students are motivated to get off to a fast start by contemplating, for a few seconds, the consequences of not doing the assignment. If it is especially hard to get started, you can always start with an easy task.

4. Work to finish rather than to put in time   Many successful college students never use time schedules. Instead, they figure out what needs to be done each day and then they study during every available time until they are finished. When they finish early, they enjoy their free time for the rest of the day. You may not have this much discipline immediately. You will eventually develop it, however, if you think in terms of completing assignments rather than putting in a set amount of time on each subject each week. For example, instead of sitting down to read history for two hours, mentally estimate that you have about six hours of history to read by Friday. Then use all available study time to complete the assignment as soon as possible. When you think not just in terms of putting in time but in terms of finishing jobs, you get a lot more done in a shorter period of time.

5. Make lists and set priorities Briefly list the things you want to accomplish each day. Number the items in order of importance, do one thing at a time, and cross them off as you complete them. Quit for the day when they are all completed. You may want to keep a week-at-a-glance appointment book so you can see what you need to do week by week as well as day by day.

6. Break big jobs into parts Look at the second item on the Time Management Worksheet (Figure 2.4). Notice in the "time required" column that a paper assignment has been broken down into manageable parts with time limits for each part. You will complete long and difficult assignments more effectively and with less stress if you deal with them in this way.

7. Make good use of your best time Some of us are most alert in the morning. Others get a surge of energy as soon as the sun goes down. Discover the times of the day when you are most alert, feel motivated, and concentrate best. Do your most difficult or most important studying at those times.

8. Make good use of class time Class is one of the best places and times to get a lot of your work for that day's class started. Under the stimulus of the classroom, you can usually accomplish twice as much as you could later on your own. Spend class time listening to the professor, writing notes, jotting down your own ideas, and asking questions. Keep your textbook handy to refer to it when the teacher does. Get to class five minutes early so that you can use that time to look over the notes you took at the last class.

When you make the most of the hour in class, you will become more interested. You can also often cut your outside study time in half and still do a good job. Students with outside jobs especially have to make the best possible use of all class time.

9. Make good use of odds and ends of time Use small amounts of time during the day for small jobs or to get started on larger assignments. A lot can be done in even fifteen minutes. Use free hours between classes to keep up with classes that require regular, spaced study, such as math, language, science, or shorthand.

10. *Make good use of study time* Study during the times you have designated for study so that you will protect your free time. Most people work faster and with better concentration if they know that they must finish within a certain time period or else cut into free time. If you get bored or have trouble concentrating during this time, switch to another activity. If you get sleepy, walk around or do some exercises.

11. *Set deadlines and rewards* It is motivating to test your ability to work against deadlines. Use the Time Management Worksheet to help you do this. Then enjoy your time off with a clear conscience.

12. *Make time for memorizing, thinking, and review* Such important learning activities take time. Set aside at least fifteen or twenty minutes out of each major study period for them.

At the Very Least . . .

This chapter has dealt with the ideal way of improving your organization. If you can't follow all of the suggestions every day, *at the very least* do this much:

1. Organize your study materials so that they are separate for each class.
2. Set up a study place that is free from external distractions.
3. Analyze how long it takes to do assignments and start allowing ample time.

SUMMARY

Your whole semester will go more smoothly and you will be able to concentrate and study better if you make some decisions and act on them before you begin attending classes. Buy separate notebooks for each class. Outfit them with paper for the first day in class. Find a place to stack books and other study materials for each class so they won't get lost. Decide where you will do your studying. Learn to manage your time so that you will meet your study responsibilities and still have time for recreation.

Exercises

A. Chapter Questions

Circle the letter of the right answer or fill in the blanks.
1. What is the cardinal principle for any system of organizing study materials?

    a. Use 8½-by-11-inch pieces of paper.
    b. Buy several spiral notebooks.
    c. Keep your notes bound together so that they won't get lost.
    d. Keep all the materials for each course separate from one another.
2. List three places mentioned in this chapter where *you* could study.
    a.
    b.
    c.
3. Which would be the best place to study when you are having trouble concentrating? _____
4. What is the main reason for making a Time Analysis Worksheet?
    a. To discover fixed time commitments and available study time.
    b. To get enough sleep.
    c. To find time for movies and recreation.
    d. To keep from forgetting to go to class.
5. What is the main reason for making a Time Management Worksheet?
    a. To keep track of assignments.
    b. To help remember due dates.
    c. To learn how much time different assignments take and then to finish them on time.
    d. To learn to break long jobs into parts.

B. Application of Skills

1. Set up the system you will use to organize lecture notes and other classroom materials and be prepared to describe your system in class.
2. Make assignment sheets for each of your classes like the example on page 17 and place them in the front of your notebooks.
3. On the Time Analysis Worksheet in Figure 2.3 write in your fixed time commitments and box in the hours when you are *most* alert and energetic and free to study. The boxed-in hours, when you need them, will be your study hours. Try to find roughly two hours of outside study time a week for each hour you spend in class.

C. Topics for Your Learning Journal

1. Write a paragraph describing the system you have set up for organizing your study materials and explain why you chose it.
2. Write a paragraph describing your study place and how you have organized it.
3. Either by yourself or as a class project, make a list of everything you can think of that interferes with your effective time management. Now make a list of everything you can think of that will help you manage your time. Finally, write a time management plan that will help you accomplish your goals in college.

PART TWO
Going to Class

3

Analyzing and Adapting to Your Classes

When you have finished reading this chapter, you will know the following:

1. How you learn best.
2. How to figure out what to do to pass each class.
3. Where to seek outside help if you need it.
4. What to do if you get in a class that is too hard for you.

Why Analyze Your Classes?

The purpose of carefully analyzing your classes is *to enable you to adapt to them better.* Classes and teachers are all different. When you adapt to each of them well, you learn well.

Part of adapting to classes involves analyzing how you learn best and then adjusting your style of learning to the way in which the class is taught. Analyze, also, the organization of the class, what your responsibilities will be, and where you can get extra help if you need it.

What Is Your Best Learning Style?

Not all people learn best in the same way. Current research suggests that most people have ways that they prefer to learn, prefer to express themselves, and even prefer to study. Such preferences are known as learning styles.

Think about yourself. How well do you learn by listening? You may be able to listen and understand problems without seeing them written out, or listen to lectures and explanations and understand them easily. Or, do you learn best by seeing? Many people must see things written down before they understand them. If you are like these people, you will want to see math problems done on the board, lectures outlined on the board but written out more fully in your notes, and handouts circulated in class. You will also better understand ideas from class when you see them written in a textbook. If you learn best by seeing, you may take notes on your telephone conversations because seeing them helps you understand what you hear. Or, do you learn best by touching, handling, or working with the material you are learning about? If you do, then you probably enjoy your science labs. It may seem natural to you to diagram or draw pictures of material you want to learn.

You also probably have a preferred way of expressing yourself. Do you express yourself best by speaking? If this is the case, you will probably be more at ease in oral than in written examinations. Or, do you express yourself best in writing? Some people find it much easier to write than to speak their thoughts.

Finally, do you prefer to study alone or with another individual or in a group? If you learn by hearing and you like to express yourself by speaking, you may find that you also like to study with other people. Or, you may prefer to study alone, writing and thinking about material you are learning by yourself.[1] People also differ in the amount of structure and control they like in their environment. It may be easy and natural for you to be well organized and to look for structure in everything you learn. Or you may be able to function without a plan, relying instead on flashes of insight, and enjoying flexibility, variety, and novelty.

One purpose of this book is to give you ideas and opportunities to practice learning in a variety of styles so that you can adapt to your different classes better since you will not always take classes where you can use only your preferred style. Work to develop a variety of learning styles.

---

[1] A number of tests have been written recently to help you analyze your learning style. They include the *Canfield Learning Styles Inventory*, Form S-A, © 1976, Albert A. Canfield, Northville, Michigan, the *Learning Styles Inventory* developed at the Murdock Teacher Center, Wichita, Kansas, and the *Kolb Learning Style Inventory*, in D. A. Kolb, I. M. Rubin, and J. M. McIntyre, *Organizational Psychology: An Experimental Approach*, 2d ed., Englewood Cliffs, N.J.: Prentice-Hall, 1974. See also Gordon D. Lawrence, *People Types and Tiger Stripes*, 2d ed. (Gainesville, Fla.: Center for Applications of Psychological Type, Inc., 1982).

How Is the Class Organized?

The best explanation of the organization of a class is usually the *syllabus,* normally distributed on the first day of class. A syllabus is a list of the topics that will be covered during the semester. It is, in effect, a table of contents for the course. Study it carefully, and fix the topics in your mind. Consult it at the beginning of each class period to see what topic will be covered that day. Read through it now and then to develop a sense of the progression of topics in the class.

Learn more about the organization of a course by listening carefully to the professor's *opening remarks.* Very often the first lecture will provide a verbal outline of the course.

In some classes there will be no syllabus and no verbal explanation of the course's organization. You will understand and learn the material better if you make an effort to organize it yourself as you learn it. Take notes in class even if they seem disorganized. Then, read rapidly through your lecture notes every two or three weeks in order to discover the sequence of major topics. Make a list of the topics and group them under headings that you create. In this way, you will write your own class outline when one is not provided. The course will then make more sense to you, and you will remember it better.

NOTES THAT YOU UNDERSTAND

What Are Your Responsibilities in the Class?

Besides listing the topics to be covered, the syllabus often states the student's main responsibilities in a class. Most professors will reemphasize these responsibilities in their opening remarks. One way or another find out what is expected of you in the class. Specifically, you need to get answers to eight questions:

1. What is the most important source of information in the class? Is it the textbook, the lectures, or both? Whichever it is, that is what you master first.
2. Are there other sources of information you will need to consult or study? For example, has the professor placed on a reserve shelf in the library books that you will be expected to read? Are you expected to read any journal articles in the library during the semester? Are you expected to conduct interviews, attend labs, or otherwise gain more information for your class?
3. What are the reading assignments? When is each due?
4. Are you expected to write any papers in the class? If so, how long are they to be, will they require library research, and when are they due?
5. Are there any other special projects and assignments you must complete? By when?
6. How many exams will there be, and when? Is there a final exam? Will it cover the entire semester or only the material taught after the last midterm exam? Will these exams be the essay, objective, or short-answer type, or some combination? Will you be examined primarily on the text, the lectures, both, or on all sources of information in the course?

7. What is the attendance policy in the class? Will unexcused absences lower your grade?
8. Is part of your grade based on your participation in class discussion?

Find out at the beginning of every semester exactly what is expected of you in each class. Then watch your time and plan ahead so that you will meet all of your class responsibilities. This is the *least* you must do to pass a course.

Is There Any Outside Help Available?

ask for help

Review or discussion sessions are sometimes run by graduate assistants who work with the professor. These sessions may be voluntary or compulsory. In any case, go to them.

Find out what is available

Many universities have tutoring services and learning labs. These services may include both individual tutoring in a particular subject and catch-up help if you have forgotten or have never learned some of the basic skills necessary to do well in college. Find out if your school has such a service, and use it. When you study with a tutor, you have to think and explain. Consequently, you learn more than when you passively sit in class. Most professors will set up office hours when they are available to discuss your points of confusion. They may also prepare bibliographies to guide your outside reading and research. They may further help you by placing the important books for the class on reserve in the library. Some professors make old exams available either in their office or in the library to help you prepare for exams.

It is also a good idea to get the name and telephone number of another class member during the first week of school. Then, if you must be absent, you can call to find out what you missed before you return to class.

What If a Class Is Too Difficult for You?

Classes usually seem too difficult when you lack the background or learning skills necessary to do well in them. Calculus will be too hard if you've forgotten or have never had trigonometry; chemistry and other college science classes will be too hard if you have a weak math background. History will seem difficult if you don't know how to take lecture notes, and so on. You may be tested during the first week of classes to see if you have sufficient background and skill to understand what will be taught. More often, however, you will not be tested.

You can do one of two things when you find yourself in a class that seems too difficult: (1) you can take advantage of all the extra help available to you (help sessions, tutors, remedial help, the help of classmates, professor's office hours) and try to pass; or (2) you can drop back and take the course or courses necessary to prepare you for the hard class. The second of these solutions is the better one. Then you can take the hard class again later when you are better prepared to cope with it.

At the Very Least . . .

This chapter has dealt with the ideal way of analyzing and adapting to your classes. If you can't follow all of the suggestions every day, *at the very least* do this much:

1. Develop different learning styles so that you can learn in every class.
2. Figure out exactly what you must produce in each class.
3. Get help when you need it.

SUMMARY

All classes and professors are different. In order to adapt to each class and successfully complete it, you need to develop different learning styles. You will understand a class and remember it better if you can see how it has been organized. You should, as soon as possible, determine all of your responsibilities in each class so that you won't leave important jobs undone. Finally, if a class is too hard, you need to seek help or drop back a level to a course you can handle.

Exercises

A. Chapter Questions

1. What is meant by an individual's "learning style?"
   a. The manner in which the professor conducts the class.
   b. An individual's preference for learning in a particular way.
   c. A manner of learning characterized by special skill and confidence.
   d. The style in which you analyze your responsibilities in a class.
2. Why is it important to analyze the organization of a course?
   a. You then see the topics and the manner and order in which they will be presented.
   b. You understand the entire course better.
   c. You remember the course better.
   d. All of the above.
3. In the following list circle *all* those items of information that are important when you are analyzing *your* responsibilities in a class:
   a. Whether or not the professor tolerates tardiness.
   b. Whether or not the professor uses the chalkboard to teach.
   c. Relative importance of class lectures and textbooks as sources of information.
   d. Whether or not the professor will fall for hard-luck excuses for absences.
   e. Number and type of assignments in the class.

    f. Number of exams, and when they are held.
    g. Attendance policy in the class.
    h. Whether active participation in class discussion is important.
4. What can you do if a class is too difficult?
    a. Drop back and take a class designed to prepare you for the harder class.
    b. Seek help from your professor during office hours.
    c. Seek tutorial help.
    d. All of the above.

B. Application of Skills

1. *Class Analysis Sheet.* Analyze your responsibilities in your classes by completing the following sheet for each class.

    1. Class _____

    2. Professor _____

    3. Office Hours _____ 4. Phone _____

    5. Other sources of help available _____

    _____

    6. What organizes the class, the lectures or the textbook? _____

    _____

    7. What are the major sources of information in the class? _____

    _____

    8. Describe the assignments (include reading, writing, special projects and due

    dates). _____

    _____

    9. How important is it for you to participate in class discussion? _____

    _____

    10. What is the attendance policy? _____

    _____

    11. What is the policy on late homework? _____

    _____

    12. What is the policy on missed homework? _____

    _____

13. How many exams are planned and when will they be given? _____

_____

14. Will the final cover only the material presented after the last midterm, or will it

cover the entire semester? _____

_____

15. What is the purpose of the course? _____

_____

16. What do I want to get out of this course? _____

_____

_____

17. What is the name and phone number of a classmate? _____

_____

2. *Questionnaire on Campus Resources.* Check all the helping resources that are available on your campus. Check also whether or not you have or might use them.

   a. Resources to help with studying and learning:

Resource	Available on Your Campus?		Will You or Have You Used?	
	Yes	*No*	*Yes*	*No*
1. Professor's office hours	___	___	___	___
2. Professor's review or help sessions	___	___	___	___
3. Teaching assistant's office hours	___	___	___	___
4. Teaching assistant's review or help sessions	___	___	___	___
5. Tutoring program	___	___	___	___
6. Writing center	___	___	___	___
7. Learning assistance center	___	___	___	___
8. Reading lab	___	___	___	___
9. Math lab	___	___	___	___
10. Organized study groups	___	___	___	___
11. Supplemental instruction group	___	___	___	___

Resource	Available on Your Campus?		Will You or Have You Used?	
	Yes	No	Yes	No
12. Study skills classes	——	——	——	——
13. Study skills workshops	——	——	——	——
14. Study skills counseling	——	——	——	——
15. Reading classes	——	——	——	——
16. Remedial math classes	——	——	——	——
17. Remedial English classes	——	——	——	——
18. Exam files	——	——	——	——
19. Reserve shelf in library	——	——	——	——
20. Organized study program in residence halls	——	——	——	——
21. Other: _____	——	——	——	——

_____

b. Resources to help you grow personally as well as solve the problems that could interfere with studying and learning.

Resource	Available on Your Campus?		Will You or Have You Used?	
	Yes	No	Yes	No
1. Academic advising office	——	——	——	——
2. Continuing orientation program	——	——	——	——
3. Financial aid office	——	——	——	——
4. Health service	——	——	——	——
5. Personal counseling office	——	——	——	——
6. Career counseling office	——	——	——	——
7. Job placement office, including part-time jobs	——	——	——	——
8. Peer counseling program	——	——	——	——
9. Self-development classes and workshops	——	——	——	——
10. Leadership program	——	——	——	——
11. Recreational or intramural program	——	——	——	——

Resource	Available on Your Campus?		Will You or Have You Used?	
	Yes	No	Yes	No
12. Cultural programs: films, lectures, concerts	____	____	____	____
13. Clubs and organizations	____	____	____	____
14. Support centers for special groups	____	____	____	____
a. Women	____	____	____	____
b. Blacks	____	____	____	____
c. Hispanics	____	____	____	____
d. Returning students	____	____	____	____
e. International students	____	____	____	____
f. Students in your major	____	____	____	____
15. Other: _____	____	____	____	____

C. Topics for Your Learning Journal

1. Write a description of how you learn best. Include what you think is your predominant learning style—hearing, seeing, or touching; how you like to study—by yourself or in groups; and how you communicate best—in writing or by speaking. Describe a learning situation that would be ideal for you and one that would be difficult.
2. In which of your classes is it easy for you to learn? In which classes is it difficult? In the latter, how can you adapt so that you will learn more easily?

4

Taking
Lecture Notes

When you have finished reading this
chapter, you will know the following:

1. Why it is important to take lecture notes.
2. How to take good lecture notes in all
types of classes.
3. How to study your notes when you have
finished taking them.
4. How to remember your notes.

Why Take Lecture Notes?

Much information that you are expected to learn in college is given in the form
of lectures. It is material the professor has worked up, and is often not readily
available in books or anywhere else. If you do not listen well and record what
you hear, you will not know this material. If you try to remember it without
taking notes, you will forget it.

Many students believe that if they sit back and listen and think during a
lecture, they will be able weeks later to remember what was said. That doesn't
work. People forget at least half of what they learn within twenty-four hours of

learning it. What is forgotten can be gradually relearned, however, if you have a record of it. The easiest and best way to get such a record is by taking good lecture notes.

Most students learn how to take some sort of notes in college by the trial-and-error method. Students who have had no instruction in note taking make two common errors: (1) their notes are so disorganized and poorly written that they are often impossible to read, and (2) the notes are skimpy and incomplete, offering insufficient information to study for an exam.

How to Take Well-Organized Notes

Outlined notes are easier to study because you can see the separate parts of a lecture. It is easier to learn parts first and then later to see how the parts fit together to form a whole lecture.

The usual outline symbols in your notes do not have to be perfectly done. When you are trying to get down a lot of material in a hurry, you cannot always remember whether to write a *1* or an *A*. Just put all main ideas close to the margin and indent all material about each idea under it. If there are several items of information about a main idea, you can either number the separate items or put a dash in front of each.

How do you recognize the main ideas in a lecture so that you can write them by the margin? There are various ways in which professors make their main ideas stand out. Sometimes they tell you in their introductory remarks, as in: "Our subject today is immigration to the United States in the seventeenth and eighteenth centuries. We shall be looking particularly at German, Scotch-Irish, and French immigration." You immediately have a title for your notes— *Immigration to U.S. in 17th and 18th Centuries*—and the three main divisions —*German, Scotch-Irish,* and *French.* During the lecture you will listen for details about these three groups of immigrants.

Professors also emphasize their main ideas by stating them slowly and then by repeating them in the same or slightly different words. Many professors also emphasize main ideas by writing them on the blackboard.

Another way to locate the main ideas in a lecture is to listen for certain phrases that speakers use to emphasize their main points. Examples of such phrases are, "Today I want to talk about . . ."; "Now we will turn to . . ."; "Next, let's take a look at . . ."; "I'm going to point out three . . . ; The first is . . . ; The second is . . ."; "The next point I want to make is . . ."; or "The first (or next, or last) point I want to discuss is as follows." These verbal clues tell you that the subject is being changed. You should indicate the change in your notes by starting a new block of material by the left-hand margin or, if the points are being numbered, by starting a new item in a list with each new number.

Some lecturers do not emphasize their main ideas in the ways mentioned above. When you can't outline your notes easily, at least skip a line whenever there is a change of subject. Later, read through your notes and impose an organization on them by writing labels and numbering sections. When a list of items is given (for example, "three ways to take reading notes"), list the three ways down the page with the title ("ways to take reading notes") at the top. Never write lists across the page with two or three items on one line. They are too hard to study that way.

How to Take Complete Notes

Your note-taking job is not done when you have written down the main ideas in a lecture. You need details, examples, explanations, and diagrams in your notes, too. Then they will make sense to you, and you will remember them longer.

Write during class, and write a lot. Fill several sheets of paper. In a fifty-minute lecture you can usually take from three to eight pages of notes. Get down as good a record as possible of what went on in class.

Try to take notes in complete thoughts rather than in isolated words or brief phrases. Look, for example, at the history notes about "The Lost Generation" on page 42. Note that the author of these notes has avoided writing isolated words and phrases that would be difficult to understand later. Instead, the ideas are expressed completely enough so that anyone can read and make sense of them. When you take complete notes, you then study in complete thoughts, and it is later easier to write in complete thoughts when you take the examination. In order to do this successfully you will have to learn to abbreviate and to leave out words that are not essential to the meaning of what is said. Make up your own abbreviations. For example, *Engl.* can stand for *English*, *M.A.* for *Middle Ages*, *bio.* for *biology.* You could write the sentence "Mencken's solution for the moral problems of the period was to legalize prostitution" as "Mencken — solution to moral prob — legalize prostitution." You have recorded enough so that when you study, you will form a complete thought in your mind even though you have not written every word.

Ten Other Suggestions for Good Note Taking

Besides outlining your notes and taking complete notes, there are other ways you can improve the quality of your lecture notes.

1. Label your notes at the top of the page with your professor's name, the course, the date, and the title of the lecture Think of your notes as chapters in a book, each with its own title. Later, when you study your notes, the titles will immediately help focus your mind on the subject of the lecture.

2. Make your notes legible Notes taken in ink on one side of the paper can be read more easily and for a longer period of time than pencil notes.

3. Be an aggressive note taker Regard note taking as hard work. Sit as close as you can to your professors so that you will be able to hear them without straining. While you are taking notes, maintain an alert physical attitude. Then your mind will usually stay alert also.

4. Start taking notes when the professor starts talking Don't sit back during a lecture and wait for something to strike you. Remember that your professors are likely to examine you on any of the material they present in their lectures. Writing down the title of the day's lecture and taking a note or two on the introductory remarks will usually get you well started so that you won't miss important points later.

5. Ignore all distractions that might interfere with your concentration Don't think about what your professors are wearing, the other students in class, the good weather outside, or anything else but the business at hand. Instead, concentrate on getting as many notes as possible during the class period.

6. Isolate the specialized vocabulary for each course as early as possible and learn it so that you and the professor will be talking the same language In order to talk about a subject your professor will use the language of that subject, though not always taking the time to define each term that is unfamiliar to you. Circle difficult words, draw a line from them out to the margin, and label them there with a *V* for *vocabulary*. This is a quick note to yourself that you must find out more about these words. Until you do, the lecture won't make complete sense.

7. Learn to differentiate fact from opinion in lectures Get the facts straight and learn them; keep them separate from the professor's opinions. Label your professor's opinions as such if you wish. It is also a good idea to insert your own opinions, questions, ideas, and reflections into your notes as they occur to you. Separate your ideas from the material presented by your professor by placing them in square brackets, thus: [ ].

When your notes are sprinkled liberally with your own reactions in square brackets, they are more interesting to study later. Such reactions also make it easier for you to come up with topics for papers and to answer those exam questions that demand original thought. Figure 4.1 shows a fragment of notes that contain fact, professor's opinion, and student's opinion.

8. Develop your own set of symbols to identify or emphasize various items in your notes It has already been suggested that a circled *V* in the margin can identify an unfamiliar term and that square brackets can be used to set off your own ideas. In addition, a circled *A* in the margin can identify an assignment slipped in without warning at the end of a lecture. A circled *B* in the margin can identify books mentioned in the lecture. A circled *P* in the margin can identify a possible paper topic that you thought of during a lecture.

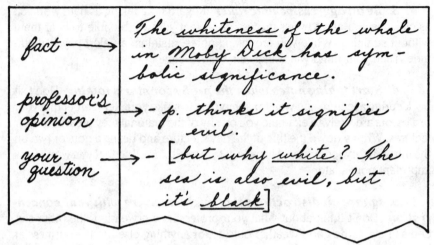

The whiteness of the whale in Moby Dick has symbolic significance.

fact ⟶

- p. thinks it signifies evil.

professor's opinion ⟶

- [but why white? The sea is also evil, but it's black]

your question ⟶

Figure 4.1 Fact and opinion in lecture notes

Questions in your own mind can be jotted down, labeled in the margin with a *Q*, and asked at the end of class. Cross-references to passages in the textbook can be indicated in your lecture notes as "see Text, p. 231."

Finally, emphasize main ideas in your notes by underlining them, and write a star next to material that is likely to be on an exam.

9. *Always take notes on discussion* Good discussion leaders come into class with a list of points that they want to make. Rather than presenting them in the form of a lecture, they draw the information from the class by asking questions. It is your responsibility in a discussion, just as it is in a lecture, to try to discover what points are being made and to record them so that you will not forget them. If you cannot outline the discussion, at least skip a line each time the subject is changed. In discussions in which you participate heavily, you probably will not have time to take notes. In such cases it is important to take summary notes on the discussion as soon as possible afterwards and certainly within twenty-four hours. In writing your summary, answer the question "What was the discussion about?" to help you isolate topics and then the question "What was said about it?" to help you get down some details.

10. *Get in the habit of always attending lectures* You will be less tempted to cut classes if you think of each class as a chapter in a book you are reading. If you cut a class, you miss a chapter and that interferes with comprehension.

What to Do with Your Notes after You Have Taken Them

If you follow the suggestions made so far for getting complete and well-organized notes, you should end up with a potentially useful set of notes. They are only potentially useful, however, until you have spent at least a few minutes with them *after* class.

At the very least you should *read and revise* the notes you have taken within twenty-four hours. During that time the class will still be fresh in your mind, and you can make certain everything in your notes makes sense to you. Remember that you will forget over half of what went on in class during the first twenty-four-hour period. If you wait for more than a day, your notes will begin to look like someone else took them. Psychologists have discovered, however, that if you go over the new material and make an attempt to set it in your mind before the first rapid forgetting has taken place, you can keep the new material in your mind for a longer period of time and you can later relearn it quickly and easily.

As you read and revise your notes, be extremely critical of your understanding. If you read a couple of lines that make no sense to you, stop and try to figure out what should be there. If necessary, find out from a classmate, or even the professor, what was said and meant at that point in the lecture. Don't leave the confusing passage as it is. It will discourage and slow you down later when you are studying your notes for an exam.

Right after class you should also attempt to straighten out the organization of your notes. If you missed some of the main heads, especially those that are the general headings for lists of items, put them in now. Underline all headings and main points that you did not have time to underline in class. If your list does not look like a list, draw a box around it, or bracket it to indicate that those points go together. Don't recopy or type your notes. This, like tape-recording notes, can be a mechanical process that does not engage your thoughts. Reading, rethinking, revising to make certain everything makes sense, and reorganizing by numbering, putting in labels, and underlining demand more mental activity. As a consequence, you understand and remember what is there better.

When you have revised and reorganized your notes, go through them quickly and write in the left-hand margin (1) *labels of the contents of your notes,* (2) *briefer notes on your notes,* and/or (3) *brief questions that will force you to reproduce the ideas in your notes as you mentally answer these questions.* Then, (4) *write a brief summary, in phrases only, at the end of the notes.*

Many students like to use notebook paper that has a wide three-inch left-hand margin. Such paper can be found in most college bookstores. The large margin provides plenty of room for labels, symbols, references to the textbook, and insights that occur to you as you study your notes. Changing the color of ink for your marginal notes and summary (red, for example) will make them stand out from your class notes. Figure 4.2 shows an excerpt from some history notes that have been marked with briefer notes and questions in the margin. Notice, especially, the use of marginal symbols and the final summary at the end.

As soon as you have written your brief labels and questions, fold your paper over so that only the left-hand margin is exposed. Then, on the basis of such a label as "Def. of lost generation" *see if you can recite, without looking,* the particulars about the origin of that term. If you can't remember, peek at your

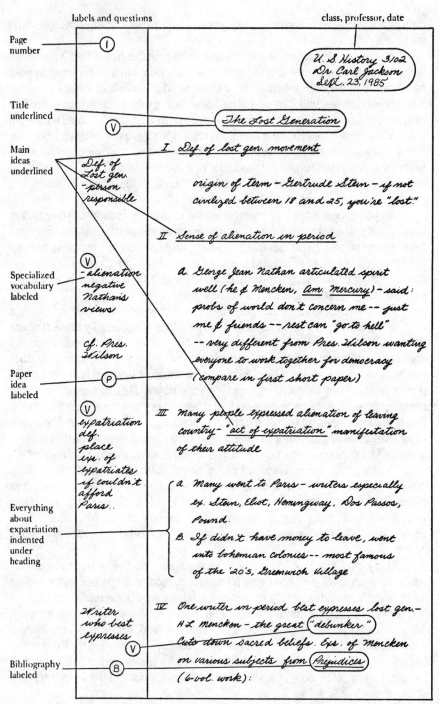

labels and questions   class, professor, date

Page number — ①

U. S. History 3102
Dr. Carl Jackson
Sept. 23, 1985

Title underlined

The Lost Generation — ⓥ

Main ideas underlined

I Def. of lost gen. movement

Def. of
Lost gen.
—person
responsible

origin of term — Gertrude Stein — if not
civilized between 18 and 25, you're "lost."

II Sense of alienation in period

Specialized vocabulary labeled

ⓥ
—alienation
negative
Nathan's
views

a. George Jean Nathan articulated spirit
well (he & Mencken, *Am. Mercury*) — said:
probs of world don't concern me —— just
me & friends —— rest can "go to hell"
—— very different from Pres. Wilson wanting
everyone to work together for democracy
(compare in first short paper)

cf. Pres.
Wilson

Paper idea labeled — ⓟ

ⓥ
expatriation
def.
place
exs. of
expatriates
if couldn't
afford
Paris..

III Many people expressed alienation of leaving
country — "act of expatriation" manifestation
of their attitude

Everything about expatriation indented under heading

a. Many went to Paris — writers especially
ex. Stein, Eliot, Hemingway, Dos Passos,
Pound.

B. If didn't have money to leave, went
into bohemian colonies —— most famous
of the '20's, Greenwich Village

Writer
who best
expresses

IV One writer in period best expresses lost gen. —
H L Mencken — the great "debunker."
Cuts down sacred beliefs. Exs. of Mencken
on various subjects from Prejudices

ⓥ

Bibliography labeled — Ⓑ

(6-vol. work):

Figure 4.2 History lecture notes

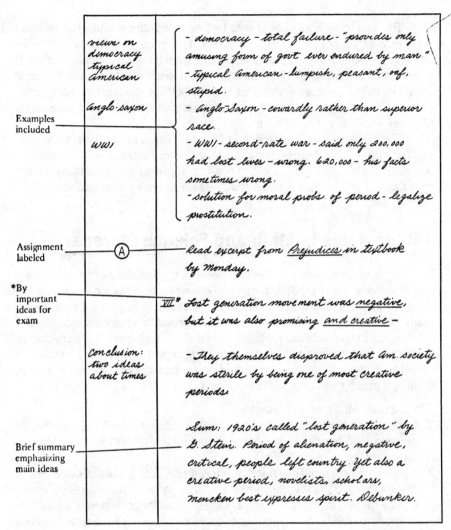

Figure 4.2 (cont.)   History lecture notes

notes, cover them up, and try again. Spend a few minutes covering your notes and reciting their contents as soon as you have put in the labels. You will find relearning the material later for an exam will be relatively quick and easy.

Use your summaries occasionally for a quick review of the course from the first day to the present. This will help you see the progression of ideas in the course so that it will make better sense to you. When you get to class early, read the summary of your last set of notes for that class. This will refresh your memory of what was said last time, and it will prepare you for the lecture to come. Finally, brief summaries of lecture notes will help you prepare for exams. You can check them when you study to make sure you don't omit anything important.

The *best* way, then, to treat your lecture notes after you have taken them is (1) go over your notes, revise, reorganize, underline main points, and make certain they make sense; (2) write labels and brief questions in the margin; (3) make a brief summary; and (4) cover up your notes; then, using your marginal notations to jog your memory, recite to yourself the contents of your notes. Follow all these suggestions as soon as possible after you have taken your notes, certainly within twenty-four hours.

The worst way to deal with your lecture notes is to put them aside after class and not look at them until you are studying for an exam. By this time your notes are "cold," and it is too late to clarify confusing passages, straighten out organization, and generally make things easier to understand and study.

Taking Notes in Math and Science Classes

You may have to modify your lecture note-taking techniques in math classes and in science classes that require problem solving. In such classes you will either be learning how to do a mathematical problem or you will be applying math to solve word problems such as those found in chemistry and physics classes. The biggest mistake most students make in taking notes in such classes is, when writing down the problems the professor puts on the board, to omit the verbal explanations that go with them. Here are six quick tips for taking notes in math and problem-solving science courses.

1. Get down what's on the board.
2. Get down the explanation that goes with what's on the board, like "factor out the *y*." Write out a reason for each step of the problem as it was done on the board.
3. If your professor moves so fast that you can't get both the board material and the explanation, leave large blank spaces in your notes. Then, within twenty-four hours, write additional explanations for each step of a problem so that you will be able to understand it when you study for exams. Number and list all the steps in each problem or process so that you can understand and learn them quickly.
4. Be careful with symbols. Ones you use in other classes to separate points, such as the dash, turn into math symbols in math classes. The best way to change the subject and separate topics in math notes is to draw a line clear across the paper from one margin to the other.
5. Label math and science notes in the left-hand column and write summaries just as you would notes from any other class. Then recite until you know them.
6. Students report that in some math and science classes they are able to copy examples and models on the board right into their textbooks. Less writing then needs to be done since the explanations are in the textbook itself. You will, of course, have to read the textbook assignment carefully before class to make this method work.

Math 3121
Dr. B. Prater
January 15, 1986

Define
Rules of
Hierarchy

Rules
1. _____

Ⓥ

2. _____
   or
   _____

3. _____
   or
   _____

4. _____
   or
   _____

__Rules of Hierarchy (Order) for Doing Arithmetic__

I. __Four Rules of Hierarchy__
   1. Do what's in parentheses first
      ex. $4 \times (3 + 2)$
      add what's in ( ) first, __then__ multiply
      $4 \times 5 = 20$

   2. Raise to a power or (take a root.)
      ex. $2^2 = 2 \cdot 2$
         $3 + 2^2$ first raise $2^2 = 4$
         Then $3 + 4 = 7$

   3. Multiply or Divide

   4. Add or Subtract

II. Apply to problems

   ex. $3 + 4 \cdot 7$ (multiply first, then add)
      $3 + 28 = 31$
   if should want to add first, have to put
   addition in parentheses.
      $(3 + 4) \cdot 7 = 7 \cdot 7 = 49$ (note change
   in answer)

Other
rules

---

work with
_____ num-
bers at
one time

ex. $3 - 2 - 7$ two subtractions can __only__
work with two numbers at a time :
   $3 - 2 = 1$, then $1 - 7 = -6$

work from
_____ to
_____

Use the __left-to-right__ rule. Work left to
right within each order.
Use rule also when choice between $\times$ or $\div$,
or between $+$ or $-$.

Figure 4.3   Math lecture notes

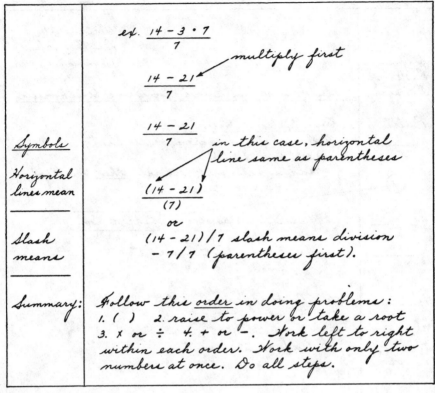

ex. $\dfrac{14 - 3 \cdot 7}{7}$

multiply first

$\dfrac{14 - 21}{7}$

<u>Symbols</u>

Horizontal
lines mean

$\dfrac{14 - 21}{7}$ in this case, horizontal
line same as parentheses

$\dfrac{(14 - 21)}{(7)}$

or

Slash
means

$(14 - 21)/7$ slash means division
$- 7/7$ (parentheses first).

Summary: Follow this <u>order</u> in doing problems:
1. ( ) 2. raise to power or take a root
3. × or ÷ 4. + or −. Work left to right
within each order. Work with only two
numbers at once. Do all steps.

Figure 4.3 (cont.)   Math lecture notes

Figure 4.3 demonstrates that the note-taking system described in this chapter works as well for math classes as it does for other classes.

At the Very Least . . .

This chapter has dealt with the ideal way of taking lecture notes. If you can't follow all of the suggestions every day, *at the very least* do this much:

1. Get complete notes in class.
2. Indicate the main topics or divisions in your notes.
3. Go through your notes after class, even if you have to do so hastily.

SUMMARY
Good lecture notes provide a record of the material your professor presents in class, material that might not be readily available in any other form. Take notes that are easy to read and easy to study. Notes should be outlined, complete, written in ink

on one side of the paper only, labeled with the course title,
professor's name, date, and subject of the lecture. Learn to abbreviate words and to use your own symbols to tag various types
of material in your notes. Be an aggressive note taker — sit close
to the professor, and don't allow distractions to interfere with
note taking. Think while you listen, identify unfamiliar words and
write down your ideas and questions. Within twenty-four hours
following class, revise and reorganize your notes, label their
contents in the left-hand margin, and cover your notes and
recite their contents until you can say them from memory.
Finally, write a brief summary, in phrases only, at the end of your
notes.

Exercises

A. Chapter Questions

1. True or false: If you listen carefully and critically to a lecture, you will not
have to take notes, and you will remember what the professor said when you
write the final exam.
2. Which of the following are used by professors to make the main ideas stand
out in their lectures? (There is more than one correct answer.)
   a. Slowing down to state a main idea.
   b. Repeating the main idea in different words.
   c. Writing the main idea on the blackboard.
   d. Using verbal pointers such as, "Now let us turn to . . ." or "Now let's
   look at . . ."
3. What types of material can the following abbreviations and symbols be used
to identify in your notes?

   a. Ⓥ _____

   b. [ ] _____

   c. Ⓐ _____

   d. Ⓑ _____

   e. underlining _____

   f. Ⓟ _____

   g. Ⓠ _____

   h. ☆ _____

   i. see text p. 281 _____.
4. How should the left-hand margin of your lecture notes be used?

    a. It should be left blank.

    b. It should be filled with questions when you are studying for an exam.

    c. It should contain only symbols and abbreviations such as those in question 4 above.

    d. It may contain symbols but should also be filled in with labels and questions on the contents of your notes within twenty-four hours after you have taken them.

5. How should the brief summary at the end of your notes be handled?

    a. Write quickly and in phrases only.

    b. Read it just before the next class to help you tune in.

    c. Read it when you are preparing for an exam.

    d. All of the above.

B. Application of Skills

1. A lecture that was delivered to new students is reproduced below. Listen to it, and take complete, well-organized notes. This lecture should be read aloud to you by either your instructor or someone else. Whoever reads it should read it slowly, as though actually delivering the lecture. That will take about ten minutes. Listen for the verbal clues that will help you identify the title and perceive the organization. If you outline this lecture accurately, your notes will take the form indicated in Figure 4.4.

Orientation Lecture[1]

There are several differences between the student who makes it in college and the student who doesn't. One major difference, and probably the most important difference, is how much the student understands about what goes on in a university learning situation. How much academic know-how does the student have? So, today, I want to look at this factor of academic know-how. I want to do what I can to provide some insight into how a student gets on at a university.

I'm going to begin by pointing out three things that the college instructor assumes about students. The first thing the college instructor assumes is that the student knows what he's doing. The college instructor assumes that the student is capable of deciding what courses he wants to take, capable of deciding whether he wants to attend class, whether he wants to do assignments. Now the instructor is going to point out certain things which should be done — certain standards in the class. He assumes that the student is capable of deciding whether he's going to do those things or not. If the student doesn't do them, he fails the course. But very few college instructors will bother the student about doing these various assignments, attending class, or anything else. That's the student's business, whether he wants to or not. It's the student's business whether he wants to stay in college or not. That's the first assumption. The student knows what he's doing.

[1] From a lecture delivered to entering freshmen by James A. Wood.

LABEL CONTENTS	
	TITLE: _____
	Introduction: _____
	_____
	I. _____
	1. _____
	_____
	2. _____
	_____
	3. _____
	_____
	II. _____
	1. _____
	_____
	2. _____
	_____
	3. _____
	_____
	4. _____
	_____
	5. _____
	_____
	III. _____
	1. _____
	_____
	2. _____
	_____
	3. _____
	_____
	Conclusion: _____
WRITE BRIEF SUMMARY	

Figure 4.4

The second assumption that the college instructor makes is that he, the instructor, is there to present material and the student is there to learn. He assumes that the student will meet him halfway. Most college instructors try to make their lectures, their courses, at least listenable, at least bearable, but they, the instructors, do not assume that they have to pound something into the student's mind. The instructor does not assume that he is going to have to make things exciting and jazzy. He does not assume that he is concerned with the student's personal behavior in class. In fact, discipline problems, in this sense, simply do not exist at the college level.

Okay, the student is there to learn. The third assumption the college instructor makes is that the student has to show some evidence of learning, some consistent performance of assignments in order to pass the course, even with a "D." The student will have to produce.

Now if you stop and think for a minute, you'll realize that what the college instructor is really assuming is that this student himself is mature enough to know what he's about, mature enough to make his own decisions, mature enough to know why he's in college. And the college instructor is there to provide a service. He's there to provide the information, he's there to distinguish between those who are understanding it and those who are not understanding it and not comprehending it.

I'm going to be negative for a moment, and I'm going to look at the major causes of student failure. I'm going to get down to a very practical level here. I'm not dealing with educational theory, or motivational theory, or any other theory. I'm dealing with the instructor who looks out at a group of freshman students, observes what's going on, and notices why some students fail. And this is going to be a kind of negative view of things.

I've singled out five of these basic, simple reasons why students seem to fail out of college in this first semester, this first year.

The first reason I've noticed is that a student will wait to be warned by someone that he's in trouble. He'll wait for the instructor to say, "You've been cutting a lot of classes. That's pretty bad." Or he'll wait for an instructor to say, "You haven't been turning in your assignments. I think we ought to look into that." As a matter of fact, in most college courses no one will ever warn the student. The wise student knows that he's going to have to perform, do well in class, and he doesn't wait for somebody to tell him that he's not doing well.

The second of these reasons why students seem to fail is that the student will put off working during the semester. In many courses there's not a great deal of day-to-day or even week-to-week work. The instructor will assign readings. He will assume that the student is doing the reading and is coming to class and comprehending the material. The student, on the other hand, puts things off, until suddenly around midterm time he's faced with an impossible amount of reading, papers to write, exams and problems that he has to work out. Sometimes it hits in the middle of the semester, sometimes it doesn't really hit until the end of the semester. Then it's often too late. The student realizes that he can't get all of it done. Therefore, facing this impossible task, he will give up.

A third reason for student failure is that a student will miss an occasional assignment and figure it will make no real difference. Let me explain something to you about grading policy in college. Very seldom will an instructor give an assignment and put a grade on it without counting that grade in your final work. And in most instructors' grading systems undone assignments do not count merely as an "F," they count as a zero. You cannot miss an occasional assignment because you don't feel like doing it. Do every assignment, even though some of it may be done relatively poorly. Be sure you do them, and do them on time.

The fourth of these mechanical causes for failure is the student doesn't really understand assignments. He doesn't take notes on assignments, and doesn't read the assignment in the syllabus. I am not talking about the student who doesn't understand the reading material and the reading assignment. I'm talking about the student who doesn't understand what the instructor is talking about when the instructor makes an assignment. An instructor will often have assignments specified in a syllabus or course schedule and he may mention them in class. If you don't understand what he is driving at, you have to ask him. An instructor may make an assignment for a major paper and it may not be due for two months. The student will not take any notes on the assignment. He'll think, "Yeah, I'll remember that." A month later, when he starts working on his paper, he doesn't know what the assignment is all about. So he does the wrong thing. In most university courses, if you write a brilliant paper on the wrong subject, it's worth exactly zero. The instructor does not want the assignment done on something that you thought he might like better than what he assigned.

The fifth and last of these mechanical causes of failure, and I suppose the most obvious, is the student who starts cutting classes. Now as I said, very few instructors will call your attention to whether you are cutting classes or not. They don't have time. They are there to teach, not to see if people come to class. Some instructors will tell you that they don't take roll, they are not interested in whether you are there or not. Now beware of this. In most of these situations where the instructor tells you that he doesn't care if you come to class, he is leaving it up to you whether you want to come or not. But he is still going to be very much aware of who is there and who isn't. Later, in a close decision on a grade, your attendance will help him decide which grade to give you.

The last section of material that I'm going to deal with is to make three very simple positive suggestions which mark the good student. I'm talking now about the student who is working pretty near his capacity, that is, his capacity in terms of the energy and intelligence that he has. The student, in other words, is a professional: he knows what he's about, and he operates efficiently in an academic situation.

I'm going to make a few simple suggestions that are basic for academic success. The first of these suggestions is to take complete lecture notes. Take lots of notes on lectures and class discussions. In many courses most of the material you'll be expected to know is given to you in these lectures. There are lots of specific techniques for taking lecture notes. The basic point that I'm making here is you can't know that material when you prepare for an examination unless you've got it in your notes to begin with. I see freshmen, sometimes half the students or more in a freshman class, who will sit and wait for me to say, "Now this is absolutely important." Sometimes even when I tell them, "I'm going to test you on this," they still don't take notes.

The professional student, on a condensed lecture, will take, on regular-size notebook paper, three or four pages of notes per class period. It's hard work. But that's where you get much of your material.

The second suggestion, positive suggestion, I'm going to make is to keep up with reading assignments. And don't just read the material passively. Try to understand what is in these reading assignments. Read the assignments, or at least scan them before they are discussed or lectured on in class, because this is usually the most efficient way to get the most out of both the lectures and the readings. The good student, the conscientious student, the person who's going to make it, is the person who will at least scan a reading assignment before going into the class; then this student will read that reading assignment afterwards.

The third suggestion I'm going to make for the good student is to review occasionally your reading notes and your lecture notes. Go back over the material you have read and your lecture notes. That will fix it in your mind. It will cause you to think about it, become a little bit involved and interested in it, and it will make the continuity in a course much easier.

Okay, these are three basic positive suggestions—take complete lecture notes, keep up with the reading, review and think about the material. I'll conclude by saying that learning is the name of the game. Really learning material is what the college academic experience is all about. I think if you try it, try to apply some of these things I've said, you'll discover that your freshman year can be really successful.

2. Now read through your notes and label them in the left-hand column as in Figure 4.2. Write a brief summary at the end. Cover the contents of your notes by doubling the paper over so that only the margin is exposed. Using your labels to trigger your memory, recite the contents of your notes until you can do so perfectly without looking. This should all take only ten or fifteen minutes.

3. Practice listening and writing at the same time by taking notes on the news on television or radio two or three times. Jot down the subject and underline it for each separate news item. Then speed write to get down as many details as possible under each item. Skip a line each time the subject is changed.

4. Use the suggestions in this chapter to take notes in one of your other classes.

Label the contents of your notes in the left-hand margin, write a brief summary of your notes at the end, and submit them to your instructor for evaluation.

C. Topics for Your Learning Journal

1. Look through a set of lecture notes from one of your most difficult classes. Make a list of everything that could be improved in these notes. Write a paragraph describing how you will take notes in that class next time you attend.
2. Either by yourself or as a class, make a list of ways to keep your mind from wandering during a class. Write your own plan for improving your concentration in classes.
3. List some examples of facts from recent classes. List some examples of opinions. How did you decide which items were facts and which were opinions?

5

Learning Specialized and General Vocabulary

When you have finished reading this chapter, you will know the following:

1. The difference between specialized and general vocabulary.
2. Why it is important to improve both kinds of vocabulary.
3. The kinds of information you can find in a dictionary or thesaurus.
4. Several ways to improve your present vocabulary.

The Difference between Specialized and General Vocabulary

During the four years or so that you are in college you will be expected to learn more about more different subjects than you probably ever will again in any similar length of time in your life. Every one of these new subjects will have its own *specialized vocabulary* (also called *key terms*) that you will have to learn in order to talk and write about it and to understand the professor. For example, your biology teacher will talk about *homeostasis* and *microbiota*. You will probably hear or see the specialized vocabulary for biology almost exclusively in biology classes, in biological discussions among professors and students, and in books and articles about biology. The same will be true of your other subjects. You may never or rarely hear or see specialized vocabulary outside of the context of the course.

It will be easier for you to deal with the specialized vocabulary for each course if you differentiate in your mind between this *specialized vocabulary* and a *general vocabulary,* which is not associated with a particular subject. Your history professor, for example, may talk about *progressivism, garrulous* old men, and *rapacious* landords during the lecture. The *specialized* term in this list is *progressivism. Garrulous* and *rapacious* could be heard in any classroom or encountered in an article in *Time.* You need to work on both your general vocabulary and the specialized vocabulary for each of your courses while you are in college. A larger vocabulary of both types makes it possible for you to think better (you think with words), to understand more, and to express yourself better both in school and after graduation.

There are some differences in the time and effort needed to learn specialized and general vocabulary. General vocabulary is comparatively easy to learn. Very often the words you select are ones you half-know already. A quick dictionary definition, perhaps even a synonym, is usually sufficient to help you learn a new word. Finally, these words usually do not have to be learned before a particular deadline in order to pass a course.

Specialized vocabulary, on the other hand, can be somewhat more difficult to learn. Certainly it is urgent that you learn it throughout a semester since you often need it in order to read and interpret exam questions. Becoming aware of some of the major problems in learning specialized vocabulary can help you learn it more easily. For instance, you may need more than a dictionary definition in order to understand a specialized term. Sometimes you will need to consult the index of your textbook and read several pages before you have an exact meaning. Or you may need to ask your professor for more information. Another problem is created when the meanings of specialized vocabulary vary from professor to professor and subject to subject. Study each new specialized word in the context in which you find it (for example, *realism* may have somewhat different meanings in art, literature, and drama courses). Finally, some specialized vocabulary may be obviously technical jargon or, to confuse you more, it may be everyday language used in a special way in a particular context (for example, *work* and *force* in physics or *spread effect* in political science). Don't trust your common sense or past experience to give you the definitions of such words. Learn their new meanings in the new contexts in which you find them.

Six Suggestions for Learning Both Kinds of Vocabulary

1. Study Your Dictionary or Thesaurus

One of the first books you should buy your freshman year is a dictionary. If you can't afford a hardback, buy a cheaper paperback edition. You will find them in your college bookstore.

When you have bought your dictionary, take a half hour to examine the front matter (that which comes before the A – Z listings) and the back matter (that which follows the listings). These pages will explain how you can make the best use of your new dictionary.

A good dictionary, you will see, does much more than define words. When you have found out what information yours contains, then keep it handy and use it regularly. You will need it to make the remaining suggestions in this chapter work for you.

The specialized vocabulary in many of your textbooks will be printed in boldface type and defined in a glossary at the back of the book. A glossary is an abbreviated dictionary that gives meanings for words as they are used in that textbook. It can be extremely useful for studying word meanings in a particular textbook.

A thesaurus, which is a dictionary of synonyms, is another useful resource for vocabulary improvement. The Preface of *Roget's International Thesaurus* (3d ed.) makes a clear distinction between a dictionary and a thesaurus: "In a dictionary you start with a word and look for its meaning. In a thesaurus you start with the idea and find the words to express it." A thesaurus can help you find dozens of synonyms and associated words to help you define words or express ideas.

2. Make Vocabulary Sheets

To make a vocabulary sheet, fold a piece of notebook paper lengthwise twice to form four columns. These four columns provide space for the four important activities necessary to learn vocabulary.

a. Find the word you need to learn and write it in the first column Set priorities in selecting words to learn. Choose *key specialized vocabulary* words and phrases that are used over and over in the course or that are the subject of an entire lecture or section in the textbook. Choose those *general vocabulary* words that are somewhat familiar to you, that interest you, or that have always bothered you because you did not know them. Even the physical act of writing them in the first column will help you begin to learn them.

b. In the second column write the word in the context in which you first found it Write only enough context to show the use of the word. Usually a phrase will do. Whenever you can, write out context that helps define the word. For example, "That the will of a popular majority should prevail in all matters is known as *populism*" tells you more about populism than "*Populism* was prevalent at the end of the nineteenth century."

c. In the third column define the word Look up the meaning of a *general* vocabulary word in the dictionary. Select the part of the definition that best fits the word as it is used in the context in which you found it. Write out the

Word	Phrase or Sentence	Meaning	Association for Remembering (use foreign or English words, diagrams, or examples)
pulverize	The storm pulverized the building.	to crush into small pieces	pulverizer
indefatigable	The little boy seemed indefatigable in the race.	not capable of becoming tired	infatigable
leonine	His hair gave him a leonine appearance.	of or like a lion	leo the lion
contagion	The contagion of laughter was too much for him, and he began to laugh also.	a spreading by contact	contagious
pensive	He was in a pensive mood and sat staring into space.	thoughtful or serious	pensar
nebulous	It was a nebulous idea, hard to grasp.	cloudlike, vague	nublado

Figure 5.1 General vocabulary sheet (Notice the context clues to the meanings of these words in the second column.)

definition in your own words. Don't copy a long, complicated dictionary definition that means nothing to you.

A dictionary definition may not be sufficient for the *specialized vocabulary* in a course. You may have to do some extra reading to understand some terms. Look for a more thorough explanation in the glossary in the back of your textbook, if there is one. Or, consult the index of your textbook, and read detailed information in the text. When you have read enough, write *in language you can understand and remember* exactly how the word or phrase is used in a particular course.

Word	Phrase or Sentence	Meaning	Association for Remembering (use foreign or English words, diagrams, or examples)
spread effect	Spread effect... capital and managerial talent spread into the less-developed regions.	prosperity spreading into areas -- wealth coming in	California
backwash effect	The spread effect is the opposite of the backwash effect.	prosperity leaving areas -- wealth flowing out	Appalachia
populism	That the will of a popular majority should prevail in all matters is known as populism.	expert and minority opinion irrelevant. The majority opinion the only one that matters -- 19th century American politics. Lost popularity end of century	the populous, the people's opinion
gerrymander	It [the first such district] was elongated like a salamander, and Gerry's opponents called it a new monster, the gerrymander.	artificially setting up unfair voting districts in a state to favor a party or a political machine	Mr. Gerry salamander

Figure 5.2 A specialized vocabulary sheet for political science

Latin Element	Meaning	Scientific Term
bi-	two	bipodal
epi-	upon	epidermis
inter-	between	intermolecular
intra-	among	intramolecular
per-	through	permeable
peri-	around	periderm
poly-	many	polyvalent
semi-	half	semipermeable
sub-	under, less	subacute
super-	above, in addition	supersaturated
trans-	across, through	transpiration
aqua	water	aqueous
homo	man	homo sapiens
pater	father	paternal
-ped, -pod	foot	biped
spir-	breathe	transpiration

Greek Element	Meaning	Scientific Term
anthropo-	man	anthropoid
astro-	star	astrocyte
auto-	self	autogamy
bio-	life	biology
chromo-	color	chromosome
chrono-	time	chronograph
cyto-	cell	cytology
eu-	well, true	euchromosome
gen-	origin, people	genotype
homo-	same	homoiothermic
hydro-	water	hydrophyte
hyper-	too many	hyperplasia
iso-	same	isomeric
-logy	study of	geology
lumin-	light	bioluminescence
micro-	very small	microbe
mono-	one	monopod
-onomy	science	astronomy
pathos	suffering	pathology
-philous	having an affinity for	acidophilous
phyll-	leaf	phylloid
-plasia/plasy	development, formation	homoplasy
-plasm	formative material	plasma
pseudo-	false	pseudomonad
-stasis	slowing, stable	hemostasis
thermo-	heat	thermocline

Figure 5.3 Latin and Greek and modern scientific terminology

Greek Numerals
(important in the metric system as well as in scientific terminology)

Greek	Meaning	Scientific Term
mono, uni	one	monopodial, unicellular
di, bi	two	dicarboxylic, biceps
tri	three	triceps
tetr, quadr	four	tetrapods, quadriceps
pent	five	pentaploid
hex	six	hexachloride
hept	seven	heptose
oct, octa	eight	octandrious
nona	nine	nonagon
dica, deci	ten	decimeter
centi	hundred	centimeter
kilo, milli	thousand	kilometer, millimeter
hemi	half	hemichordate
multi	many	multicellular

Figure 5.3 (cont.)   Latin and Greek and modern scientific terminology

d. Associate the word or term with any other familiar English or foreign word, object, diagram, example, or experience; write that association in the fourth column to aid your memory It doesn't matter how far-fetched the association, so long as it helps you remember. Bilingual students have two languages to draw on for associations. If you know Spanish, for example, *carne*, the Spanish word for meat, will help you remember that *carnivorous* means "meat eating," or *verde* will help you remember that a *verdant* forest is green.

Figure 5.1 shows an example of a *general* vocabulary sheet made by a student whose first language was Spanish. Notice that several of the words she wrote in the fourth column are Spanish words. Spanish is a Romance language derived from Latin. For vocabulary improvement, knowing any Romance language can be almost as useful as knowing Latin. These languages can provide you with clues to the meanings of thousands of difficult English words.

Figure 5.2 shows an example of a *specialized* vocabulary sheet for a political science course.

3. Notice How Words Have Been Formed

It is useful to know the meanings of a few Latin and Greek prefixes, suffixes, and roots. Over 100,000 English words have bits and pieces of Latin and Greek in them. You can often get a pretty good idea of what a word means without looking it up if you know the meaning of its Latin or Greek components and if you also study the context in which find it.

It is especially useful when studying science to know a little Latin and Greek. Scientists draw on these languages when they need new names for things. Figure 5.3 provides some examples.

Word	Phrase or Sentence	Meaning	Association for Remembering (use foreign or English words, diagrams, or examples)
biolumin-escence	The biolumin-escence of the firefly.	light produced by organisms	bio--life (biology) lumin--light (luminarios) <u>light from life</u>
transpire	Tremendous quantities of water are transpired from the leaves.	passage of vapor from a living body through a membrane or pores	trans--across spir--to breathe
cytoplasm	The cytoplasm of a plant cell.	material of cell exclusive of nucleus	cyto--cell; (all "cyto" words have to do with cells) plasm--formative material plasma--fluid in blood. <u>cell fluid</u>
pseudopodia	The extensions which form the body of the ameba are pseudo-podia and are used in loco-motion.	temporary projection of a cell. function: locomotion and ingestion	pseudo--false, fake pod--foot (podiatrist) <u>false foot</u>

Figure 5.4 A specialized vocabulary sheet for biology

If some of the terms you have to know for your science courses "look like Greek" to you, it is because they are. Memorizing the meanings of the Greek and Latin elements in Figure 5.3 will give you clues to the meanings of many of these otherwise difficult-to-remember terms. The list is not exhaustive. When you get into your first science courses, you will add to it.

A specialized vocabulary sheet for biology is shown in Figure 5.4. All the words on this sheet are made up of Latin and Greek parts. Having been previously memorized by the students, these parts are now listed as aids to memory in column 4.

Example 1   An *outline* of related terms for geology

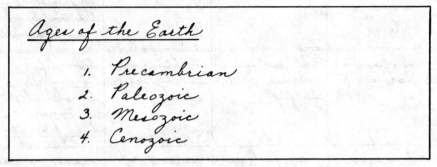

Ages of the Earth

1. Precambrian
2. Paleozoic
3. Mesozoic
4. Cenozoic

Example 2   A *diagram* of related words for English

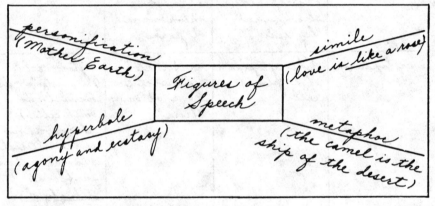

personification
(Mother Earth)

simile
(love is like a rose)

Figures of Speech

hyperbole
(agony and ecstasy)

metaphor
(the camel is the ship of the desert)

Figure 5.5   Words grouped according to categories

4. Group Words in Categories

It will help you learn a lot of specialized vocabulary if, whenever possible, you group related words in categories provided by the course itself. Or, you can group words around a Greek or Latin word part that all the words have in common. When you group, you can make either *outlines* or *diagrams,* whichever helps you most. Figure 5.5 provides two examples of words grouped according to categories, and Figure 5.6 shows two ways words can be grouped around a common Greek word part.

Diagrams such as the one in Figure 5.6, example 2, sometimes make relationships clearer than lists or outlines because each subitem is connected to the major, organizing item by a line. The relationships among the parts are then obvious. Of course, outlines also show relationships by ordering groups of related words in lists under main topics. Use whichever is best suited for the material you are trying to learn. Either way helps you see relationships that will, in turn, help you to remember.

Example 1 A list of *plasm* words for biology

> *Plasm* .... formative material
> cytoplasm ...... cell material
> endoplasm ..... inner material in cell
> sarcoplasm ..... flesh material
> ectoplasm ...... outer material in cell
> protoplasm ..... first material (in the living nucleus)

Example 2 These same words can be grouped in the form of a diagram, which might be easier for you to study.

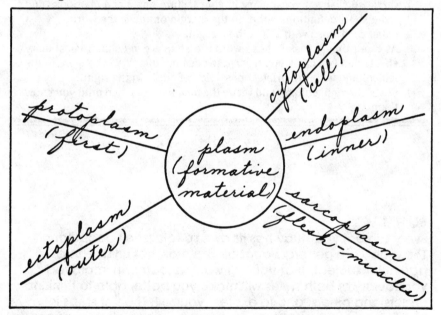

Figure 5.6 Words grouped according to a common Greek element

5. Make Vocabulary Cards

You may prefer to isolate and learn both specialized and general vocabulary words by putting them on three-by-five cards. Write the word and the context in which you found it on the front of the card. Using language easy to understand and remember, write a brief definition on the back of the card. Use these as flash cards to help you memorize the meanings.

6. Use Short, Frequent Practice to Learn Vocabulary

Many introductory courses in college are predominantly courses in specialized vocabulary. You will need to master this vocabulary quickly to pass the courses in which it is taught and, more important, to use it in upper-division courses. Short, frequent practice done out loud is by far the best way to accomplish this. You usually have to be exposed to a new word repeatedly over a period of time before it becomes a part of your active, usable vocabulary.

At the Very Least . . .

This chapter has dealt with the ideal way for improving vocabulary. If you can't follow all of the suggestions every day, *at the very least* do this much:

1. Circle specialized vocabulary in your lecture notes and textbooks and write short definitions either in the margin or above the word.
2. Label each word with a *V* in the margin.
3. At exam time transfer these words to simple two-column vocabulary sheets that you can study from at the last minute. Write the word in the left column with the briefest possible definition in the right.
4. Cover the right column and recite the meanings out loud until you know them.

SUMMARY

Every subject you study has its own specialized vocabulary. There also are general vocabulary words, not unique to a particular subject, that you will want to learn. An improved vocabulary of both types will make you better able to think, to understand others, and to express yourself. The first steps in improving your vocabulary are buying a good dictionary and learning how to use it. A thesaurus can also be useful. Then isolate the words you want to learn, examine them in context, find a definition that you can understand, and, finally, associate the new word with something already familiar to you. To make vocabulary easier to learn, you can organize the words and the information about them on four-column vocabulary sheets. Or you can group them in categories around a common Greek or Latin word part. Short, frequent practice done out loud is the best way to learn new words. Two-column vocabulary sheets can help with your final studying for exams.

Exercises

A. Chapter Questions

1. What does *specialized* vocabulary refer to?
   a. Words and terms used in talking and writing about a particular subject.
   b. Words you have heard many times but can't define.
   c. Words you can understand in context but can't define.
   d. Words you have to look up in the dictionary.
2. True or false: When the words are familiar, you can usually rely on your common sense to figure out the meanings of specialized vocabulary.
3. List the information you would write in the four columns of a vocabulary sheet:

   a. column 1 _____

   b. column 2 _____

   c. column 3 _____

   d. column 4 _____
4. Knowing some Latin and Greek elements is especially useful in the study

   of _____.

B. Application of Skills

1. If you don't already have a dictionary, buy one. List five types of information that your dictionary contains in the front matter (that which comes before A–Z listings) and the back matter (that which follows the listings).
2. Look up the word *mesomorph* in your dictionary and list *four types of information* given about this word.
3. Look up the word *study* in the index to a thesaurus. Select the synonym or related word listed under it that interests you most. Turn to the numbered section and list five synonyms for the word you selected.
4. Reorganize the information in Figure 5.5, example 1 (ages of the earth) into a diagram form. Then reorganize the information in Figure 5.5, example 2 (figures of speech) into outline form. If you can do this successfully, you have demonstrated that you understand the relationships among the pieces of information in each of these examples.
5. Look up in your dictionary the meanings of the words on the diagram in Figure 5.6. Notice how knowing the meanings of Greek word parts (as written in parentheses on the diagram) helps you understand and remember the dictionary definition.

6. To make it easier to learn, group the following material on diagrams similar to those in example 2 in Figures 5.5 and 5.6.

> ### *Group 1*
> Naturalistic (observe nature)
> Experimental (experiment)
> Three psychological approaches
> Correlational (observe specific variables)
>
> ### *Group 2*
> Endomorph (fat)
> Body types
> Mesomorph (average)
> Ectomorph (thin)

7. Make specialized vocabulary sheets like those in Figures 5.2 and 5.4 for each course you are taking. Remember that the easiest way to do this is to fold the paper lengthwise twice to make the four columns. In addition, make one sheet for general vocabulary (use Figure 5.1 as an example). If you have organized your notes in folders, keep these sheets in the left-hand pocket. If you use a spiral or looseleaf notebook, keep them at the front of your notes, right behind the assignment sheets. Your vocabulary sheets should be easily accessible. At least once a week, cover the meanings, and recite the words and meanings out loud until you know them.

C. Topics for Your Learning Journal

1. Either by yourself or as a class, list some specialized vocabulary words you have encountered recently. List some general vocabulary words. Describe the systems you will use to learn both types of vocabulary. How are they similar? How are they different?
2. Write a television advertisement that is designed to sell a specialized vocabulary word from one of your classes.

6

Participating
in Class
Discussion

When you have finished reading this
chapter, you will know how to do the
following:

1. Prepare for class discussion.
2. Listen and concentrate in class
   discussion.
3. Speak effectively in class discussion.
4. Participate even when you are scared.

Prepare for Discussions

If a reading assignment is to be discussed, read it before class, underline
important material in it, jot main points in the margin, and bring it to class with
you. Refer to Chapter 9 for more information on how to mark a textbook so that
you can later find material in it easily. During the discussion keep your textbook
open and refer by page number to specific passages and ideas in it that support
what you say.

   If you have been assigned a topic for discussion that you are to think about
rather than read about, jot down some ideas about it before you go to class.
Enter into every discussion with a full mind. Then your contributions will be
worthwhile.

Ten Tips for Active Participation in Class Discussion

1. Tune in quickly Focus on and write down the topic for discussion. This is the title for your discussion notes. Continue to concentrate on it.

2. Be an active listener Assume an alert physical posture in order to keep mentally alert. Think about what you hear, relate it to what you already know, anticipate what is coming next. Jot down questions and observations so that you will be ready when it's your turn to speak. Maintain eye contact with the speaker.

3. Try to stay objective Recognize that there is room for both fact and opinion in discussion. Continue to listen, even if you disagree. Withhold judgment of another opinion until you have heard the entire argument. If you wish to speak in opposition, do so politely and logically, using evidence and examples. Do what you can to prevent other participants from indulging in emotional tirades, also, by continuing to use reason and evidence whenever you have the opportunity to speak.

4. Stay on the subject You should know the general subject for discussion and know exactly what point about the subject is being discussed before you start talking. When you talk, try to make all of your remarks relevant to the subject. Your remarks should be brief and to the point. Then let someone else take the floor. If you want to speak again, allow several others to contribute before you make your next remarks.

5. Take notes on the main points Try to write both main points and some details either during the discussion or right after it. Skip lines or number the main points to keep them separate. See page 40 for additional suggestions about taking notes on discussion.

6. Ask questions occasionally It is appropriate to ask questions that (1) call for more information, (2) clarify factual material or unclearly stated opinions, or (3) help participants discover the value in what is being discussed.

7. Help keep the discussion clear and understandable You can often help clarify a vague point in a discussion by making additional observations or giving examples. This helps everyone understand what is going on better. Whenever you have an urge to relate a personal experience, make sure that it will contribute to the discussion. Then keep it brief, interesting, and to the point.

8. Stop and summarize when necessary You can help maintain the flow of a discussion, especially when someone has spoken too long or is getting off the point, by interjecting a summary and then introducing a new idea. Such a contribution is not overly long, it reminds everyone of what has been said so far in the discussion, and it gives the group a new problem to talk about that will get them back on the subject. Then the discussion grows and stays organized.

9. Don't talk too much If you are naturally talkative and assertive, it may also be natural for you to want to establish yourself in the group by talking, joking, or even showing off. Curb this tendency so that everyone gets an equal chance to participate. If someone else dominates the discussion day after day without contributing much, complain privately to the professor after class.

10. Participate even when you're scared If you are naturally shy, it may also be natural for you to withdraw from a discussion or to appear bored or even angry that you are there. Curb these tendencies by forcing yourself to raise your hand and say something in every discussion class as soon as you can. It's always easier to speak again after you have once spoken. No one but you will know that you are nervous. Soon you will be caught up in the ideas being discussed, and you will lose your self-consciousness. You will then enjoy class more and learn more, too, because you will be actively involved in what is going on. An incidental advantage, not to be ignored, is that class time will go faster if you are involved in the discussion.

There are some students who are very shy in a class discussion. If you fall into this category, make certain you listen well, formulate your own silent contributions, and at least make brief, occasional remarks. Contribute short answers like "yes" and "no," and raise your hand when the professor asks how many agree or disagree. Ask a question occasionally. Don't worry about not contributing more than this. You will still learn from the class if you are listening and thinking. The ones who don't learn are the ones who tune out completely.

At the Very Least . . .

This chapter has dealt with the ideal way for participating in class discussion. If you can't follow all of the suggestions every day, *at the very least* do this much:

1. Prepare for discussion even if only a few minutes.
2. Listen and think.
3. Make brief contributions.
4. Take some notes.

SUMMARY
Read and think about the material to be discussed before you go to class discussions. In the discussion itself begin to concentrate immediately, be an active listener, stay objective, take some notes, stay on the subject, ask some questions, give examples and observations, summarize blocks of material when

you can, and keep the discussion moving. Don't dominate the discussion. Say something in each discussion class at the first opportunity. Concentrate and pay attention in discussions whether or not you continue to contribute much.

Exercises

A. Self-Evaluation

Use the following list to evaluate the quality of your participation in class discussion. Do you:

		Yes	No
1.	Prepare ahead of time and go into a discussion with a full mind?	___	___
2.	Bring your textbook and refer to it when it is the subject of discussion?	___	___
3.	Focus your mind immediately and keep it focused?	___	___
4.	Take notes on the main points?	___	___
5.	Stay objective and listen even when you disagree?	___	___
6.	Think about what you hear, relate it to what you know, and anticipate what is coming next?	___	___
7.	Stay on the subject when you speak?	___	___
8.	Ask questions occasionally?	___	___
9.	Contribute examples and observations?	___	___
10.	Avoid relating long, boring personal experiences?	___	___
11.	Avoid dominating the discussion?	___	___
12.	Contribute something, even if only a "yes" or "no" answer, to every discussion?	___	___
13.	Refer to what other people have said when you talk, so that they know you have heard and thought about their contributions?	___	___
14.	Get people back on the subject when necessary by summarizing what has been said and then introduce a new point?	___	___
15.	Break the sound barrier in each class as soon as you have the opportunity and something to say?	___	___
16.	Use the discussion techniques described in this chapter in all discussions outside of the classroom, including those with friends, on the job, or in meetings?	___	___

If you have marked more than two of the above as No, you need to work to improve your participation in class discussion. If you have marked all but questions 13 and 14 as Yes, you are learning in discussion classes even if you do not say a great deal.

B. Application of Skills

Prepare five questions for discussion on Chapter 5. Put the best questions on the board. From these the class should select two or three questions to discuss. The authors of the questions should lead the discussion.

C. Topics for Your Learning Journal

1. How do you usually feel when you are a member of a group and expected to contribute to class discussion? Confident? Scared? Bored? Hostile? Why do you feel this way?
2. Are you satisfied or dissatisfied with your usual performance in class discussion? Pinpoint why you are satisfied or dissatisfied. Jot down some ideas that will help you become a better discussion participant.

PART THREE

Reading the Textbook

7

Surveying Books and Chapters

When you have finished reading this chapter, you will know the following:

1. How understanding a book or chapter's organization can help you learn and remember material from it.
2. Some purposes for surveying.
3. How to survey a textbook.
4. How to survey a chapter.

The Organization of Books and Chapters

Authors work out a plan for arranging the material in their books and chapters before they begin to write. If authors did not consciously arrange their materials in a logical order according to a well-thought-out plan, you would have trouble reading, understanding, and remembering their ideas. Look, for example, at the following list of ideas that have not been placed in any particular order:

Those who erase the blackboard too soon
Those who use big words
No pictures or examples
Problems students face
Difficult textbooks

Five or six steps, none of which are clear
Not enough time to do them well
Assignments
Some professors
Long paragraphs

This list is not only confusing; it would also be difficult to remember if you had to memorize it. The ideas, presented as they are, do not follow a logical sequence. Furthermore, there is no quickly apparent relationship between one item and the next.

The human mind has a natural tendency to want to see relationships among items in a list of this sort. Look at the list a few minutes, and you will begin to see that some of the items on it can be grouped together under headings. Furthermore, there is one item on the list that can, in fact, be used as the title. Once you have discovered the title, the other items fall into a pattern:

Problems Students Face
  I. Difficult textbooks
      A. Long paragraphs
      B. No pictures or examples
  II. Some professors
      A. Those who use big words
      B. Those who erase the blackboard too soon
  III. Assignments
      A. Five or six steps, none of which are clear
      B. Not enough time to do them well

Compare this list with the original, jumbled list. Arranged as it now is in a logical sequence, it is easier to read, to understand, and to remember.

When the authors of your textbooks organize their ideas in logical sequence, they are deliberately making it easier for you to understand and remember those ideas. They organize their ideas in outlines, but they do not write in outline form. It would be dull if they did. Part of the challenge and pleasure of reading is learning to discover the author's original outline.

Aids to Discovering Organization

1. The table of contents The major aid to discovery of the outline of a book is the table of contents. It lists, in sequence, the major ideas and, sometimes, the subideas to be developed. Materials in your textbooks are usually arranged either according to topics or in chronological order. When they are arranged topically, you need to discover *what topics will be covered,* to consider *why the author has placed them in that particular order,* and to note *how much space is alloted each topic.* When they are arranged chronologically, as are history books, biographies, diaries, books of directions, and lab manuals, you need to know *how much time is covered* and *where the breaks in time occur.*

Take a look at the table of contents of this book. Notice that the major topics are placed in a roughly chronological order. You get started first (Part 1). Then you normally go to class (Part 2) before you read the textbook (Part 3). And you usually do both before you take exams (Part 4) and do written assignments (Part 5). Under each of these major headings are the chapter titles, which represent the topics to be developed under each of the major headings. This book, then, combines the chronological and topical patterns of organization.

2. The introduction Another way authors sometimes clarify the organization of their books is to insert a brief explanation of their organizational plan in the preface or introduction. This explanation, plus the outline of the book provided by the table of contents, will usually give you a pretty clear idea of the way the book has been put together. Sometimes, in fact, the table of contents doesn't really make sense to you until you have read the accompanying explanation in the introductory material.

An explanation of the organizational plan is only one type of useful information that may be found in the prefatory material. Other information, some or all of which may be found in introductions and prefaces, includes (1) the author's explanation of why he or she wrote the book; (2) a list of the topics to be developed in the book; (3) a statement of personal bias if the book takes up a controversial topic; (4) why this approach to the material was used, particularly if it is different from the traditional approach; (5) a description of the author's background and authority for writing on the subject; (6) definitions of key terminology; (7) background information to help you place the information in the book in a context; and (8) useful tips on how to read the book.

Take a look now at the Preface to this book and make a list of the items of information that will help you read and use it. Be selective in your reading of any preface and skip over information, such as the acknowledgements, that will not help you with your reading of the book itself.

3. Familiar chapter organization Authors very often clarify the organization of chapters by using familiar organizational schemes. It will help you at the outset to recognize that most chapters and many lectures and essays have three main parts: (1) an introduction, (2) a main body, and (3) a summary or conclusion:

Part I	Introduction. May include — purpose sentence — list of main points
Part II	Main Body — development of material mentioned in introduction
Part III	Summary (restatement of main ideas) or Conclusion (emphasis on a major idea)

You will need to notice these three parts of the chapter when you make a survey.

Why Survey Books and Chapters?

The main object of surveying both books and chapters is to learn something about them immediately so that it will be easier to read later. Surveying a **book** provides you with an outline of its contents and overall plan as well as the purpose and slant of the author. You will, furthermore, discover any special aids that have been included in the book to help you read it.

There are other reasons why you might survey a book, however, besides simply preparing yourself to read it. You should survey any unfamiliar book before you take research material from it. For example, you wouldn't want to quote an author's opinion about capital punishment before you were sufficiently familiar with the book to know whether the author supports it or opposes it.

You might also survey a book when you are in a bookstore and are in doubt about whether or not to buy it. Fifteen minutes or less of surveying will usually yield enough information to enable you to make a decision.

There are some books that you should know something about in order to be a liberally educated person. Yet you may not want to read them all the way through. For instance, Gibbon's *Decline and Fall of the Roman Empire* is a work you have perhaps heard mentioned many times and feel you should know something about. A half hour's surveying may yield as much information as you are ever likely to need about this particular work.

There are also several reasons for surveying a **chapter.** First, surveying provides you with a *quick mental outline* of the main ideas. When you have such an outline in mind, you will be able to *concentrate* better when you start to read because you will know, in its broad outline, what the chapter is about. Another reason to survey is for review. After you have read an extremely complicated chapter or article, it may be a jumble in your mind. Go back and survey it to get its organization clear. Then you will be able to understand and remember the main points for a much longer period of time. You should always survey journal or magazine articles before you take research materials from them. In order to quote responsibly and intelligently you need to know something about the context of a quotation you wish to use. Finally, whenever you are about to listen to a professor lecture on a chapter, or when you are about to take a test on a book or a chapter that you have not read, survey it. Surveying, naturally, will not be as effective as reading, but it will be a lot better than not looking at the material at all.

How to Survey a Book

Begin each semester by surveying your textbooks. Here is a six-step method for surveying a book in about fifteen or twenty minutes.

1. Read the title Surveying demands intense concentration. Begin to concentrate by focusing on what the title suggests about the book's contents and the author's approach to the subject. Titles like *The Movies* or *Crystals* explicitly name the subject. *The Picture History of Astronomy* tells you both the subject *and* that the author will develop it chronologically and through pictures. The title *Art in Movement* is suggestive rather than explicit. Nevertheless, you should stop for a moment to consider what the title might suggest about the contents of the book. Consider, also, how much you already know about the subject.

2. Read the table of contents Look for the topics the author will cover. Notice the order in which they will be presented. Take long enough to understand, if possible, not only the order, but also the relationships among the various topics of the book and the reasons they are presented in the order they are.

3. Read all introductory and prefatory material Move through this material rather quickly, looking for information that will help you read the book. Whenever you encounter useful information, slow down and read it carefully. By the time you have examined the introductory material and the table of contents, you should have in mind an ordered list of the topics to be developed in the book. You also want to gather as much other information as will help you do a more informed job of reading.

4. Look at the first and last chapters of the book They are important. In the first chapter authors often introduce the subject in greater detail. In the last chapter they either summarize what has been said or present material that they particularly want to emphasize. Look at the *titles* of these chapters, read the *introductory paragraphs*, the *final paragraphs,* and look at the *headings* and *subheadings*.

5. Read the first paragraph of each of the other chapters This will give you a sense of the progression of ideas in the book and will show how they are introduced in each new chapter.

6. Look to see if there is an index, glossary, or any other built-in aids to help you read the book An index, placed at the back of the book, gives an alphabetical listing of the topics covered in the book. It is more complete than the table of contents. Use it to find material on a specific topic or to check whether or not specific topics are covered. A glossary, also usually located at the back of the book, provides definitions of the technical terms used by the author. These definitions can also be placed in the margins or at the bottom of textbook pages. Other aids might include charts, diagrams, or special tables of information.

Notice what you have now accomplished:

1. You know what the book is about and what major topics will be discussed in it.

2. You know something about the author's purpose for writing the book and how you should read it.
3. You know what kinds of special reading aids have been supplied to make your job easier.

How to Survey a Chapter

It should take you only five to ten minutes to survey a chapter. There are six steps involved:

1. Read the title It tells you the subject of the chapter. Prepare to read by recalling what you already know about the subject to help you understand the new material. If the title communicates nothing (for example, "Dividends, Retained Earnings, and Treasury Stock," a chapter title in an accounting text), find out something about it immediately by looking up unfamiliar terms in the glossary, a dictionary, or the index. Then make a note or two by the title so that you will know, in a broad sense, what the chapter is about.

2. Read the chapter objectives and introduction Textbook authors frequently begin chapters with learning goals or objectives that serve the same purpose as an introduction. The list of items at the beginning of each chapter in this book is an example. Read such information carefully. These lists highlight the main ideas of each chapter for you before you begin to read. If there are no objectives, read the first paragraph and look for a purpose sentence. Underline it so that you will know the author's main intent in the chapter. Also, look for a list of the main points to be covered in the chapter. Get them well in mind by underlining them and numbering them.

3. Read the summary (if there is one) A summary is a restatement of the most important ideas in the chapter. It should be read first as a preview of those ideas and last as a final check on your understanding of the ideas.

Lists of terms and/or questions at the end of a chapter can perform the same function as a summary: They can highlight the important ideas in the chapter. Read them as a preview and as a final check just as you would a summary. If there is no summary or exercises, read the concluding paragraph to see which idea the author particularly emphasizes by placing it last.

4. Read the headings and subheadings Read all headings and subheadings, which may be set in boldface type or in italics, to help you discover the main ideas and their sequence. If there are no headings, read the first sentence in each paragraph to help you discover the main ideas in the chapter. Number and letter the headings and subheadings as in an outline, so that you can see the relative importance of ideas. Create chunks by drawing lines across the page at the end of each section. Write one or two question words next to each heading and think about how it develops the subject of the chapter.

Examples of such words are *who, what, when, where, why, how much, how many, how significant,* and *what does this have to do with the subject of this chapter?* Now try to recite the main topic of each main chunk. You should be able to hold seven or eight of these topics in your short-term memory while you read. As you read, focus on the headings and questions again. They will help you keep your mind on the subject as you read.

    5. Study all visual materials. As you leaf through the chapter stop to study all tables, graphs, diagrams, pictures, and their titles or captions. Such study can help introduce you to many of the major ideas in the chapter.

    6. Circle or box in all of the words or terms that are in italics or bold type These are key terms you will need to know in order to understand the author. Identify them now and make them stand out from the text so that your eyes will not slide over them later as you read.

    Notice what you have now accomplished:

1. You have divided a difficult whole into manageable parts.
2. You have thought about the meaning of each part by itself and also how it relates to the whole.
3. You have in mind the main topics and the order in which they will be discussed.
4. You have recalled what you already know about the subject.
5. You have a rudimentary understanding of the organization of the chapter. You are now ready to read to fill in the details and to get a fuller understanding of both the parts and the whole.

At the Very Least . . .

This chapter has dealt with the ideal way for surveying books and chapters. If you can't follow all of the suggestions every day, *at the very least* do this much:

1. Survey new textbooks at the beginning of each semester. At least look at the table of contents and the introduction, and examine a typical chapter to see how it is organized.
2. Before reading a chapter, at least read the title and headings, and notice visuals, key vocabulary, and the material at the end.
3. Remember that it is better to survey reading material before a class or exam than not to look at the material at all.

SUMMARY

Perceiving the organization and format of a book or chapter before you read it can help you understand and remember it later. It is also useful to know something about the purpose and slant of the author. Get this information by surveying. For books, read the title, study the table of contents, read the preface or introduction, look at the first and last chapters, read the introductions to the other chapters, and look for any built-in aids to help you read the book. Surveying is useful not only for textbooks but for any book you have neither the time nor, perhaps, the desire to read clear through. For chapters or articles, read the title, read the introduction, read the summary, read heads and subheads and jot down question words, study visual material such as pictures or graphs, and circle or box in important words and concepts. The object of surveying a chapter is to get an idea of the subject matter and organization and to fill your mind with as many questions about that subject matter as possible before you begin to read. Surveying books and chapters involves slightly different procedures. Memorize the steps to avoid confusion.

Surveying in Brief

These lists are intended to help you memorize the steps in surveying *books* and *chapters*. Noting the similarities and differences in the two processes will help you learn them.

Surveying Books
1. Read the title
2. Read the table of contents
3. Read the preface or introduction
4. Survey the first and last chapters
5. Read the first paragraph of each of the other chapters
6. Look for built-in reading aids

Surveying Chapters or Articles
1. Read the title
2. Read the introduction
3. Read the summary
4. Read the headings and subheadings
5. Study all visual materials
6. Circle key terms

Exercises

A. Chapter Questions

1. Why do most authors organize their ideas before they write?
    a. They don't. They organize as they write.
    b. To make it easier for the reader to understand and remember their ideas.
    c. To help them discover what they want to write about.
    d. To make certain they will have enough to write about.
2. What part of a book should you study first in order to discover an outline of the ideas in it? _____
3. Which is characteristic of books that are arranged topically?

a. They are the easiest to read.
b. They have the simplest type of organization.
c. They have all of the material in the book organized under specific topics.
d. They must have their topics in a particular order.
4. Which is *not* a step used in surveying a chapter?
a. Read the introduction.
b. Read the summary.
c. Study the table of contents.
d. Study visual materials.
5. Which of the following are listed as reasons for surveying? (More than one answer is correct.)
a. To become familiar with the contents of a book or chapter before you read it.
b. To become familiar with an article before you quote from it.
c. To review a chapter that has been difficult to understand.
d. To use when you have run out of time and can't read an assignment in detail.
e. To use as a substitute for reading long assignments.

B. Application of Skills

1. Look at your textbooks and see if one of them is organized topically. Which one is it? _____

2. Is one of your textbooks organized chronologically? Which one? _____

_____

3. Use the following survey sheet to help you survey this book or one of your other textbooks.

Survey Sheet for a Book

1. What is the title? _____
2. What do you already know about the subject as stated in the title?

_____

3. Read the table of contents and list the major divisions or parts in the book. _____

_____

4. Is the book organized chronologically, topically, or does it follow some other organizational plan? _____

_____

5. Read the introduction and preface. Who is the author, and what do you now know about him or her? Mention qualifications and background,

biases, unusual approach, or any other information about the author that you find in the introduction or preface. _____

_____

6. List three items of useful information in the preface or introduction that will help you read the book. _____

_____

7. Look at the first chapter of the book. What is its title? _____

_____

8. Look at the last chapter of the book. What is its title? _____

_____

Why do you think the author decided to place it last? _____

_____

9. Read the first paragraph of each of the other chapters. List three major ideas that are developed in the book. _____

_____

10. Look to see if there is an index, glossary, or other built-in aids to help you read the book. List these aids. _____

_____

11. Assume that you have just been asked to describe this book in fifty words or less. What would you say about it?

4. Use the following survey sheet to help you survey the next chapter or a chapter in one of your other textbooks.

Survey Sheet for a Chapter

1. What is the title? _____

2. What do you already know about it? _____

_____

3. Are there chapter objectives or learning goals? Yes ____ No ____.

   If yes, what are they? _____

_____

4. Read the first paragraph. Is it an introductory paragraph? Yes _____
   No _____. If yes, what information does it give about the subject and
   organization of the chapter? _____

   _____

   _____

5. Is there a summary? Yes _____ No _____. If yes, list three important
   items that are described in the chapter. _____

   _____

6. List all other material that follows the summary. _____

   _____

7. If there is no summary or other ending material, such as questions or
   exercises, read the last paragraph. What idea is emphasized in this final

   paragraph? _____

   _____

8. Read the headings and subheadings or the first sentence of each paragraph. Briefly list the main ideas that are developed in the chapter.

   _____

9. Look at all visual materials in the chapter. What ideas in the chapter do

   these materials illustrate? _____

   _____

10. Circle or box important key words or terms and list three of them.

    _____

    _____

11. Assume that you have just been asked to describe this chapter in fifty
    words or less. What would you say about it?

C. Topics for Your Learning Journal

Survey all of the textbooks you will be reading this semester. Record your
reaction to each of them. Which will be easiest and most interesting to read?
Which will be most difficult? What can you do to make the difficult textbooks
more interesting to read?

8

Reading the Chapter

When you have finished reading this chapter, you will know:

1. How to recognize general and specific ideas.
2. How to read paragraphs and sections of material.
3. How to recognize and read main ideas, subideas, supporting material, and transitions.
4. How to read a difficult textbook assignment.

Read in Units and Know What to Expect

Surveying helps you divide a chapter into units. You will read with better comprehension and concentration if you then read in units. Concentrate first on understanding paragraphs and then longer sections. This will help you later to understand the whole. You will read units more easily if you have some idea of what to expect as you read.

You can expect every unit, whether it is a paragraph, a section, or even a whole chapter, to have a subject and to contain both *general* and *specific* ideas about that subject. You can, furthermore, expect to be able to tell the difference between the general information, or *main ideas,* and the specific information, or *subideas,* and the *supporting material.* You can also expect to encounter various kinds of *transitional material* that either explain relationships among ideas or change the subject entirely. The rest of this chapter will heighten your awareness of the back-and-forth movement between *general* and *specific ideas* and will help you learn to locate *main ideas, subideas, supporting material,* and *transitions* in everything you read. Being able to recognize a main idea, spot a transition, and understand how subideas and supporting material develop main ideas will enable you to see how ideas are developed and related to each other and will enhance your comprehension of what you read.

Recognizing General and Specific Ideas

In all communication writers and speakers present a general idea, support that idea with specific materials, and then go on to present another general idea. Figure 8.1 shows a conventional outline that visually represents such a pattern of ideas.

The most general ideas on the diagram in the figure are the main ideas. They are outlined at the Roman numeral level (I, II). Read the two main ideas. Notice that by themselves they are abstract, almost meaningless. They don't tell you much. Subideas are more specific than main ideas and are outlined at the A, B level. They tell you more about the main idea. Many paragraphs contain only a main idea and one or more subideas. When this is the case, it may be the author's judgment that no additional explanation is required. Or the author may continue development of the idea in the same or in later paragraphs with any of various types of specific supporting material. Such material is entered on an outline at levels 1, 2 or a, b.

The pattern just described can be found both in paragraphs and in longer sections of material that contain more than one paragraph. The authors of the textbook *Biology* begin a paragraph: "Adaptations may be broadly classed as anatomical, physiological or behavioral."[1] This sentence, which states the general subject of the paragraph, is called the topic sentence. You have, at this point in your reading, a topic in mind (three types of adaptations) that provides you with a mental focus for reading the remainder of the paragraph. You need to know more, however, before you will understand or remember the idea and terms presented in this sentence. These authors continue their paragraph with material at the subidea level: "Anatomical adaptations are those involving the physical structure of the organism." The authors are aware that the reader may

[1] Karen Arms and Pamela S. Camp, *Biology* (New York: Holt, Rinehart and Winston, 1979), p. 9.

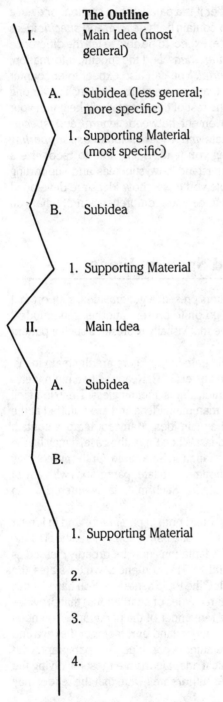

The Outline	Example
I. Main Idea (most general)	In college you will have to develop two types of vocabulary.
A. Subidea (less general; more specific)	One of these is a specialized vocabulary
1. Supporting Material (most specific)	You will need to know what your biology professor means by *D.N.A.*
B. Subidea	You will also need to develop a general vocabulary.
1. Supporting Material	If someone calls you *ingenuous*, you will know what he means.
II. Main Idea	You will need a method for developing both types of vocabulary.
A. Subidea	A method that won't work is reading and listening to new words without looking them up.
B.	A method that will work better has four steps. Let's look at these specific steps.
1. Supporting Material	Consciously *look* for a word you don't know.
2.	Record the *context* in which you found it.
3.	*Look it up* in the glossary or dictionary.
4.	*Associate* it with something familiar to you.

Figure 8.1   A typical pattern of ideas

still not understand what is meant by *anatomical adaptations*. Thus, the next sentence in the paragraph is an example: "For instance, a penguin's flippers are an anatomical adaptation that permits it to swim." They continue the paragraph with another subidea followed by examples. Look at the entire paragraph and notice how it moves from the general main idea in the topic sentence to the subidea level, then to the supporting material level, and then back again to the subidea and supporting material levels:

Adaptations may be broadly classed as anatomical, ⎫ ◀ *Topic sentence –*
physiological, or behavioral. **Anatomical** adaptations ⎭   *main idea*
are those involving the physical structure of the orga-   ◀ *Subidea*
nism. For instance, a penguin's flippers are an anatomi-   ◀ *Example*
cal adaptation that permits it to swim. An organism's
physiology is all of the internal workings of its body: ◀ *Subidea*
the biochemistry of its cells and the processes that allow
it to digest food, exchange gases, excrete wastes, reproduce, move, and sense and respond to the outside
world. An example of an extreme physiological adaptation to temperature is seen in the ability of the blue-
green bacterium *Synechococcus* to live in hot springs at
temperatures up to 80°C (175°F), which would destroy
all biochemical activity in most other organisms. An
example of an impressive **behavioral** adaptation is the
ability of a kangaroo rat to eat the leaves of the desert   *Examples*
saltbush. No other animal can eat this plant since its
leaves are full of salt crystals. The kangaroo rat flakes off
the salt-filled outer layer of the leaf with its front teeth,
and then eats the salt-free inner part. This ability to
prepare its food is a behavioral adaptation that allows
the kangaroo rat to eat a food which is completely
unavailable to other animals.[2]

The main ideas, subideas, and supporting material in this paragraph are stated briefly and compactly. If the authors had decided that more explanation was needed, they could have added further examples and explanations and divided this material into three or four paragraphs. The pattern of ideas would remain the same whether explained briefly in a paragraph or expanded into a larger section of material.

Adequate comprehension of any textbook paragraph, section, or chapter requires an understanding of both main ideas and details. As you read, both the general and specific material becomes interrelated in your mind until you are finally able to say or write what the chapter is about by describing both its broadest ideas and its most specific details. To help you achieve such comprehension, it is useful at this point to think separately about how to locate *main ideas, subideas, supporting material,* and *transitions.*

[2] Ibid.

Locating Main Ideas

One way to discover the main idea in the material you are reading, is to stop at the end of a paragraph or section of material and ask yourself, "What was most of this paragraph or section about?" The answer to that question will help you discover the main idea in that unit of material.

Another way to discover main ideas is to locate topic sentences. The topic sentence is usually a general statement that gives control and direction to the rest of the paragraph or section by stating what it will be about. It is most often placed at or near the beginning of a paragraph or section unit so that you will have an idea to which you can relate the more specific material that follows. Topic sentences may also, however, be located in the middle or at the end of a unit of material. Or, there may not be a topic sentence at all. In this last case, you will usually be able to locate a phrase or to come up with a sentence of your own that states what most of the material is about.

The following are some examples of topic sentences. Notice that in each case a main idea is introduced but that you will need more information in order to understand it in detail.

> The problem of preserving peace is the most serious and most urgent problem that moral philosophy has to deal with.[3]

> Symbols, formulas, and equations are used in chemistry to convey ideas quickly and concisely.[4]

> The question of what holds a community together has interested sociologists and political scientists since the early 1920s.[5]

a. Locating Main Ideas in Paragraphs

Read the next paragraph that comes from a chemistry textbook and locate and underline the topic sentence. What is this paragraph about? Jot the main idea in the margin.

> Atoms can unite (bond together) to form molecules. A **molecule** is the smallest particle of an element or a compound that can have a stable existence in the close presence of like molecules. One or more of the same kind of atom can make a molecule of an element. For example, two atoms of hydrogen will bond together to form a molecule of ordinary hydrogen, and eight sulfur atoms will form a single molecule. Subscripts in a chemical formula show the number of atoms involved: H_2 means a hydrogen molecule is composed of two atoms, and S_8 means a sulfur

[3] Gerald Runkle, *Ethics. An Examination of Contemporary Moral Problems* (New York: Holt, Rinehart and Winston, 1982), p. 441.

[4] Mark M. Jones, David O. Johnston, John F. Netterville, and James L. Wood, *Chemistry, Man, and Society*, 4th ed. (Philadelphia: Saunders College Publishing, 1983), p. 12.

[5] James E. Grunig and Todd Hunt, *Managing Public Relations* (New York: Holt, Rinehart and Winston, 1984), p. 272.

molecule is composed of eight atoms. The noble gases, such as helium, He, have monatomic molecules (monatomic = one atom).[6]

You are correct if you decided that the first sentence in this paragraph is the topic sentence. It introduces the main idea that molecules are made up of atoms. The rest of the paragraph explains and gives examples to prove and clarify this idea.

Now look at another paragraph that comes from a political science textbook. Until you read the paragraph carefully, you might think that the first sentence is the topic sentence. There is, however, another sentence in this paragraph that states what most of it is about better than the first sentence. Locate it and underline it. Then jot the main idea in the margin.

The Constitution came into force on June 21, 1788. Two years later the first census reported a population of 3.93 million people living in 888,881 square miles. Much has changed since 1790. By 1977, the U.S. population had reached 216 million, the thirteen states had increased to fifty, and the United States had an area of 3.615 million square miles. More important, the world has become much more complex. Problems that are common today — nuclear weapons, disarmament, pollution, poverty, racial and sexual discrimination — were not major issues requiring government solutions 190 years ago. The transformation of society has understandably raised serious questions about the current political relevance of the Constitution. Some critics have even viewed the Constitution as an archaic force that is inherently undemocratic because nobody alive today ever explicitly agreed to it.[7]

In this paragraph the next-to-the-last sentence is the topic sentence. The last sentence is at the subidea level. The rest of the paragraph contains supporting material — statistics, examples, facts, and contrasts. The main idea could be stated something like this: "Constitution outdated because of changes since 1788."

b. Locating Main Ideas in Sections of Material

So far you have looked at topic sentences in paragraphs. Topic sentences are also used to state the main ideas in longer sections of material that contain more than one paragraph. All of the paragraphs that make up a section will then contribute to the development of the main idea. Read the following section of material about children's roles in household purchasing. Underline the topic sentence and jot the main idea of the section in the margin.

The role of the children in purchasing evolves as they grow older. Children's early influence is generally centered around toys to be recommended to Santa Claus

---

[6] Mark M. Jones, David O. Johnston, John T. Netterville, and James L. Wood, *Chemistry, Man, and Society,* 4th ed. (Philadelphia: Saunders College Publishing, 1983), p. 12.

[7] Robert Weissberg, *Understanding American Government* (New York: Holt, Rinehart and Winston, 1980), p. 41.

and the choice of cereal brands. Younger children are also important to marketers of fast-food restaurants. Even though the parents may decide when to eat out, the children usually select the restaurant.

    As children gain maturity, they increasingly influence their clothing purchases. One study revealed that teenagers in the thirteen to fifteen age group spend an average of $12 per week. At sixteen to nineteen, their average weekly expenditures increase to $45. Teenage boys spend most of their funds on food, soft drinks, candy, gum, recreation, hobbies, movies, records, gasoline, and car accessories. Teenage girls spend most of their money on clothes and gifts.[8,9]

You are correct if you underlined the first sentence and recognized that this section is about children's purchases from childhood through the teenage years. Note, furthermore, that the first sentence states the main idea of the section but that each of the paragraphs develops a subidea that explains more about the main idea. The section could be outlined like this:

I. **Children's purchasing power evolves**   *Main idea*

    A. Small children's purchases   *Subidea*
                                    (paragraph 1)

    B. Teenager's purchases   *Subidea*
                                      (paragraph 2)

    This section of material has an *overall main idea* that is the subject of the entire section. In reading and studying these paragraphs, you would think of them as a unit, tracing the evolution of children's purchasing power as they grow older.

    In reading a textbook chapter, you need to learn to discover the *relative* importance of ideas in the paragraphs. Determine whether each paragraph you read introduces one of the few major ideas in the chapter or whether it supports and develops one of these major ideas.

Locating Subidea and Other Types of Paragraphs

Subidea paragraphs that support and develop major ideas very often begin with sentences that indicate those paragraphs will give further information about ideas that have already been introduced. Here are a few examples of sentences that occur at the beginning of subidea paragraphs.

---

[8] "Keeping Up . . . with Youth," *Parade*, December 11, 1977, p. 20. See also James U. McNeal, "Children as Consumers: A Review," *Journal of the Academy of Marketing Science*, Fall 1979, pp. 346–59; George P. Moschis and Roy L. Moore, "Decision Making among the Young: A Socialization Perspective," *Journal of Consumer Research*, September 1979, pp. 101–12; and George P. Moschis and Gilbert A. Churchill, Jr., "An Analysis of the Adolescent Consumer," *Journal of Marketing*, Summer 1979, pp. 40–48.

[9] Louis E. Boone and David L. Kurtz, *Contemporary Marketing*, 4th ed. (New York: CBS College Publishing, 1983), p. 189.

Aside from being a pleasant daydream, this little experiment should have proved that it's possible to communicate without using words.[10]

There is a third way to deal with lawbreakers: rehabilitation.[11]

The example shows that light waves have relatively short wavelengths.[12]

Each of these sentences suggests that you look back to read what has gone before as well as to read ahead. In the first example you will want to know what "little experiment" is being described, in the second, you will want to know what the other two ways of dealing with lawbreakers are, and, in the third, you will want to go back and study the example.

Besides *main idea paragraphs* and *subidea paragraphs*, there are three other types of paragraphs that can help you locate main ideas. The *introductory paragraph*, which appears at the beginning of a chapter or major section of material, may list the main ideas that will be developed. The *summary paragraph* at the end restates the main ideas. *Transitional paragraphs* frequently summarize a main idea that has been discussed to that point and then introduce you to the next idea.

Locating Supporting Material

Supporting material is used by authors to make main ideas clear, interesting, and memorable. Sometimes it is also used to prove an idea. Supporting material is not difficult to locate because it is usually the most interesting material that you read. It is usually familiar, close to, or even a part of the experience you bring to your reading. It is also easy to imagine, visualize, or sense.

The following is a list of types of supporting material that authors use. When you learn to recognize supporting material, you won't get it confused with main ideas and subideas, and you can better comprehend what you read.

1. *Examples* or *specific instances* may be long, brief, made-up, or real.
2. *Comparisons* show how one thing is like another (Skilled college students are like unskilled college students in their common desire for a diploma).
3. *Contrasts* show how one thing differs from another (Skilled students are different from unskilled students in that they use a method to read a textbook).
4. *Statistics* and other *factual material* (75 percent of the students who do not attend class regularly receive grades of C or worse).
5. *Graphs* (Statistics can be effectively illustrated by graphs.)

[10] Ronald B. Adler, Lawrence B. Rosenfeld, and Neil Towne, *Interplay: The Process of Interpersonal Communication,* 2d ed. (New York: Holt, Rinehart and Winston, 1983), p. 112.

[11] Gerald Runkle, *Ethics: An Examination of Contemporary Moral Problems* (New York: Holt, Rinehart and Winston, 1982), p. 356.

[12] Jerry D. Wilson, *Technical College Physics* (Philadelphia: Saunders College Publishing, 1982), p. 330.

6. *Quotations* from authorities (Professor Smith admits, "I tell students they don't need to attend my class if they don't want to. I know, however, that if they don't come, they won't pass").

7. *Vivid description* (The student took the exam from the professor's hand, quickly looked at the grade, gave a sigh of relief, and began to smile).

If you do not consciously look for and recognize supporting material as you read, it is easy to commit a very common reading (and listening) error—you remember items of supporting material and either never notice or forget the main idea these items were meant to support. The reason this error is so common is that supporting material stands out more. When you encounter supporting material, look to see what main idea it supports. Total and accurate comprehension requires that you locate both types of material as well as understand their relation to each other.

Locating Transitions

Authors (and speakers) use transitions to indicate that they are moving from one major section to another or from one idea to another. The word *transition* derives from the Latin word *transire,* which means *to go across.* A transition quite literally takes you from one idea "across" to the next. You might think of transitions as signposts that signal where the narrative has been and where it is going next.

Besides signaling a change of subject, transitions are also used by authors to emphasize main ideas so that they are easier for readers to spot. Sometimes transitions also state relationships between ideas (such as "These are the problems the student faced; now, how did he solve them?" or "What was the result of cutting class? Just this . . ."").

The following are some examples of types of transitions used by college textbook writers and by other writers and speakers as well.

1. Heading and subheadings   Headings and subheadings fulfill two of the functions of the transition. They show you that the author is moving from one idea to another by marking a break in the text. Furthermore, they emphasize the main idea of the coming section by stating that idea.

2. Preoutlines or advanced organizers   Preoutlines, also called advanced organizers, may be used to set out the pattern of ideas in an entire selection, or in the next two or three paragraphs. Here is an example of a preoutline used at the beginning of a chapter about calculators. It not only states the main ideas in the chapter, it also mentions how calculators will be dealt with in future chapters.

In this chapter, we begin by looking at some of the general features of scientific calculators (Section 1.1). Then we will consider how some of the simpler arithmetical operations are carried out with a calculator (Sections 1.2 – 1.6). This chapter concludes with a brief discussion of a few of the things that a calculator will *not* do for you. In later chapters, we will see how a calculator can be used to deal with exponential numbers (Chapter 4) or to find logarithms and antilogarithms (Chapter 5).[13]

Preoutlining provides you with a mental outline of the material you are about to read and helps you anticipate what the author might say. Stop and number the ideas in a preoutline (try it in the example above) and then skim ahead to see where the discussion of each of the ideas begins and ends.

3. Enumeration with or without a key phrase Enumeration (signaled by such words as *first, second, third; one, another; finally* or *last*) is often used to separate and emphasize items in a list of ideas. It can also be used with a key phrase to identify the subject of a list ("The first *way in which college differs from high school is* . . ."). Such transitions will help you mentally list items as you read. Be sure you also assign a heading to each list.

4. Connective paragraph transitions Entire paragraphs may function as transitions by separating and stating the relationship between two major sections or two chapters. The paragraph below functions as a transition from one main idea to the next in a textbook on communication.

> So far we've talked about how becoming a better listener can help you to understand other people more often and more clearly. If you use the skills presented so far, you should be rewarded by communicating far more accurately with others every day. But there's another way in which listening can improve your relationships. Strange as it may sound, you can often help other people solve their own problems simply by learning to listen — actively and with concern.[14]

5. Internal summaries Writers and, even more often, speakers pause occasionally within the main body of their material to restate several main ideas. Read such sections carefully, noticing exactly what is being summarized and how important it is in the overall material. When you have finished reading the summary, get set for a new idea.

6. Transitional words and phrases By recognizing the following words and phrases as transitional, you will follow the author's train of thought more easily.

a. *Next, soon, after, later, after a time,* or *much later* signal a change in time. *At another place, near, above, beneath,* or *on the other side* signal a change

---

[13] William L. Masterton and Emil J. Slowinski, *Mathematical Preparation for General Chemistry,* 2d ed. (Philadelphia: Saunders College Publishing, 1982), p. 1.

[14] Ronald B. Adler, Lawrence B. Rosenfeld, and Neil Towne, *Interplay: The Process of Interpersonal Communication,* 2d ed. (New York: Holt, Rinehart and Winston, 1983), p. 159.

in place. When you read such transitions, move mentally with the author to another time or place.
b. *At the other extreme, consequently, the result of all this, by contrast, in comparison,* and *on the contrary* are used to separate ideas as well as to state the relationships between them.
c. *Let us now turn, today I want to talk about, the purpose of this chapter,* and *one . . . another* all signal that a new idea is about to be introduced and that you should shift your attention to what will be the new subject.
d. *For example, for instance, to quote, to illustrate,* and *to be specific* take you from the main idea or the subidea level to the specific supporting material level in a paragraph or series of paragraphs.
e. *In conclusion, to summarize, finally,* or *let me end with* all signal that you are about to be presented with a concluding point or a restatement of main ideas.

7. Paragraph linking   Paragraph linking involves the repetition of words and phrases, usually in the topic sentences, to lead smoothly from the ideas in one paragraph to another. Here is an example from a psychology text. The repeated words and phrases that link the ideas from one paragraph to the next have been underlined. Notice how they help you keep your mind on the subject by emphasizing it:

Eustress

In an interview with Hans Selye, published in the March 1978 issue of *Psychology Today,* the man who "invented" the concept of physiological stress talks at length about **eustress,** or "good" stress.

According to Selye, not all stress is bad. We shouldn't try to avoid all stress, for that would be impossible. Rather, we should recognize what our typical response is to stress—and then try to adjust our lifestyles to take advantage of what that typical response is.

Selye believes that some of us are what he calls "turtles"—that is, we prefer peace, quiet, and a tranquil environment. Others of us are "racehorses," who thrive on a vigorous, fast-paced way of life. The optimum amount of stress we may require to function best is what Selye calls *eustress.*[15]

Why Notice Transitions?

Becoming adept at spotting transitional material is one of the best ways to speed up your textbook reading and improve your comprehension. Whenever you spot a transition, you should slow down and read it well. It will map out the ideas to come. You can usually then read through those ideas more rapidly. As you read, use the transitions to help you form a mental outline of ideas. Then, jot

---

[15] James V. McConnell, *Understanding Human Behavior,* 4th ed. (New York: Holt, Rinehart and Winston, 1982), p. 315.

those ideas in brief outline form in the margin of your book. Once you see the outline written out, you will be able to understand and remember what you have read more easily.

How to Read a Difficult Textbook Assignment

Everything you read is a fusion of main ideas and subideas, supporting material, and transitions. If you can now recognize these four types of material, then you have the basic skills necessary to tackle any reading assignment, no matter how difficult it may at first seem. The only other major aid to comprehension you will need is a dictionary or glossary to help you with the unfamiliar words and concepts.

Some assignments will seem particularly difficult when the ideas and vocabulary are new and unfamiliar. Read such assignments through to the end. Draw a line next to the passages that you do not understand and circle the words you do not know. But keep reading. Take some risks and guess occasionally at the meaning. When you reach the end of the chapter, go back and look up the meanings of the words that you still do not know and reread the difficult passages to see if you now understand them better. Finally, reread the entire chapter. As you read, pay attention to the back-and-forth movement between general and specific ideas. Read transitions to help you locate the most important ideas. Notice also how these ideas are developed and explained with subideas and supporting material. Taking some notes while you read will also help your comprehension and concentration. The next chapter will explain how.

At the Very Least . . .

This chapter has dealt with the ideal way for reading a chapter. If you can't follow all of the suggestions every day, *at the very least* do this much:

1. Look for topic sentences both in paragraphs and longer sections of material.
2. Note the repeated movement from general ideas to specific material.
3. Mentally connect supporting materials to the main ideas they support.
4. Use transitions to help you locate the main ideas and understand their organization.

SUMMARY
Survey to understand the overall organization of a chapter. Then read to locate main ideas and details. As you read a textbook, your mind will constantly be switching from general statements, which mean little by themselves, to the details and explanations

that accompany them. In a single chapter not all of the ideas in all of the paragraphs are of equal importance. An author usually introduces a major idea and then spends several paragraphs developing it. Your job as a reader is to discover which ideas are the major ones in the chapter, to locate where they are introduced, and to understand the kinds and purposes of the materials that are used to develop them. Learn to differentiate main ideas from subideas and supporting material so that your focus of attention will not be diverted from the major line of thought. Learn to recognize transitions so that you will know when an author is switching the discussion from one idea to another. Recognizing transitions also helps you understand relationships among ideas and makes it easier for you to form mental outlines as you read. Read difficult chapters the first time through to the end. Then reread, paying attention to the main ideas and how they are developed.

Exercises

A. Chapter Exercises

1. To better understand how writers and speakers move from the general to the specific, unscramble the items below and write them in the blanks. Write the main idea, the subideas, and the supporting material to show what you would expect if you were to read this paragraph in its original form.

    _3_ There may be four hundred other students with you in the class.
    _1_ In college you will have to take lecture notes.
    _4_ The professor will seem impersonal and far away.
    _2_ One place you will have to take these notes is in the large lecture hall.
    _5_ You will have to work hard to get good notes.

    I. _In college you will have to take lecture_
       A. _One place you will have to take these notes is in the large lecture hall_
          1. _There may be four hundred other students with you in class_
          2. _The professor will seem impersonal and far away_
       B. _You will have to work hard to get good notes_

2. Which of the following is the best example of a topic sentence that introduces a new unit of material?
   a. Look back at the last exercise in order to understand this principle better.
   b. Math and language, for example, should be studied daily.
   c. Another subject that requires regular study is biology.
   d. All subjects do not need to be studied in exactly the same way.
3. Match the types of paragraphs with their descriptions.

   1. ____D____ subidea paragraph

   2. ____C____ main idea paragraph

   3. ____B____ introductory paragraph

   4. ____A____ summary paragraph

   5. ____E____ transitional paragraph

   a. Restates the main ideas.
   b. May list the main ideas that are to be discussed.
   c. Presents a major idea and tells more about it.
   d. Supports and develops a main idea stated in a previous paragraph.
   e. Concludes the discussion of one idea and opens discussion of the next idea.
4. Which of the following are kinds of supporting material? Circle the correct answers.
   a. examples
   b. subideas
   c. statistics
   d. main ideas
   e. quotations
   f. vivid description
   g. comparisons and contrasts
   h. pictures and graphs
5. Test your understanding of the specialized vocabulary in this chapter. Match the following types of transitions with descriptions of how they make main ideas more clear.

   a. internal summaries
   b. preoutlines
   c. heads and subheads
   d. enumeration and key phrases
   e. connective transitions

   1. number and identify items in a list
   2. link two major sections of material
   3. restate main ideas in the middle of a chapter or lecture
   4. set off main ideas from the text
   5. list ahead of time what is to be discussed

B. Application of Skills

Before you begin to read the following section of material from a marketing textbook, look at the title and answer these questions.

1. What do you already know about this topic? _____

economic reasons

2. What are two questions you could ask about this topic? _____

Why?   What -percentage?

Now read the material and answer the remaining questions at the end.

Why Women Work

1. At the beginning of the twentieth century, only one woman in five worked outside the home. By 1985, more than 51 percent of the nation's adult female population will be part of the work force. Three of five married women work.

2.   For most women, the primary motivation for working is economic. William Lazer and John E. Smallwood report that 90 percent of working mothers in sales, clerical, and blue-collar occupations and 71 percent of women employed in the professions worked for economic reasons.[16] Although unprecedented increases in the cost of living have forced the emergence of many two-income households, equal employment legislation has also played a role in stimulating increased female employment by opening job opportunities in traditionally male-dominated occupations.

3.   A third factor in stimulating female employment is the social acceptability of women with careers. Women are increasingly represented in the college classroom, and account for almost half the students receiving college degrees each year. Approximately one-third of all students in the nation's Master of Business Administration (MBA) degree programs are women. Such academic preparation helps to move well-qualified women into middle- and top-management positions.[17]

3. What is this section of material about? ___ *reasons for women*

working

4. Indicate the main idea and the subideas on the outline.

I. ___ *Why Women Work* ___

A. ~~Percentages~~ *Economic Reasons* ___

[16] William Lazer and John E. Smallwood, "The Changing Demographics of Women," *Journal of Marketing*, July 1977, p. 19. See also Mary Joyce, "The Professional Woman: A Potential Market Segment for Retailers," *Journal of Retailing*, Summer 1978, pp. 59–70; and Suzanne H. McCall, "Meet the 'Workwife,'" *Journal of Marketing*, July 1977, pp. 55–65.

[17] Louis E. Boone and David L. Kurtz, *Contemporary Marketing*, 4th ed. (New York: CBS College Publishing, 1983), pp. 115–16.

B. _Economic Reasons_   _Social Acceptability_

C. _Social Acceptability_   _Equal Employment_

5. Is there a topic sentence that states the main idea or did you have to infer

the topic after reading the section? _infer the topic sentence_
If there is a topic sentence, underline it.

6. What type of paragraph is paragraph 1?
  a. introductory
  b. summary
  c. main idea
  d. subidea
  e. transitional

7. What type of paragraph is paragraph 3?
  a. introductory
  b. summary
  c. main idea
  d. subidea
  e. transitional

8. In the first column below list three bits of supporting material. Identify their types in the second column.

Supporting material   **Type**

a. _3 of 5 women work_   _STATISTICS_

b. _women to men employment_   _Comparisons_

c. _7% women wanted economic_   _quotations_

9. What type of transition is used? _Narrated_

List the three transitional words or phrases that helped you locate the three subideas.

a. _Primary_

b. _Although_

c. _Third Factor_

Before you begin to read the following section of material from an ethics textbook, look at the title and answer these questions:

10. What do you already know about this topic? _____

_____

11. What are two questions you could ask about this topic? _____

_____

Now, read the material and answer the remaining questions at the end.

The Values of an Athletic Program

1. The athletic program is expected to bring publicity to the school, attract students, foster student unity, and encourage alumni giving. "The traditional American affinity for sports and reverence for education combined to form an unbeatable attraction. Every Saturday, educated sports heroes performed for an appreciative audience. Fanfare, combat, and hope of victory assured public identification and loyalty."[18] The most conspicuous function of athletic competition is to enhance the image of the institution.

2.   We may want to question the appropriateness of this public relations function. Publicity is not necessarily a good thing. If this publicity is scandalous (or even negative), the school has not benefited. There is a university on the banks of the river that sponsors a "Mississippi River Festival" every summer. The "festival," for the most part, consists of rock concerts. Unfortunately, since these festivals have been plagued with violence, rape, drunkenness, drug dealing and usage, and automobile accidents, the publicity has been counter to the kind the festival was designed to produce. With respect to athletics, the public is finding out more about the universities than they would wish.

3.   Does athletic fame attract students? Perhaps it does, but it would be a stupid engineering student who chose Georgia Tech over M.I.T. because of its athletic prowess. Some serious students are "turned off" by a school's athletic record. Notre Dame, which has an excellent academic program, is unjustly viewed by many as simply a sports mill. Does athletic success foster student unity? Here again, the case is not clear. Often students' enthusiasm is tepid in comparison with that of alumni and townspeople—especially when they have difficulty in getting tickets, have to pay a handsome price, or are relegated to seats in the end zone.

4.   Does athletic success arouse public support? Do legislators tend to reward successful schools with more generous appropriations? They may have done so in the past, but today, with the closer scrutiny of tax dollars, there are signs that funds will be more available for activities closer to the heart of the academic mission.[19] What about alumni giving? Certainly alumni will contribute money for *athletic* purposes in the case of a few successful universities, but the overall record for alumni giving exhibits no such pattern. A careful study of 138 "big-time" schools from 1960 to 1976 yielded this conclusion: "Our statistical analysis has revealed that there is simply no relationship between success or failure in football and basketball and in-

---

[18] Christine H. B. Grant, "Institutional Autonomy and Intercollegiate Athletics," *Educational Record* (Fall 1979), p. 411.

[19] If taypayers are now willing to reduce expenditures for athletics and other "frills" in the high schools, they may do so also for universities—even the "successful" ones.

creases and decreases in alumni giving."[20] "In the final analysis, however, the lack of any relationship between success in athletics and increased alumni giving probably matters a great deal less than the fact that so many people believe that such a relationship exists."[21,22]

12. What is this section of material about? _____

_____

13. Indicate the main idea and the subideas on the outline.

I. _____

    A. _____

    B. _____

    C. _____

    D. _____

14. Is there a topic sentence that states the main idea of this section or did you

have to infer the topic after reading the section? _____
If there is a topic sentence, underline it.

15. In the first column below list four bits of supporting material in this section. Identify their types in the second column.

Supporting material   *Types*

    a. _____   _____

    b. _____   _____

    c. _____   _____

    d. _____   _____

16. What type of transition is used in this section? _____

_____

List five sentences that function as transitions.

    a. _____

    b. _____

[20] Lee Sigelman and Robert Carter, "Win One for the Giver? Alumni Giving and Big-Time College Sports," *Social Science Quarterly*, September 1979, p. 293.

[21] Ibid. See Frederick Klein, "Bring in the Brawn: Recruiting of Athletes Intensifies as Colleges Seek Prestige, Money," *Wall Street Journal*, April 11, 1967, p. 1.

[22] Gerald Runkle, *Ethics: An Examination of Contemporary Moral Problems* (New York: Holt, Rinehart and Winston, 1982), pp. 280–81.

c. _____

d. _____

e. _____

17. Locate a section of material in one of your textbooks in which a major idea in the chapter is introduced in the first paragraph and developed in two, three, or more paragraphs. It may be introduced by a heading or subheading as in the exercises above. State the main idea of this material and then list, in phrases only, five or six items of information used to develop this idea.

18. Copy a paragraph from one of your textbooks that contains a good example of a transition and underline it. Include enough context so that it will be clear why the material you have underlined is transitional. It may be a heading or subheading, preoutline, enumeration, connective transition, or internal summary. Describe the function of the transition you have located. Does it emphasize and separate ideas? Which ideas? Does it state a relationship between ideas? What is it?

19. Copy a paragraph from one of your textbooks that contains supporting material and underline it. Answer the questions: What type of supporting material is it? What main idea does it support?

20. Locate an example of paragraph linking in one of your textbooks. The passage should be two or three paragraphs long. Copy the passage and underline the repeated words and phrases that link the ideas from one paragraph to the next. Write a brief outline of the ideas in the passage.

C. Topics for Your Learning Journal

1. Further clarify your understanding of main ideas and supporting materials by writing a paragraph or section of material yourself. Choose one of the following topic sentences, make a list of at least three items of supporting materials to develop it, and write the paragraph or section.

   a. My neighborhood has changed (very little or a great deal) in the time I have lived there.

   b. High school, for me, was (the best or the worst) experience in my life.

2. Clarify your understanding of transitions by writing a three- to five-paragraph essay on a topic of your own choice in which you use three different kinds of transitions described in this chapter. Begin by making an outline of ideas. Then use transitions to make your ideas clear to your reader. Label each transition you use in the margin of your paper.

   If you have trouble thinking of a topic, use one of the following as a "starter" sentence.

   a. There are some major differences between high school and college.

   b. It is not always easy to work and go to college.

9

Taking
Reading Notes

When you have finished reading this chapter, you will know how to do the following:

1. Mark a textbook so that you can review it quickly for a discussion or an exam.
2. Take reading notes when you do not want to write in the book.
3. Take reading notes on math textbooks and imaginative literature.

How to Mark a Textbook

The biggest problem with textbook reading is to keep your mind on it. One good way to keep your mind on it is to take reading notes. Note taking also prepares you for class. Read the textbook and take notes on it before you go to class to make the most efficient use of class time.

In Chapter 1 you were shown a method for marking a textbook to help you concentrate. It was suggested that you follow the example in that chapter by continuing to mark this book, as well as your other textbooks, in the way demonstrated. If you have followed that advice, you should be good at marking textbooks by now.

If you have not followed that advice, this chapter will review the system presented in Chapter 1 and provide you with additional suggestions to make that system work effectively for you.

One advantage of owning your own textbooks is that you can make notes in the books themselves. Marking in the text takes less time than other note-taking systems. Your notes are next to the text and can be brief—a mere reminder of what is in the text itself. Preexam review is fast and efficient. You can quickly and easily find passages during class discussions. You can maintain a high level of concentration while you read.

Plan to keep a well-marked textbook instead of selling it after the course is over. Such a book is a valuable reference tool that you can use in future classes

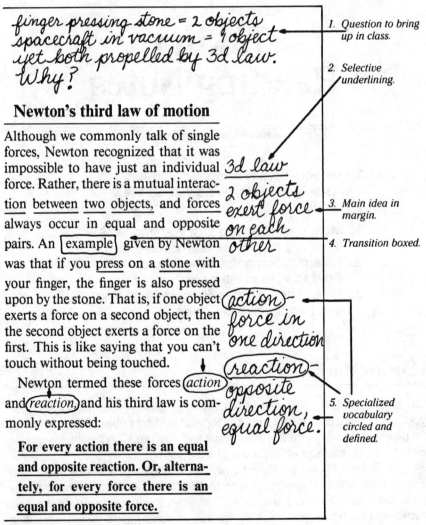

Figure 9.1 How to mark a section of a textbook chapter

This third law may seem contradictory to the second law, but it is not. The <u>second law</u> is concerned with a <u>force</u> *cf. 2d law* acting on a given body of mass *m* and its <u>resulting acceleration</u>. The force pair of the third law acts *on different bodies.* Consider the third law in the familiar context of firing a <u>rifle</u>. . . . When the charge explodes, the <u>bullet</u> is accelerated down the barrel. It is acted upon by a force (an action), as evidenced by its acceleration. The reaction force acts on the rifle and it is accelerated in the opposite direction, which gives rise to the backward recoil or "kick" of the rifle. According to Newton's third law

$$F_{action}' = -F_{reaction}$$

ex.

6. *Examples identified.*

where the minus sign indicates the opposite direction to the action. . . .

Newton's third law is incorporated in many applications. . . . Exhaust gases from burned fuel are accelerated out the back of <u>rocket and jet aircraft engines,</u> and the rockets and aircraft are accelerated forward by the reactive forces.[1]

ex.

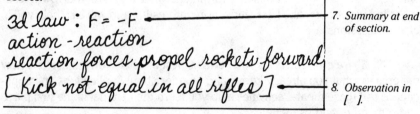

3d law : F = −F
action − reaction
reaction forces propel rockets forward
[Kick not equal in all rifles]

7. *Summary at end of section.*

8. *Observation in [ ].*

Figure 9.1 (cont.) How to mark a section of a textbook chapter

and refer to after you leave college to refresh your memory. The following ten suggestions will help you mark your textbooks so that they will be of immediate and lasting value to you. Figure 9.1 illustrates a section of a textbook that has been marked according to these recommendations.

[1] Jerry D. Wilson, *Technical College Physics* (Philadelphia: Saunders College Publishing, 1982), pp. 97–99.

1. Underline selectively Make conscious decisions about what to underline, and limit the amount. Too much underlining is difficult to study later and often becomes a mechanical process that requires little thought. Underline only the words and phrases that most accurately state what a chunk of material is mainly about.

2. Box transitions and number important ideas Making transitions stand out in the text helps you locate the ideas. When you box such words as *first, second, for example, next,* or *finally,* you not only locate important ideas more easily, you also see how they relate to each other.

3. Circle specialized vocabulary Write brief meanings in the margin if you need to. You will need to know this vocabulary to understand the textbook, understand the instructor, and take the exams.

4. Jot main ideas in the margin At the end of a paragraph, stop and ask yourself, "What was most of that paragraph about?" Write the answer in as few words as possible in the margin. This is an especially useful technique for short, dense assignments that are difficult to understand, such as those in philosophy, physics, or chemistry.

5. Label examples When you encounter an example, determine what main idea it exemplifies and label it. It will help you understand the main idea when you study later.

6. Write your own ideas in square brackets If you are reading actively, concentrating and understanding, you will also be thinking. Jot down the ideas that occur to you as you read either at the top or the bottom of the page and put them in [square brackets] to indicate that they are your own. Your recorded ideas will make later study more interesting and will also help you in class discussions.

7. Write questions as you read Questions help you think, relate new material to what you already know, and wonder about implications and applications. All these mental activities help you learn the material in the first place and remember and use it later.

8. Write brief summaries at the end of each section of material, and, later, at the end of chapters and the book Use the white space throughout the book to write summaries. Write them in brief phrases only. They should answer the questions "What was this about?" and "What did the author say about it?" Summarize after you have finished reading and in your own words as much as possible. Don't read and write at the same time, or you will end up with too many notes.

9. *Make outlines of obvious major ideas in the margins* Outlines are a visual representation of ideas and their relation to each other. At times obvious transitions will make the ideas in a passage stand out. When you encounter such material, write brief outlines of the ideas in the margins. Look at pages 88 and 92 in the last chapter for examples of such outlines.

10. *Make maps* Outlines force you to isolate and organize important ideas so that you can visualize them and thereby understand and remember them. Writing ideas in *map form* accomplishes the same thing. You can map major sections, chapters, or even entire books. Maps are also called "graphic post-organizers."

How to Make a Map

There are three steps in making a map.[2] First, write the subject of the material you are mapping in the middle of a piece of paper. Draw a box or a circle around it so that it stands out.

Second, locate the main ideas that support and develop the subject and write them on lines attached to the center subject.

Finally, attach enough supporting details to each of these lines so that the whole map will make sense to you when you study it later.

Figure 9.2 shows an example of a map of the ideas in the section about transitions in Chapter 8 of this book. Notice that brief phrases are written on the map to help you remember the ideas and details in the chapter. Imagine, now, that you must review this part of Chapter 8 for an exam. It would be easier to study and remember this map than it would be to reread and remember the chapter.

You may make maps in any way that helps you to see the author's pattern of ideas. Other mapping schemes might look like those in Figure 9.3. The map in Figure 9.4 helps you associate the laws of motion with an object in motion. This literal visualization can make these laws even easier to remember than a more abstract map.

To make effective maps it is essential that you first read and understand the material. Do not map it until you do understand it. Sometimes you will finish reading with a clear pattern of ideas in mind, and you will be able to map them with no trouble. Other times, especially when there are no obvious transitions and when there is no introduction or summary, it is difficult to identify the pattern of ideas. In this latter case skim back through the material and pick out six or seven ideas that seem to be main points in the material and map them with their details. Do your best to map what appears to be important. Include

[2] For a more detailed explanation of mapping see the essay by M. Buckly Hanf, "Mapping: A Technique for Translating Reading into Thinking," *Journal of Reading XIV* (January 1971): 225–30. See also John R. Hayes, *The Complete Problem Solver* (Philadelphia: The Franklin Institute Press, 1981), pp. 114–16.

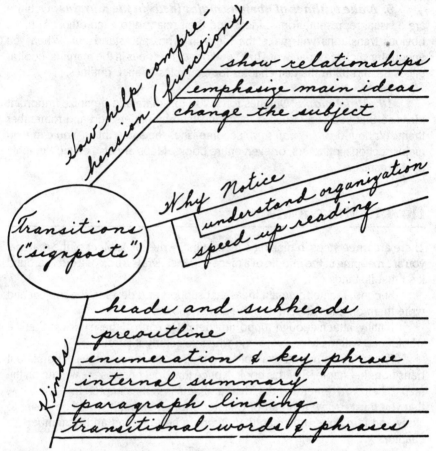

Figure 9.2   A map of ideas in the section about transitions in Chapter 8

examples if the material is hard to understand and remember without them. Use maps to study for exams. Other types of exam study sheets will be explained later in Chapter 11.

What If You Don't Want to Write in Your Books?

Some students can't bring themselves to write in books. Either they want to resell them, or they have been so conditioned in school not to write in books that it is nearly impossible for them to do so. It is *best* to mark in your books if you own them and can bring yourself to do so.

If you can't or won't mark in your text, however, there is an alternative. Buy five-by-eight note cards, and when you finish reading the chapter, summarize or map it on the card instead of in the book itself. Take notes in your own words and phrases. Get down main ideas and a few important details. As a

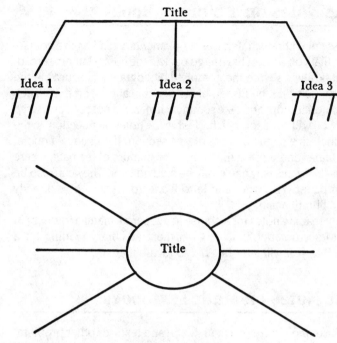

Figure 9.3   Other schemes for mapping

rough guide, spend only 10 – 20 percent of your time taking notes and 80 – 90 percent of your time reading. Then insert these cards in the book at the beginning of each chapter. Paper-clip them in if you are afraid of losing them. When you need to review or find a passage quickly, use these cards to help you. They will work nearly as well as marking in the book itself.

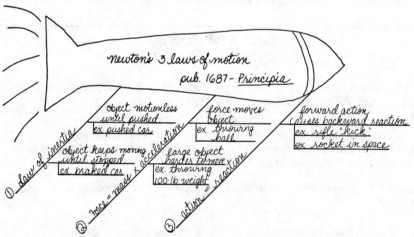

Figure 9.4   A map that uses a visual image to make abstract ideas easier to remember

How to Take Notes on a Library Book

If you have been assigned library material as supplementary reading in a course, take a few notes so that you will not have to go back to the library later to reread. In taking these notes, always write the complete bibliographical source at the top of the page—author, title, publisher, place of publication, and date. Then read a section of material, stop, and take summary notes. Do not read and write simultaneously, or you will write too much. Next to the notes on a section, in the margin, write the inclusive page numbers of that section. If you copy a quote, put it in quotation marks and write in the margin the number of the page where you found it. Notes taken this way can easily be studied later. They can also be used in a research paper. You will be able to work from your notes directly without visiting the library again.

File the library reading notes for a course in a separate manilla folder or in a separate part of your notebook. Then label them as library reading for a specific course so that you will later be able to locate them easily.

How to Take Notes on Math Textbooks[3]

You will probably take more notes on math texts (and texts for other problem-solving courses, such as chemistry and physics), than you will for any other sort of textbook. Plan to take notes as you read on the following three types of material:

1. On five-by-eight cards write strategies for solving problems. Some textbook authors occasionally provide such strategies that can be copied exactly (see Figure 9.5). If the author of your math text does not provide explicit strategies, you will need to construct your own. The examples are the best place to look when constructing strategies. These strategy cards need to contain a

---

BASIC PRINCIPLES FOR
SOLVING INEQUALITIES

Performing any one of the following operations on an inequality produces an inequality with the same solutions as the original inequality.

1. Add or subtract the same quantity from both sides of the inequality.
2. Multiply or divide both sides of the inequality by a *positive* quantity.
3. Multiply or divide both sides of the inequality by a *negative* quantity and *reverse the direction of the inequality.*[4]

Figure 9.5 A strategy card (Information supplied by textbook author—copy exactly)

[3] Adapted from material prepared by William J. Dodge.

[4] Thomas W. Hungerford, Richard Mercer, and Sybil R. Barrier, *Precalculus Mathematics* (Philadelphia: Saunders College Publishing, 1980), p. 21.

Solving Radical Equations

1. Rewrite the eq. so that a single radical is isolated on one side of the eq.
2. If the isolated radical is $\sqrt[p]{\cdots}$, raise both sides to the pth power (to eliminate the radical)
3. Simplify the new eq. If radicals remain, go to 1; otherwise solve as usual.
4. Check answers in original equations! (critical for radical eq.)

Figure 9.6   A strategy card constructed by a student

title and a list of the steps used to solve a particular type of problem. Figure 9.6, for example, shows a strategy card for solving radical equations. In most cases, the strategy card will contain a verbal description of how some particular problems are solved.

2. You will also find it useful to write math rules, laws, or theorems on *fact cards*. These facts must be learned word for word. It is easier to learn them when they are on cards that you can carry around with you or tack up over your desk or some other place where you will see them frequently. Figure 9.7

Fraction Facts

$$\frac{a}{b} = a/b = a \div b \quad \text{``a divided by b''}$$

$$b = 0 \text{ is forbidden} \quad \frac{0}{b} = 0 \quad \frac{b}{b} = 1$$

$$-\frac{a}{b} = \frac{-a}{b} = \frac{a}{-b}$$

$$\frac{a}{b} \pm \frac{c}{d} = \frac{a \cdot d \pm b \cdot c}{b \cdot d} \quad \text{``invert \& multiply''}$$

$$\frac{a}{b} \cdot \frac{c}{d} = \frac{a \cdot c}{b \cdot d} \qquad \frac{a}{b} \div \frac{c}{d} = \frac{a}{b} \cdot \frac{d}{c} \quad \frac{a \cdot d}{b \cdot c}$$

Figure 9.7   A fact card, example 1

shows the type of information that you might put on a card for an algebra course in which the topic is fractions.

In mathematics many theorems are stated, "If (hypothesis), then (conclusion)." To understand such a statement, carefully examine the hypothesis to see the significance of each part of it. Remember that the *theorem only applies* when the *entire hypothesis is satisfied*. It may help you to understand a theorem if you rephrase it in equivalent form: "If not (conclusion), then not (hypothesis)." Figure 9.8 provides examples of fact cards using these ideas.

3. The third type of information you should extract and write out as you read your math texts are the *specialized vocabulary and symbols along with their definitions*. Like the theorems, these definitions must be learned exactly, word for word. You will probably find it easiest to learn these words, symbols, and definitions if you write them out on sheets of paper, as in Figure 9.9.

It will help you to understand and remember the definition in Figure 9.9 if you ask yourself what the negation or denial of the definition says: "What are nonequivalent equations or inequalities?" If you have difficulty answering this question, ask your instructor. This is a good type of question to ask during class discussion.

Now take a final look at Figure 9.9. When you have written a definition, read it to make certain that you understand every word. If you have forgotten what "solution sets" are, for example, look up that term immediately in the index or on your definition list so that the definition you have just written will make complete sense to you.

Strategy cards, fact cards, and definition lists are the permanent notes you will be taking as you read math textbooks. These do not represent the only

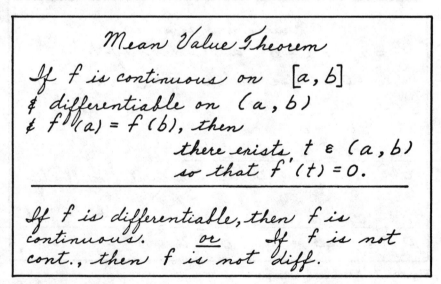

Figure 9.8 A fact card, example 2

sum	*any expansion that has the form A + B (addition)*
term or addend	*either of A or B in the above sum*
equivalent equations or inequalities	*two equations or inequalities in one variable are equivalent if they have equal solution sets.*

Figure 9.9 A definition sheet for mathematics

writing you will need to do as you read math, however. Keep plenty of scratch paper handy as you read so that you can write out in detail examples of problems you encounter in the text. It is always tempting simply to read through these examples. Try writing them out, however, and you may find that you don't understand them as well as you thought. If the author says, "It is clear that . . . ," make certain that it is *clear to you* and write down *why* it is clear by referring to a definition or theorem. Any questions you can answer about examples as you rewrite them should be brought up during class discussion. Remember that the examples are models of what you will be doing later in the exercise set. If you don't learn how to do the models first, you will have trouble working the exercises later.

When you work the exercises at the end of the chapter, you will then use all of the notes you have written out: strategy cards, fact cards, definition sheets, and the examples of the problems you have copied. All this material will help you understand how to do the final exercise set. Always do these assigned exercises whether or not they are graded each time by your instructor.

How to Take Notes on Novels, Short Stories, Plays, and Poems

You can mark up all literature you read. Summarize novels, for example, chapter by chapter. Five or six phrases jotted down at the end of each chapter to identify plot action and characters make review an easy and quick affair. If you have any major insights or ideas of your own about the novel, write them out in some detail on the flyleaves of the book. They may turn out to be good topics for future papers or points to bring up in class discussion.

You can take notes on short stories and plays, too. Mark the main characters and their identifying characteristics as they are introduced, write a plot summary at the end, and then try to write out the major themes or ideas developed.

Take more thorough notes on a poem. Go through the poem first and underline all words and allusions that you do not understand. Look them up and write in the meanings. Then read the poem again and write, in your own words, a summary of what you think it says. Take these summaries to class and listen to the professor discuss the poems. During class discussion, you may find that you have badly misread a poem; if so, change your summary on the spot so that it won't mislead you when you are studying for an exam.

At the Very Least . . .

This chapter has dealt with the ideal way for taking reading notes. If you can't follow all of the suggestions every day, *at the very least* do this much:

1. Underline selectively.
2. Write brief summaries at the end of major sections of material.

SUMMARY

Taking reading notes will help you improve your concentration while doing reading assignments. Reading notes will also help you locate important material later in class discussion and in exam preparation. Underline selectively, box transitions, circle specialized vocabulary, write your own ideas and questions at the top of the page, jot down main ideas in the margin, and write summaries at the end of each section and at the end of the chapter. Finish your note-taking activities by making outlines or maps of the main points. If you do not want to write in the book, take summary notes or make maps on five-by-eight cards and insert them at the beginning of chapters. Take summary notes on library books as well. Record the page numbers on which the material was found and a complete bibliographical reference in case you ever want to use these notes in writing a research paper. Adjust your note-taking system somewhat to make it work well for mathematics textbooks and imaginative literature.

Exercises

A. Chapter Questions

1. When should you read a textbook assignment?
   a. Just before an exam.
   b. After the class in which it is discussed.
   c. Before the class in which it is discussed.

   d. During the class in which it is discussed.

2. What was recommended about underlining in the text?

   a. Underline most of the text to help you concentrate.

   b. Highlight the text with a yellow marker.

   c. Avoid underlining and take summary notes instead.

   d. Make decisions about what to underline and do so sparingly.

3. What is a map as it was described in this chapter?

   a. A visual representation of a body of land.

   b. A visual representation of the ideas in a section or chapter.

   c. An outline of the important ideas.

   d. A summary of the important ideas.

4. How do you take notes on library books?

   a. Summarize sections of material.

   b. Never write in the book.

   c. Include page numbers and bibliographical information.

   d. All of the above.

5. Circle all of the answers below that would help you take notes on math
   textbooks.

   a. Write on cards step-by-step strategies for solving problems.

   b. Write rules, laws, and theorems on cards.

   c. Write definitions of symbols and specialized vocabulary on sheets of
      paper.

   d. Underline extensively.

B. Application of Skills

1. Read and mark the following section of material from a marketing textbook
according to the recommendations made in this chapter. This section contains obvious transitions that emphasize the main ideas. Box them. Circle
specialized vocabulary. Underline selectively. Summarize the main ideas, in
phrases only, in the blank space provided at the end. Remember that your
summary should answer the questions "What was this passage about?" and
"What did the author say about it?"

Collecting Primary Data

   1. The Survey Method Some information cannot be obtained through observation. The researcher must ask questions in order to obtain information on
attitudes, motives, and opinions. The most widely used approach to collecting
primary data is the survey method. Three kinds of surveys exist: telephone,
mail, and personal interviews.

   2. *Telephone interviews* are inexpensive and fast for obtaining small quanti-
ties of relatively impersonal information. Since many firms have leased WATS
services (telephone company services that allow businesses to make unlim-
ited long-distance calls for a fixed rate per state or region), a call to the most
distant state costs no more than an across-town interview.[5]

   [5] William Lyons and Robert F. Durant, "Interviewer Costs Associated with the Use of
Random Digit Dialing in Large Area Samples," *Journal of Marketing,* Summer 1980, pp. 65–69.

3.   Telephone interviews account for an estimated 55 to 60 percent of all primary marketing research. A national survey revealed that one woman in five had been interviewed by telephone in 1980, as compared with one in seven only two years earlier. The percentage of men who had participated in telephone interviews had grown from one in ten in 1978 to one in seven in 1980.[6] Telephone interviews are, however, limited to simple, clearly worded questions. Also it is extremely difficult to obtain information on respondents' personal characteristics, and the survey may be prejudiced by the omission of households without phones or with unlisted numbers.

4.   One survey reported that alphabetical listings in telephone directories excluded one-third of blacks with telephones and one-fourth of large-city dwellers and that they underrepresented service workers and separated and divorced persons. In addition, the mobility of the population creates problems in choosing names from telephone directories. As a result, a number of telephone interviewers have resorted to using digits selected at random and matched to telephone prefixes in the geographic area to be sampled. This technique is designed to correct the problem of sampling those with new telephone listings and those with unlisted numbers.[7]

5.   *Mail interviews* allow the marketing researcher to conduct national studies at a reasonable cost. Whereas personal interviews with a national sample may be prohibitive in cost, the researcher can contact each potential respondent for the price of a postage stamp. Costs can be misleading, however. For example, returned questionnaires for such studies may average only 40 to 50 percent, depending on the length of the questionnaire and respondent interest. Also, some mail surveys include a coin to gain the reader's attention (such as the illustration in Figure 4.4), which further increases costs.[8] Unless additional information is obtained from nonrespondents, the results of mail interviews are likely to be biased, since there may be important differences in the characteristics of respondents and nonrespondents. For this reason, follow-up questionnaires are sometimes mailed to nonrespondents, or telephone interviews are used to gather additional information.[9]

6.   In 1980, the U.S. Bureau of the Census conducted the largest mail survey in history when it mailed census questionnaires to 80 million house-

[6] "Marketing Research Industry Survey Finds Increase in Phone Interviewing," *Marketing News*, January 9, 1981, p. 20.

[7] Reported in A. B. Blankenship, "Listed versus Unlisted Numbers in Telephone-Survey Samples," *Journal of Advertising Research*, February 1977, pp. 39–42. See also Roger Gates, Bob Brobst, and Paul Solomon, "Random Digit Dialing: A Review of Methods," in *Proceedings of the Southern Marketing Association*, New Orleans, La., November 1978, pp. 163–65; and Donald S. Tull and Gerald S. Albaum, "Bias in Random Digit-Dialed Surveys," *Public Opinion Quarterly*, Fall 1977, pp. 389–95.

[8] Stephen W. McDaniel and C. P. Rao, "The Effect of Monetary Inducement on Mailed Questionnaire Response Quality," *Journal of Marketing Research*, May 1980, pp. 265–68; and Robert A. Hansen, "A Self-Perception Interpretation of the Effect of Monetary and Nonmonetary Incentives on Mail Survey Respondent Behavior," *Journal of Marketing Research*, February 1980, pp. 77–83.

[9] Kevin F. McCrohan and Larry S. Lowe, "A Cost/Benefit Approach to Postage Used on Mail Questionnaires," *Journal of Marketing*, Winter 1981, pp. 130–33; and Jacob Hornik, "Time Cue and Time Perception Effect on Response to Mail Surveys," *Journal of Marketing Research*, May 1981, pp. 243–48.

[handwritten margin note: 1980 Census]

holds. A number of questions were raised, including the difficulties of developing an accurate population count utilizing mail questionnaires. Another sensitive subject concerned confidentiality of answers. The 85 percent response rate was a pleasant surprise to Census Bureau officials and to researchers throughout the world who rely upon mail surveys to obtain research data.

7. ***Personal interviews*** are typically the best means of obtaining detailed information, since the interviewer has the opportunity to establish rapport with each respondent and can explain confusing or vague questions. Although mail questionnaires are carefully worded and often pretested to eliminate potential misunderstandings, such misunderstandings can occur anyway. When an employee of the U.S. Department of Agriculture accidentally ran into and killed a cow with his truck, an official of the department sent the farmer an apology and a form to be filled out. The form included a space for "disposition of the dead cow." The farmer responded, "Kind and gentle."[10]

[handwritten margin note: Pers inter, "Best"]

8.   Personal interviews are slow and are the most expensive method of collecting survey data. However, their flexibility coupled with the detailed information that can be collected often offset these limitations. The refusal to be interviewed and the increasing difficulty of hiring interviewers to call on respondents at night present additional problems in utilizing this technique.[11]

WRITE SUMMARY:

[handwritten: These paragraphs explained the different types of surveys including their advantages and disadvantages. Results of other Polls were given and advice about the do's and don'ts.]

2. Map the ideas in this section of material in whatever map form you would like to use. Look back at pp. 110 and 111 to review the possibilities.

C. Topics for Your Learning Journal

1. Reflect about the ideas for taking reading notes presented in this chapter and then list each class you are taking this semester along with a description of the most appropriate and useful note-taking techniques for each of them.
2. If you haven't already, try making a map. Write an explanation of how this activity helps you learn and remember textbook material.

[10] "About That Cow," *Wall Street Journal,* June 28, 1972.

[11] Louis E. Boone and David L. Kurtz, *Contemporary Marketing,* 4th ed. (Hinsdale, Ill.: The Dryden Press, 1983), pp. 93–95, 109–110.

10

Thinking about and Remembering What You Have Read

When you have finished reading this chapter, you will know the following:

1. How your memory operates.
2. How to use some major aids to thought and memory: organizing, associating, reciting, and elaborating.
3. How to use ten additional aids to help you think and remember.
4. How to monitor your own learning.

The Problem of Forgetting and Some Solutions

By the time you have surveyed a chapter, read it, and taken notes on it, you may think that you have completed a reading assignment. You haven't quite. The material you have just read, at this point, is confined to what psychologists call your short-term memory. Information in the short-term memory decays quickly or is soon replaced by newly learned material. You will forget more than half of what you have just read within twenty-four hours and most of the rest of it within a week unless you take some immediate steps to transfer it to your long-term memory. Once material becomes a part of your long-term memory, much of it can be recalled immediately and the rest of it can be relearned comparatively quickly. The techniques described in this chapter are designed to help you transfer newly learned material to your long-term memory where it will remain for the rest of your life. It is usually of some comfort to students to learn that no one, no matter how brilliant, can remember effortlessly.

You have already been provided with some solutions to the problem of forgetting. You have learned in past chapters how to produce efficient *external memory aids* such as lecture notes, vocabulary sheets, and reading notes. Since you create these aids to memory yourself, you will be able to find your way around in them easily, looking up information that you have already forgotten. They will also be useful to you when you use *internal memory aids* to help you think about and commit to memory the information that you have written in these notes.[1]

You have already been introduced to some internal memory aids that were built into the study systems presented in preceding chapters. In Chapter 4 you were introduced to a system for lecture note taking that involves *organizing* the notes in the first place, *labeling* and *summarizing* their contents in your own words in the margins and at the end, and *reciting* their contents until you can do so from memory. In Chapter 5 you were given some systems for remembering vocabulary. It was suggested that you make vocabulary sheets and write an *association* for remembering the word in the fourth column of these sheets. It was further suggested that you *organize* related words in outlines and diagrams. In Chapter 9 you were shown how to *summarize* your reading notes and also how to *organize* them in outlines on maps in order to make them easier to think about and remember.

Organizing, associating, and *reciting* are all activities that help you think about and remember new material. This chapter will describe how you can expand your use of these, along with one other major aid to thought and memory, *elaborating*. It will also provide you with ten additional suggestions for improving your understanding and memory.

Organizing As an Aid to Memory

Information in your long-term memory is remarkably well organized in an elaborate internal filing system. New information is efficiently sorted, filed, and stored until you need it. You can store and retrieve new information more efficiently if you work to organize it first because material that goes into your memory already organized is easier to get back out. All of the study systems presented in this book that function as external aids to memory stress organization as their key feature.

---

[1] I am indebted to John R. Hayes, *The Complete Problem Solver* (Philadelphia: The Franklin Institute Press, 1981), pp. 71–111, and Laird S. Cermak, *Improving Your Memory* (New York: McGraw-Hill, 1976), for some of the ideas in this chapter.

In organizing material that you want to learn, you can group or rearrange it according to topics, by the sequence or order in which it took place, or by some established organizational pattern such as problem-solution, cause-and-effect, or even alphabetically. You can, for example, mentally list five topics, or divide the material into three blocks of time, or note that the author listed one problem and three solutions. It will be even easier to remember if you show visually how you have grouped and rearranged the material. For this purpose use *lists, charts, diagrams, outlines,* and *maps.* In the next chapter you will learn how to organize material on *study sheets* to help you prepare for exams. The process you go through to organize material to be learned forces you to select what is important, to see relationships among the bits of material, and finally, to arrange it in an order that makes sense to you. The organizing activity itself helps you to learn much of the material as you work with it. Other suggestions in this chapter for thinking and remembering will help you finish the job.

Associating the New with the Old

The more you know about a subject, the easier it is to learn more. Conversely, if you know nothing at all about a subject, it is relatively difficult to get started learning it. You automatically use the information you already have in your memory to help you interpret and understand new material. One purpose of education is to fill your memory with information on a wide variety of topics to help you learn through association during the rest of your life.

Consciously use the knowledge, experiences, and ideas that you already have in your mind to help you think about and learn new material. If you are studying a subject that is brand new to you, be patient at first. Once you start learning the new material, over a period of time it will become easier to learn more about it because you will now have something in your memory with which to associate it.

Use any familiar material to help you learn the new, including ideas, knowledge, experiences, attitudes, judgments, places, occurrences, people, songs, pictures, numbers, words. It doesn't matter how far-fetched the association is, if it helps you remember. Associate a new concept in physics with something you have observed in your life experience. Or, in a history class, memorize a few important dates such as 1066 (The Battle of Hastings), 1492 (Columbus), 1603 (King James Bible), 1776 (the American Revolution), and 1861–1865 (the American Civil War). You can then remember other historical events by associating them with these familiar dates. Example: The French Revolution occurred about 10 years *after* the American Revolution, or Queen Elizabeth died a few years *before* the publication of the King James Bible.

Reciting and Using the Active Ways of Studying

One of the best ways to improve your memory of written material is to cover up what you are trying to learn, look away, and recite it to yourself. First, however, you should have read and marked the chapter and have written brief summaries, in your own words, at the end of each section. Now, go back and read through all your underlinings, marginal notes, and summaries. This enables you to get a sense of the whole chapter. Then, immediately and, section by section, look away from the book and see if you can recite the main points in each section. As you recite, think about the material you are learning. Explain it to yourself in your own words. As often as possible, visualize what you are learning either in the form of graphs and diagrams or in actual images and pictures. Effective recitation is more than just memorizing. When done well, it results in a thorough understanding of new material.

Use the active ways of studying — speaking and writing — when you recite. Reading and listening are relatively passive, and you will not learn as well if you rely on them. Here are some ways you can use speaking and writing to help you remember more:

1. As soon as you have finished reading your assignment, get together with another member of the class. Repeat and explain to that person the main points in the chapter until you can do so from memory.
2. When you study with someone else, make sure that you do at least half of the talking. The one who mainly listens doesn't learn as much.
3. When you recite the contents of your lecture notes or a textbook chapter, do it out loud. You will remember more that way than if you read silently.
4. Whenever you encounter a new word or a difficult concept, say it out loud. Hearing it will help you to understand and remember it.
5. Write any material you are trying to memorize as many times as is necessary. It is far better to write the conjugation of a foreign-language verb three times than read it in the book ten times.

Memory experts say that you should spend more than half of the time it takes to complete a reading assignment on recitation.

Elaborating and Thinking about Newly Learned Material

Research suggests that rehearsing or reciting material over and over without thinking about it, as you might a telephone number until you finish dialing it, will keep it in your short-term memory for a time but will not result in permanent learning. You must do more than rote recitation to transfer new material to your long-term memory. Actively thinking about and elaborating on the material is required. Such mental activity can be done concurrently with reading, note taking, summarizing, organizing, associating, and reciting. Elaborating involves thinking about the implications, applications, and exceptions to what you are learning. It involves making inferences, creating images, making associations, thinking of your own examples, and asking questions about new material. It involves seeing new relationships, new combinations, or alternate solutions to problems. Here is an example of a bit of important information from a chemistry book, first, in a simple, unelaborated form:

Avogadro's number: 6.02×10^{23}

Here is the same information accompanied by some elaboration that the textbook author has supplied for you:

The Mole Concept

We mentioned earlier that an organized table of relative atomic masses can be obtained by weighing equally large numbers of atoms of different elements. . . .

The specific large number used by chemists is 6.02×10^{23}. This number, known as Avogadro's number and symbolized N, can hardly be described as being merely "large." The term "large" does not begin to describe the enormity of 10^{23}. An analogy that might suggest a picture of Avogadro's number would be to try to imagine how much of the earth's surface could be covered by 6.02×10^{23} marbles. The answer is that the entire surface of our planet could be covered by Avogadro's number of marbles to a depth of more than 50 miles!

Avogadro's number of particles is called a *mole,* from the Greek word meaning "pile" or "mound." Although Amadeo Avogadro did not experimentally determine the number that bears his name, he has been so honored because his studies of gas behavior indirectly led to the finding of the number. . . .

Avogadro's number of anything may be specified as one mole; 6.02×10^{23} atoms of lead is a mole of lead atoms; 6.02×10^{23} molecules of carbon dioxide is a mole of carbon dioxide molecules; and 6.02×10^{23} sneakers (perish the thought) is a mole of sneakers. However, the *internationally recognized standard for a mole is the number of atoms in 12.000 grams of carbon-12.* This number of atoms is, of course, Avogadro's number.[2]

Notice that the author has elaborated on Avogadro's number by helping you visualize marbles to understand how large this number is, by explaining the derivation of the word *mole* to help you remember its meaning, and by inviting you to imagine a mole of sneakers. The effect of this visualizing and associating makes this abstract number more interesting and meaningful to you and, consequently, easier to remember. Such elaboration is not usually done for you, so you need to make some effort to do it for yourself. Some of the suggestions that follow will help you think and elaborate as well as remember.

Ten More Suggestions to Help You Remember

1. Decide to remember A conscious decision to focus your attention so that you can concentrate and remember is necessary if any of the other suggestions in this chapter are to work well. You will make this decision more easily if you generate an interest in what is to be remembered. You may have

---

[2] Stanley M. Cherim and Leo E. Kallan, *Chemistry, An Introduction,* 2d ed. (Philadelphia: Saunders College Publishing, 1980), pp. 69–70.

known people who can remember batting averages but can't remember the parts of speech because they were interested in baseball and not interested in grammar. When you have to remember material that is not interesting, try to think of some reasons why it is important. Ask, "What is the value of this material to me?" and come up with a positive answer. Then, think of anything else you know that might be related that could help you understand it.

2. Visualize what you read and hear as often as possible Create mental images and draw your own pictures and diagrams in the margins of your textbook (and in your lecture notes) whenever the material lends itself to such treatment. A complex diagram or graph in a textbook is always difficult. Understand and remember complicated visual material by tracing over it with a pencil or your finger. This helps you see the parts so that the whole will make better sense to you. Visualize when you are reading imaginative literature, too. Re-create in your mind the verbal pictures that authors create. Imagine some movement or action in the pictures you create and they will be even easier to remember.

3. Make up examples of your own They will help you understand and remember difficult material. If you can't remember the difference between an igneous rock and a metamorphic rock, carry an example of each of them in your pocket until you can. Do whatever you can to make the abstract concrete and familiar.

4. List and number items to remember Words, technical terms, and foreign-language vocabulary can be listed in one column with the meanings in another. Numbering the items in a list will also help you to remember them unless, of course, there are too many. You will, for example, more easily remember six steps for surveying a textbook, ten ways to remember, and six ways to improve vocabulary than you would if these items were unnumbered. Simplify such lists so that each item is represented by one word. Select ones that are easy to remember.

5. Relate new material to what is important to you What does the material have to do with you and your past or potential experience or with what you value? Make new material even more memorable by imagining yourself personally active or involved with it. For example, if you are taking a theatre class, imagine yourself on the stage, or, if you are in a computer class, imagine yourself operating a computer. Use your senses: Imagine saying, seeing, hearing, tasting, and feeling.

6. Look for chunks, label them, and memorize the labels The short-term memory can hold five to nine items of information at one time. One way to remember a long and detailed body of material is to break it into nine or less chunks, to create simple, short labels for these chunks, and then to rehearse these labels until you know them. These labels will help you recall the details that you also need to know because details cluster around major concepts through a process of association. For example, try chunking the last four chapters on textbook reading. You could find and label seven chunks: (1) survey book; (2) survey chapter; (3) main ideas; (4) supporting material; (5) transitions; (6) notes and summaries; (7) think and remember. As you located and labeled these chunks you would also review the details that you would use to explain them. Just before an exam or class discussion, however, you would memorize the seven brief labels. They, in turn, would help you remember the details necessary to write or speak intelligently and completely about reading textbooks.

7. Make up rhymes or sentences to help you remember Rhymes can aid memory because they are easy to remember themselves. Think of the ones about "*I* before *e* except after *c*" and "Thirty days hath September." If you are not good at rhymes, you can compose sentences such as "Mary Visits Every Monday and Just Stays Until Noon Period" to help you remember the order of the planets: Mercury, Venus, Earth, Mars, Jupiter, Saturn, Uranus, Neptune, and Pluto. Beware of composing rhymes and sentences, however, that are more difficult to remember than the material itself.

8. Take off the first letter from each word in a list you want to remember and memorize the letters Make words of these letters when you can. *Nec* could help you remember the naturalistic, experimental, and correlational approaches to psychology. *TISH V.W.* can help you remember the steps in surveying a chapter — title, introduction, summary, headings, visuals, words. You will find this method of remembering especially useful if you tend to panic in exams. Having a few made-up words and letters in your mind will give you something to grab quickly when you start the exam. You will feel more sure of yourself.

9. When you want to remember something in the morning, go over it just before you fall asleep at night One reason you forget is that other things capture your attention, interfere with what you have just learned, and cause you to forget. When you are asleep, there is less of this interference. Unless you are too drowsy, the last few minutes before you go to sleep is a prime time for fixing material to be remembered in your mind.

10. Review every week or two by reading through the summaries you have written in your lecture notes and textbooks This review will help you see the sequence of ideas being developed in a book or series of lectures. Seeing this sequence will help you understand and learn the material. You may feel at times that you are overlearning material as you review it again and again during a semester. You should not worry about this. Reviewing to the point of overlearning will guarantee that material is imprinted in your long-term memory, ready to retrieve for a future class or an exam.

Monitor Your Own Learning

Think for a moment of some new reading material in the past that was important to you and that you had to struggle to understand. Examples might be reading the instructions for installing a car stereo, hooking up a video cassette recorder, cutting out and sewing an article of clothing, cooking a meal, filling out income tax returns, or completing your college application forms. In such cases you worked with the material, using a number of mental activities, until you finally understood it. You may have thought about it, reworded it, reorganized it, or associated it with what you already knew. You may have taken some notes, drawn pictures, traced over diagrams, or made simple lists out of the complicated ones. You might also have thought of some of your own examples, talked to yourself until you finally "got" it, or asked someone else to explain it to you. In other words, you worked with the material until you were confident that you understood it. Furthermore, your *internal monitoring system* let you know when you understood the instructions well enough to do the tasks.

You can consciously use similar processes and the same internal monitoring system when you read and learn textbook and lecture material. Consciously use a variety of learning processes, such as those described in this chapter, and then monitor your understanding of new material. You have finished studying when you know you can successfully report on it, discuss it, or take an exam on it. To do this successfully you will have to evaluate continuously what you need to learn, what you already know, and what you still have to learn. You can do this by testing yourself as you read and study. Ask questions and try to answer them, look away and recite important information, or stop and see if you can explain the implications or importance of a major concept. If you find that you cannot, stop immediately to think about and recite what you don't know. You can learn to become critical of your own memory and understanding and to improve on them when they seem inadequate. Such activity results in immediate and permanent learning and leads to the development of methods for further learning that will make you an educated person for life.

At the Very Least . . .

This chapter has presented some ideal ways of thinking about and remembering what you have read. If you can't follow all of the suggestions every day, *at the very least* do this much:

1. Find the organization in material you want to learn, or reorganize it yourself.
2. Look away and recite what you have just read from time to time.
3. Think about and elaborate on material you are learning. Discuss it with others.
4. Read through all of your notes occasionally as a review.

SUMMARY

Surveying, reading, and taking notes on a reading assignment do not finish the job. You also need to think about the new information and commit it to your long-term memory. Organizing, associating, reciting, and elaborating are some useful major aids to learning and remembering. Also effective are writing and speaking while you study, deciding to remember, visualizing, making up your own examples, listing and numbering, personalizing new material, chunking, making up such aids as sentences and nonsense words, going over material to be remembered just before falling asleep, and, finally, reviewing. It is also important to learn how to monitor your own learning so that you will know when you have mastered an assignment.

Exercises

A. Chapter Questions

1. Label the following activities with an *i* for *internal memory aid* or with an *e* for *external memory aid*.

   a. _____ taking lecture notes

   b. _____ making vocabulary sheets

   c. _____ associating

   d. _____ elaborating

   e. _____ visualizing

   f. _____ reciting

   g. _____ summarizing

   h. _____ outlining

   i. _____ mapping

2. Which of the following was not discussed as a major aid to thinking and remembering?
   a. Elaborating on material to be learned
   b. Reciting by either speaking or writing
   c. Organizing ideas so that you can understand them
   d. Managing time so that you have an opportunity to remember

3. What is reciting?
   a. Reading and reviewing
   b. Looking away and saying material from memory
   c. Underlining and writing summaries
   d. Reorganizing material on maps

4. How does association help you remember?
   a. It helps you see the pattern of ideas.
   b. It makes unfamiliar material easier to understand by linking it to familiar material.
   c. It helps you locate the important points.
   d. It helps you create summaries and maps.
5. Which of the following is *not* an example of elaboration?
   a. Deciding to remember
   b. Visualizing
   c. Thinking of examples
   d. Making associations and comparisons

B. Application of Skills

1. Look at the following list for fifteen seconds, one second for each item. Count "one and, two and," and so on. Now look away and write as many of these items as you can from memory.

1. evening	9. going to bed
2. writing a paper	10. studying
3. calling a friend	11. going to classes
4. talking to adviser	12. drinking coffee
5. going to work	13. eating breakfast
6. morning	14. taking a nap
7. afternoon	15. going to the library
8. watching television	

Since the short-term memory holds at the most seven to nine items, you were probably not able to remember all fifteen of these. Now organize all of the items under the three time chunks in the list. List the activities in the order in which you might do them.

morning	*afternoon*	*evening*
1. _____	1. _____	1. _____
2. _____	2. _____	2. _____
3. _____	3. _____	3. _____
4. _____	4. _____	4. _____
5. _____	5. _____	5. _____

Now visualize yourself engaged in each activity. Put some action and movement into the mental images you create. Look at the reorganized list again for fifteen seconds and again look away and see if you can now write these items from memory.

2. Think of some familiar associations to help you remember the following information from a psychology textbook.

According to a 1980 survey made by Elizabeth and Geoffrey Loftus, most people think that Long-term Memory is much like a "video recorder," and that you can *always* recover an item if you try hard enough. As the Loftuses note, though, the experimental data don't support this viewpoint. Indeed, a large number of scientific studies suggest that most of us totally forget much of what we've experienced in the past. And, judging from the bulk of the laboratory studies on this subject, once an item is lost, it's probably gone forever.[3]

3. Suppose you are studying the Constitution for a political science class. How would you elaborate on the first amendment to help you remember it?

Amendment 1. Congress shall make no law respecting an establishment of religion, or prohibiting the free exercise thereof; or abridging the freedom of speech, or of the press; or the right of the people peaceably to assemble, and to petition the Government for a redress of grievances.

4. Visualize the following descriptive material from a metallurgy textbook and draw a simple picture of it.

Hardness Testing

Everyone is familiar with denting a piece of metal by hitting it with a hammer. The hardness of a metal is tested in a similar manner. An accurately ground steel ball or diamond point is pressed into the metal sample, under a known load (or pressure), by a hardness testing machine. Gauges then measure the size of the resultant dent in the metal sample. Hardness tests are among the most important and reliable means of testing a metal for its capability of doing a certain job. The dents made in hardness testing usually do not destroy the metal part for use. Hardness is not a true or basic property of a material but, rather, it is a measure of the material's resistance to penetration or denting.[4]

5. Practice what you have learned about reading textbooks on a book from one of your other classes. First, survey the book and write a brief description of it. Then survey a chapter. Underline main points, jot main ideas in the margin, and write section summaries. Now, reread your marginal notes and summaries, and, finally, make a map of the major points, noting also some of the major details developed in the chapter. Write a paragraph of your own mental elaborations on what you have learned.

C. Topics for Your Learning Journal

1. Select an idea or item of information from another class that has particularly interested you recently. Elaborate on it in writing by relating it to what you already know, thinking of examples or comparisons, visualizing it if possible, and, finally, considering its value, significance, or usefulness.

[3] James V. McConnell, *Understanding Human Behavior,* 4th ed. (New York: Holt, Rinehart and Winston, 1983), p. 376.

[4] Donald V. Brown, *Metallurgy Basics* (New York: Delmar Publishers, 1983), p. 89.

PART FOUR
Taking Exams

11

Preparing for an Exam

When you have finished reading this chapter, you will know how to do the following:

1. Make the best use of your study time just before an exam.
2. Organize the material you have to study.
3. Make study sheets to help you prepare for an exam.
4. Use other study methods to help you prepare for an exam.

Plan Your Study Time

In the last chapter you learned a number of techniques and activities to help you think, learn, and remember. All will help you prepare for exams both during the semester and the final study session that precedes the exam. This chapter explains additional study activities that will help you organize and learn material during the final study session.

The activities described in this chapter will only work, however, if you provide time to use them. One difference between high school and college is the time and effort necessary for effective exam preparation. Instead of the hour or two you may have spent studying for a high school test, you will now need ten, twelve, or even twenty hours to prepare for a college examination. Make a Time Management Worksheet to help you plan your exam study time. Look back at page 21 for a reminder on how to do this. Allow ample time to study for each exam and then add a couple of hours for possible interruptions and distractions. Now, get off to a fast start and work to finish your studying within the time you have allotted.

How to Get Started — The Table of Contents Sheet

For most courses you will have accumulated a lot of information from several sources by exam time. You may have, for example, a stack of lecture notes, anywhere from 50 to 450 pages of marked-up textbook assignments, handouts from class, notes on library reading, returned papers and other written assignments, old exams the teacher has let you see, vocabulary sheets, notes on review sessions, and finally, some ideas and insights of your own. This is a lot of material. When you get it all together and take a good look at it, your first question will probably be, "Where do I start?"

First, go to the source of information that has been the basis of organization, or backbone, of the course. In some courses the textbook provides the organizational framework, and the lectures clarify and amplify the text. In other courses the lectures are central, and the textbook and other materials are assigned to give additional information and other points of view.

Using this prime source of information and organization together with the syllabus, if one is available, you can begin to study for an exam by making your own brief table of contents of the material on which you will be examined. Don't confuse your own table of contents with the table of contents in your textbook. You might get some ideas from the latter, but it may not name all of the topics you have covered during the semester. On your table of contents sheet you will list the major chunks of information developed in the course in the order they were presented.

Making a table of contents is a simple process that should not take you more than five or ten minutes. The purpose of it is to permit you to see all the parts of a course as an organized whole. You will also be able to see exactly what has to be studied, and you will then not omit anything. You may find that the class syllabus functions as a table of contents to the course because it lists the topics and the order in which they are covered. Rewrite the syllabus as a simple, brief list. This active reprocessing of the class topics will help you get a grasp of the course far better than simply rereading the syllabus.

Examples of table of contents sheets made by students that have proved to be effective guides for study appear as Figures 11.1, 11.2, and 11.3. Notice that all these sheets are short, containing heads and subheads only. They contain no detail. Rather, they give an overall picture of what has been presented in the course and what needs to be studied for the exam. They pave the

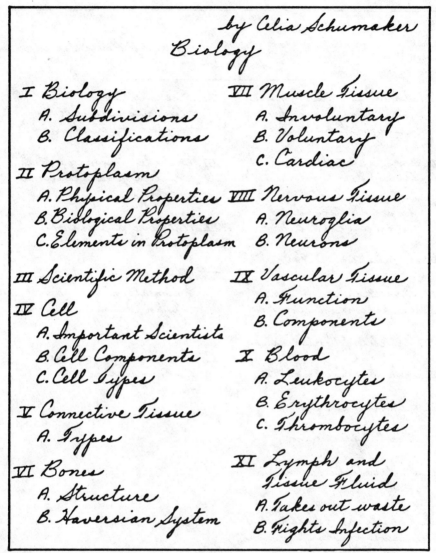

by Celia Schumaker
Biology

I Biology
  A. Subdivisions
  B. Classifications

II Protoplasm
  A. Physical Properties
  B. Biological Properties
  C. Elements in Protoplasm

III Scientific Method

IV Cell
  A. Important Scientists
  B. Cell Components
  C. Cell Types

V Connective Tissue
  A. Types

VI Bones
  A. Structure
  B. Haversian System

VII Muscle Tissue
  A. Involuntary
  B. Voluntary
  C. Cardiac

VIII Nervous Tissue
  A. Neuroglia
  B. Neurons

IX Vascular Tissue
  A. Function
  B. Components

X Blood
  A. Leukocytes
  B. Erythrocytes
  C. Thrombocytes

XI Lymph and Tissue Fluid
  A. Takes out waste
  B. Fights Infection

Figure 11.1   Example 1: Table of contents sheet for biology

way for the second and most important step in the final study process, the making of study sheets.

The Second Step—Study Sheets

The next step in studying for an exam is to make a detailed study sheet for each item listed on your table of contents. Notice on the table of contents sheets for biology, reproduced in Figure 11.1, that the sixth item is "Bones." Having made

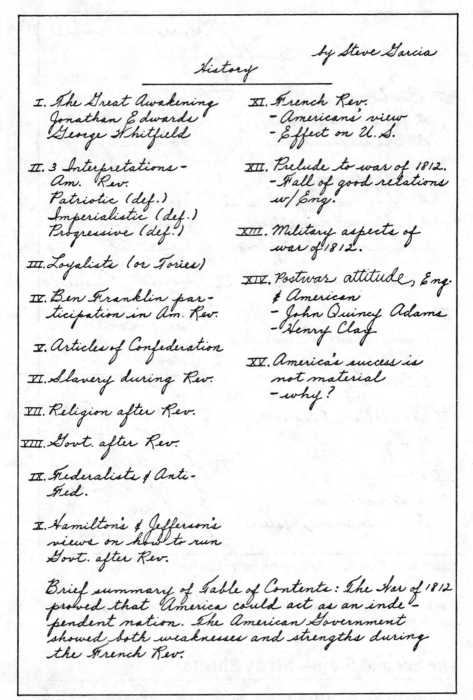

History — by Steve Garcia

I. The Great Awakening
Jonathan Edwards
George Whitfield

II. 3 Interpretations –
Am. Rev.
Patriotic (def.)
Imperialistic (def.)
Progressive (def.)

III. Loyalists (or Tories)

IV. Ben Franklin participation in Am. Rev.

V. Articles of Confederation

VI. Slavery during Rev.

VII. Religion after Rev.

VIII. Govt. after Rev.

IX. Federalists & Anti-Fed.

X. Hamilton's & Jefferson's views on how to run Govt. after Rev.

XI. French Rev.
– Americans' view
– Effect on U.S.

XII. Prelude to war of 1812.
– Fall of good relations w/ Eng.

XIII. Military aspects of war of 1812.

XIV. Postwar attitude, Eng. & American
– John Quincy Adams
– Henry Clay

XV. America's success is not material
– why?

Brief summary of Table of Contents: The War of 1812 proved that America could act as an independent nation. The American Government showed both weaknesses and strengths during the French Rev.

Figure 11.2 Example 2: Table of contents sheet for history

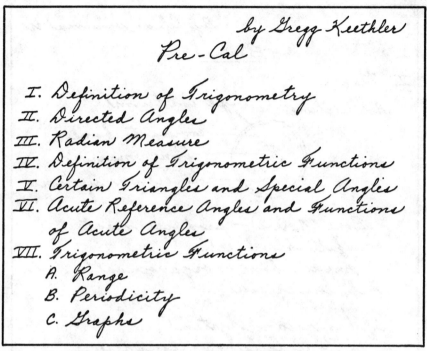

Figure 11.3   Example 3: Table of contents sheet for preparation for calculus

a quick list of the topics she wanted to study for her biology test on her table of contents sheet, this student then made study sheets for each of the topics on her list. On her "Bones" sheet (Figure 11.4) she wrote out the material about bones that she thought she should learn for the exam. Figures 11.5 and 11.6 show two other examples of detailed study sheets. Their topics are drawn from the table of contents sheets for history and for math, which you just looked at in Figures 11.2 and 11.3.

Now that you've looked at these examples, you can begin to see what characterizes good study sheets. Note first of all that they contain lots of ideas, all in *brief form*. Use a summary process, and write only enough so that when you glance at one of the words or phrases on the sheet, a host of related ideas and details will flood into your mind. If a phrase does not call forth a number of details, you may have to write a bit more about that subject in order to trigger your memory. One of the purposes of these sheets is to set the associative processes of your mind in motion.

Although the study sheets produced here are neat enough so that anyone can read them easily, yours need only be neat enough so that you can read them easily. Write big, write fast, and use only one side of a sheet of paper. You have to be able to read study sheets quickly.

Finally, *outline or map* your study sheets as much as possible. Make the main points stand out clearly by underlining or circling them. Write a list of

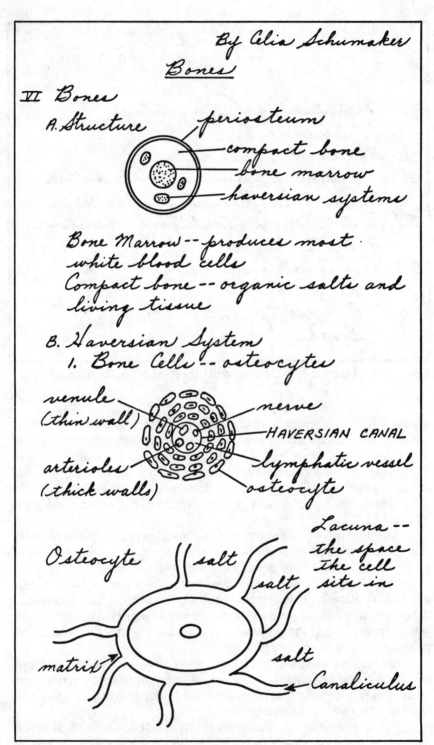

By Celia Schumaker

Bones

II Bones
  A. Structure

  periosteum
  compact bone
  bone marrow
  haversian systems

Bone Marrow -- produces most
white blood cells
Compact bone -- organic salts and
living tissue

B. Haversian System
  1. Bone Cells -- osteocytes

venule
(thin wall)

nerve

—HAVERSIAN CANAL

lymphatic vessel

arterioles
(thick walls)

osteocyte

Lacuna --
the space
the cell
sits in

Osteocyte   salt

salt

matrix

salt

Canaliculus

Figure 11.4   Example 1: A study sheet for biology

by Steve Garcia

The Great Awakening

The Great Awakening

A massive religious revival, where screaming and swooning in the aisles became common. All people are damned and there is little they can do to salvage themselves.

A. Jonathan Edwards
1. Rejected Puritans' covenant theology
2. Established Princeton & Dartmouth, 1700's
3. "Sinners in the hands of an angry God" -- famous sermon
4. He was center of Rev.
5. Sermons were against "man can save himself" theory
6. Want a religion of the "heart & senses"

B. George Whitfield -- arrives in Phil. (1739) era.
1. Methodism occurring in England
2. "Willingness to resist authority of leaders brings guilt to the people"--era of materialism
3. Clergy was hostile toward revivalists
4. Great Awakening leans toward democracy
5. Revolution splits the churches
6. Protestant churches arise in midst of Rev.
7. Revivalists had no faith in established hierarchies.

Summary: The beginning of the American Revolution along with the Great Awakening can be considered as a radical democratic movement to the left.

Figure 11.5 Example 2: A study sheet for history

items down the page and number each item. Remember that it is easier to learn and remember material when you can see it in an organized body. If it is easier for you learn from maps than from outlines, then map sections of material on your study sheets as you learned to do in Chapter 9.

Where do you get the material for study sheets? Just as you did with your table of contents, start by drawing material from the primary organizing princi-

by Gregg Keethler

<u>Acute Reference Angles and Functions of Acute Angles</u>

Definition: <u>Reference angle Ø of Θ</u> = smallest angle between terminal side of Θ and X axis.

* Theorem I: Any trig. function of an angle Θ in any quadrant is the same (except possibly for sign) as the same function of the acute reference angle Ø of Θ.

Definition of trig. functions for acute angles:

$$\sin \theta = \frac{opposite}{hypotenuse} \qquad \cos \theta = \frac{adjacent}{hypotenuse}$$

$$\tan \theta = \frac{opposite}{adjacent} \qquad \cot \theta = \frac{adjacent}{opposite}$$

$$\sec \theta = \frac{hypotenuse}{adjacent} \qquad \csc \theta = \frac{hypotenuse}{opposite}$$

Definition: If a and b are 2 angles such that $a + b = \pi/2$, then a and b are <u>complementary</u> angles.

<u>Cofunctions</u>: sine and <u>cosine</u>
tangent and <u>cotangent</u>
secant and <u>cosecant</u>

Cofunction identities: For $0 < a < \frac{1}{2}\pi$

$$\sin a = \cos (\tfrac{1}{2} \pi - a) \qquad \cos a = \sin (\tfrac{1}{2} \pi - a)$$
$$\tan a = \cot (\tfrac{1}{2} \pi - a) \qquad \cot a = \tan (\tfrac{1}{2} \pi - a)$$
$$\sec a = \csc (\tfrac{1}{2} \pi - a) \qquad \csc a = \sec (\tfrac{1}{2} \pi - a)$$

Figure 11.6 Example 3: A study sheet for preparation for calculus

ple in the course — the lectures or the textbook. Then turn to other sources for more information. But remember to keep everything organized according to the headings you have written at the top of your study sheets. The purpose of study sheets is to help you synthesize material from lectures, texts, and other sources such as notes on library books and articles, handout sheets, returned papers, and notes on review sessions. Finally, by all means add your own thoughts and insights in square brackets as they occur to you. Put down your own examples, your applications, comparisons, and diagrams so that you will be ready for those questions on the exam that ask you not only to reproduce the material you have learned, but also to tell what you *think* about it.

Making study sheets won't guarantee you success on every exam. You have to learn to make study sheets that are *complete* and that will supply you with the information you need to do well on an exam. Some students, especially those with sketchy lecture notes, make sketchy study sheets, and find when they take the exam that they don't know enough. Use your internal monitoring system to evaluate your study sheets as you make them. If they are sketchy or incomplete and you feel that they won't work, go back to the textbook or ask to look at a classmate's notes. Add information until you know the study sheet will help you learn what you need to know.

Adapt Study Sheets to Different Types of Exams

Learn as much as possible about each exam before you take it so that you can devise special study sheets for special types of exams. Some ways to learn about an upcoming exam are to: (1) attend the classes that precede it to get exam information; (2) attend review sessions; (3) analyze old exams, if available, in exam files in the library or learning center; (4) analyze all of the exams you have taken so far in the course. In analyzing such exams, notice how the professor expects you to think about the material in the course. In a sense, instructors act as your guides. Make some effort to be sensitive to their approach. You will gain added insight into their approach and expectations if you analyze their favorite key direction words. Directions that ask you "to take a position and defend it," "to argue," "to evaluate," or "to judge" call for different thinking and study activities than questions that ask you "to list," "to explain," or "to define." Check, also, to see if you should expect primarily essay or objective questions, or a quantitative, problem-solving type of exam. Armed with this information, adapt your study sheets to help you prepare for specific types of exams. Here are some variations on the standard study sheet. The first two are particularly useful in preparing for objective exams. The third will help you prepare for quantitative exams, and the last three will help you prepare for essay exams.

1. Vocabulary study sheets You will encounter questions that demand a knowledge of specialized vocabulary in virtually every exam you take. Here are some examples of such questions:

From biology: Which phylum do true bacteria belong to?
    a. cyanophyta
    b. schizophyta
    c. protista
    d. sarcodina
    e. bacillariophyceae

From chemistry: Is the conversion of chlorine to chloride an oxidation or reduction process?

From math: Explain the difference between *K-selection* and *K-combination.*

From history: What was the "Puritan ethic?"

Prepare for such questions by making vocabulary study sheets that list the specialized vocabulary in the left column and brief meanings in the opposite column. Then cover up the meanings until you can recite them. Don't go into an exam without knowing the specialized vocabulary. You are likely to have difficulty interpreting the questions let alone answering them.

2. Identification study sheets   Make identification study sheets to help you prepare for matching questions or questions that ask you to "identify." Here are examples of such questions.

From history: Identify:
            The Magna Charta
            Mary, Queen of Scots
            The Great Awakening

From biology: Identify:
            The Scientific Method
            The Classification System

From literature: Identify:
            Othello
            Desdemona
            Iago

Such questions require study sheets that are set up in the same way but that are more detailed than vocabulary study sheets. Write the important people, events, processes, or procedures in the left column and, in the right, some words and phrases that will help you later to compose short, detailed answers or to find the matching answer from a jumbled list.

3. Quantitative study sheets   Quantitative exams that require you to read and solve word problems and apply math skills call for different types of study sheets. Here is an example of a question from a quantitative exam:

From chemistry: Calculate the number of molecules in a 5.0 gram sample of water.

To answer such questions you should make study sheets that include units of measurement and their equivalents, formulas, equations, and practice problems. Making strategy cards, fact cards, and definition sheets as described in Chapter 9, pages 112–115, will also help you prepare for quantitative exams.

4. Question-and-answer study sheets The standard study sheet, with the topics written at the top, helps you organize and learn material for both objective and essay tests. When you have finished making them, go back and write simple but comprehensive global questions for each major topic at the top of blank pieces of paper. Now, without looking at the study sheet, list in words and phrases all of the information you would use to answer these questions. When you have finished, look back at the study sheet and add information you missed. Figure 11.7 is an example of such a question along with its answer material.

Later, in the exam, no matter how a question on the topic might actually be phrased, you will be able to answer it by recalling information from your question-and-answer study sheet.

5. Comparison-and-contrast study sheets Comparison and contrast questions are favorites of some professors. Since it is hard to come up with all the material you need for these questions in the exam itself, you should prepare ahead of time by making comparison-and-contrast study sheets. Remember that *comparison* asks you to show *similarities,* and *contrast* asks you to show *differences*. Here is an example of a question that asks you to contrast.

> *From history:* Write a brief essay contrasting the climate, geography, and economics of the three sections of English colonies in America as they developed by the eighteenth century.

Describe the great awakening
religious revival
swooning, screaming
all damned — can't be saved
Jonathan Edwards's sermons
George Whitfield
radical democratic movement
to left

Figure 11.7 A question-and-answer study sheet about the material on the study sheet in Figure 11.5

Prepare for such questions by writing two or more topics that could be compared or contrasted at the top of each study sheet. Then list the similarities and differences. In listing similarities, note that only one list is necessary. Imagine putting the two items you are comparing side by side, looking for characteristics that they *both* share, and making one list. In contrasting, however, you slide the items apart and make two lists to show their differences. Reread the history question above about the English colonies. To help you anticipate and study for this question, you could have made a study sheet entitled: *3 sections of English Colonies in 18th Century.* The similarities would be a single list of the features all three sections share. The differences would require three lists, each headed by one of the three colonial sections. The three lists would show their differences in such areas as climate, geography, and economics. In the exam, you would mentally refer to this sheet while composing your answer.

6. Mental elaboration study sheets Most professors like to write some questions that call for your original thoughts on various subjects. Here are some examples of such questions:

> *From philosophy:* What attitudes do you believe are essential attributes of yourself? Are these attributes the kind of things that might survive your bodily death?
> *or*
> Give a brief statement of what you think philosophy is and what some of the tasks of philosophy are. What views of philosophy would you *reject* and why would you reject them?

> *From a management course:* On the basis of the readings in class and your own opinion, do you believe that collective bargaining is or is not on the way out? Why? Should it be adversarial?

These questions call for extensive reflection, and you will be better prepared for them if you have made some mental elaboration study sheets. Label them with the major topics in the course as you would standard study sheets. Then start thinking and jot down your thoughts. Think of real-life examples and applications, of consequences or effects, of solutions, of how you personally might be influenced or changed. Associate, compare, and contrast new material with material already familiar to you. Think of arguments for and arguments against. Make value judgments. Write down your thoughts and your beliefs. All this will help you get ready for the questions that direct you to *argue, evaluate, judge, take a position, defend,* or *tell what you think* or *believe.*

How to Use Study Sheets

By the time you have finished making your study sheets, you will have done a considerable amount of studying. You may find that you know almost everything you have written on your sheets already. Put away all your other notes and books and finish learning what is on these sheets. The best way to do this is to look at a brief point on a study sheet and then, looking away, see how much additional information you can think of that has to do with that point. If there are lists to be learned, look away from the sheets and repeat to yourself the items on the list until you know them. If you repeat the material out loud, you will learn it even faster.

Go over your study sheets more than once. You learned in Chapter 10 that a particularly good time to study them is just before you go to sleep on the night before the exam because there will be no interference from other learning while you sleep. Go over them again when you wake up. Try to spend an hour with them just before the exam. If you have two exams in a row, use the time between exams, even if it's only ten minutes, to read rapidly through the second set of study sheets. You will then go into your exams with a full and orderly mind.

You may decide to study with a group of other students. Group study will work for you only if you have already studied quite a bit and can be an active contributor to the group. Write out your study sheets and spend some time with them first. Then meet with others, and make sure you do your share of talking. Those students in the group who write and talk learn the most. Those who listen learn the least. If you don't get a chance to talk in the group, it is better to study alone and talk to yourself.

Why Do Study Sheets Work?

The chairman of a chemistry department was baffled recently by a group of students scoring between 50 and 60 percent on an examination. He decided to give them another chance by giving them the exact same exam again. One week later, with plenty of warning, he gave the same students the exam they had taken the week before. The class average edged its way up to a mere 75. He said that they all could have had 100 percent simply by taking the time to look up the answers to the questions, memorize them, and write them on the exam. When he asked them how they had studied, most said that they had "read through the first exam a couple of times."

Many students think that reading something through two or three times will result in their learning the material. It doesn't, because reading is a passive way of studying. So is listening. Reading and listening involve mainly the short-term memory, and information is lost quickly. Writing and speaking, on the other hand, are the active ways of studying. In order to make study sheets, you have to write. In order to study from them, you have to speak, even if you are only mumbling to yourself. Writing and speaking are learning activities that move material from the short-term memory to the long-term memory.

Think about the other learning activities involving the long-term memory that you employ when you make study sheets. Study sheets force you to get all the different materials for a course *synthesized* and *organized* so that you can retain it in your long-term memory more easily. They force you to *elaborate* and *associate*. They also provide you with something to *visualize* during the exam itself. You visualize the study sheet that contains information about the question, and you then answer the question more easily. Finally, study sheets force you to *recite* by looking away and either writing or speaking the material to be learned until you know it.

If you master your study sheets and still feel nervous, think of possible test questions, jot down ideas for them, and actually write out answers to some of these questions. It may also help you calm down to get a tutor or to study with another student just before the exam. Often, you need reassurance from another person. Have the tutor or other student read your answers and go over them with you. They should tell you what you did well and where you need to improve.

Allowing plenty of time to study so that you don't feel rushed will also help you control negative feelings. As you plan your study time, plan, also, where and when you will take each exam and what materials you will need, such as examination booklets and pens. Use positive self-talk as you study. You *have* learned a great deal already in the course and you can learn the rest of it for the exam. It will help to remind yourself of those facts as you study so that you will enter the exam confident, prepared, and ready to do your best.

At the Very Least . . .

This chapter has dealt with the ideal way of improving your exam preparation. If you can't follow all of the suggestions, *at the very least* do this much:

1. Read through your lecture notes and make some study sheets.
2. Survey the book and make additional study sheets.
3. At least one hour before the exam, stop, put away books and lecture notes, and recite from your study sheets until exam time.

SUMMARY

Get yourself organized to study for an exam by first making a Time Management Worksheet and then by making a one-page table of contents on which you list the blocks of material that will be on the test. This sheet shows you exactly what you will need to study and prevents you from accidentally omitting any important material. It should take five or ten minutes to make it. The second and most important step in studying for an exam is to make study sheets for each item on the table of contents. Draw material for these sheets from lectures, textbooks, and other sources, and organize and synthesize them by topic. Outline the material as much as possible, and write it so that you can read it quickly and easily. Make variations of the standard study sheet to help you prepare for different types of exams:

vocabulary, identification, quantitative, question-and-answer, comparison-and-contrast, and mental elaboration study sheets. Use active ways of study that involve the long-term memory in using study sheets. Include some positive self-talk to improve confidence and motivation.

Exercises

A. Chapter Questions

1. What is the table of contents sheet that you start with in exam preparation?
  a. A copy of the table of contents of your textbook
  b. A copy of the syllabus
  c. A list of the major chunks of information in the course in the order in which they were presented
  d. A list of the professor's lectures
2. What are study sheets made up of?
  a. All details about a subject that have been mentioned in the course.
  b. Those details and information about a subject that you think might be on the exam.
  c. All diagrams and pictures the professor has put on the blackboard.
  d. All definitions given in lectures.
3. Circle the following statements that accurately describe study sheets.
  a. They are neat.
  b. They are outlined.
  c. They are brief — phrases only.
  d. They are written in complete sentences.
  e. They are as detailed as you need them to be.
  f. You write them quickly, on one side of the paper only.
  g. They should have some of your own ideas on them.
4. Which of the following was *not* mentioned as a special type of study sheet?
  a. Comparison-contrast sheets.
  b. Specialized vocabulary sheets.
  c. Sheets with questions at the top and material to answer the questions below.
  d. A list of the main topics covered in the course.
5. Circle the statements that were mentioned as ways to control preexam anxiety.
  a. Make study sheets and use them.
  b. Use positive self-talk.
  c. Figure out where and when each exam is.
  d. Stock up on beer and snacks.
  e. Make the exam important to you by relating it to your goals.
  f. Study through the night and up to exam time.
  g. Make up questions and answer them.

B. Application of Skills

1. Make a table of contents sheet for the topics and subtopics covered so far in this book. Or, if you are using this book as supplementary material in a class, make a table of contents sheet for the material you have studied in this book so far.
2. Make standard study sheets entitled "How to Prepare for an Exam," "How to Read a Textbook," and "How to Take Lecture Notes." Then make question-and-answer study sheets on the three topics.
3. Make a comparison-and-contrast study sheet entitled "Surveying a Book and Surveying a Chapter."
4. Make a mental elaboration study sheet entitled "How to Think about the Material for an Exam."
5. Make a table of contents sheet and study sheets to help you prepare for the next exam you will take in any of your other classes.

C. Topics for Your Learning Journal

1. Write some examples of positive self-talk that would help you while preparing for an exam.
2. List the courses you are presently taking and the types of exams you expect in them. Then describe the types of study sheets that would help you prepare for each type of exam.

12

Taking an Exam

When you have finished reading this chapter, you will know the following:

1. How to take objective exams.
2. How to take the quantitative exams given in math and other problem-solving classes.
3. How to plan and write an essay exam.
4. How to combat test anxiety.
5. How to avoid the most common errors students make in taking exams.

The Objective Exam

The main characteristic of objective exams is that nearly all the material you will be working with is printed on the exam itself. You will not have to search your mind for all of the information needed to answer the questions, as you do with essay exams. In many instances all you have to do is recognize the correct answer. For example, in a true-or-false test you recognize which statements are true and which are false. In a multiple-choice test you recognize which of several answers is correct. In a matching test all the material is there — your job is to rearrange the presented material so that it is accurate. In a fill-in question you read the supplied context for a clue to the missing word you are being asked to supply.

Because the material is there to recognize, arrange, or complete, students often believe that objective exams are easier than essay exams — and consequently they do not need to study for an objective test. They believe that they can go in, guess, and do well enough. But guessing is never good enough. *You need to study for objective exams just as much as for other exams.* The best way to do so is to organize your ideas on study sheets, and then go over these sheets until you know the material.

Here are examples of each of the four major types of objective exam questions. They are straightforward questions with no tricky wording and with nothing to throw you off. Your chances of answering these questions correctly by guessing, however, are slim.

A True-False Question

T   F   The language spoken in England from 1150 to 1500 (the language of the *Canterbury Tales*) is called Old English.

The answer is *false*. The language of this period is called Middle English. If you don't know this fact, you can't answer the question.

A Fill-In Question

The country in which the Renaissance had its first great expression was _____.
The answer is *Italy*. If you have made a study sheet on the Renaissance, you will know this fact.

A Matching Question

Draw lines from the names of the people in the first column to their areas of specialization in the second column.

1. Doré   1. Social worker
2. Tolstoy   2. Engineer
3. Brunel   3. Painter
4. Engels   4. Illustrator
5. Millet   5. Novelist

Go ahead and guess on this one and see how you do. Compare your answers to the correct ones: 1–4; 2–5; 3–2; 4–1; 5–3. Unless you already knew why these people are remembered by history, you probably didn't come out very well on your guessing.

A Multiple-Choice Question

In what century did the Protestant Reformation begin?
a. 16th   c. 18th
b. 19th   d. 17th

The correct answer is *a*. The question is not a tricky one. You either know the answer or you don't. If you have studied from a complete study sheet on the Reformation, you will know the answer.

It is important, then, to study thoroughly for an objective exam. But sometimes, even when you study a great deal, you can still have trouble with these exams. The sample questions you have just read are simple and straightforward. Objective exam questions can, on the other hand, be confusing, tricky, or put together in an unexpected way. So here are some *test-taking strategies* to help you take objective exams.

1. *Read through the whole exam rapidly,* answering only the questions you know quickly. Put a mark in the margin by all questions that you are not absolutely sure of so that you will be able to find them easily when you come back later to answer them.

2. *Go back to the unanswered questions. Read each of them with a pencil in hand, circling the key words that identify the information asked for in the question. Underline all words like* only, all, always, never, sometimes, *or* which is not. These words can have a big influence on the way you interpret the question.

After you have marked the question as suggested, attack it from two angles. First, look at the encircled words and think of what you know about each of them. Visualize your study sheets and your lists of key terminology. Bring your knowledge to bear on the question. Second, analyze the question for tricky wording by carefully considering the qualifying words you have underlined and how they influence the meaning of the question.

3. *If you are stuck on a multiple-choice question, read the question again, stop and think of the answer, and then look for it.* In a good multiple-choice question all of the answers are plausible. Sometimes you can read through the answers and become confused. It may help to stop and think of the correct answer, and then read through the choices again.

4. *Sometimes in answering a difficult multiple-choice question a process of elimination will help you* at least to narrow down the choices. Here is an example of how you can use this process:

How is supporting material used by authors?
   a. To move smoothly from one idea to the next.
   b. To help the reader distinguish the main points.
   c. To clarify a main point and make it more interesting.
   d. To show the relationship between a major point and a detail.

Now, perhaps for the moment at least, you may not be able to remember why authors use supporting material and, consequently, cannot use suggestion 3 above. So you move through the choices. Answer *a* is a description of the function of a transition, so you eliminate it. Answers *b* and *d* are also functions of the transition. You are sure of that much. So, by the process of elimination, answer *c* must be correct.

5. *Don't automatically eliminate the choices "all of the above" or "none of the above."* Here is an example of a question in which "all of the above" is the correct answer.

Which of the following is an example of humanitarian reform in the 19th century?
a. Abolishment of slavery
b. Prison reform
c. Children's hospitals
d. All of the above

If you use the process of elimination and can't eliminate anything, choose "all of the above" as your answer. If, on the other hand, you find that you can eliminate every answer, and "none of the above" is the last answer, choose it.

6. *Always find out if you can mark more than one choice in answering multiple-choice questions.* Students often take for granted that all multiple-choice questions have only one correct answer. Some students fail exams because they assume this when, in fact, more than one answer can be circled for each question. Instructors will usually tell you in the directions printed at the top of the exam if more than one answer can be marked. If there are no instructions, and you have reason to believe that more than one answer could be chosen, ask your professor. Here is a question in which two of the choices are correct. See if you can figure out which ones they are:

Which of the following are part of the process of surveying a book?
a. Read the table of contents.
b. Read the introduction.
c. Read a sample chapter from the middle of the book.
d. Quickly glance at each page.

Both *a* and *b* are correct answers.

If you have read all the questions on the test as carefully as possible, if you have circled the key words, underlined and analyzed the qualifying words, used the process of elimination to arrive at answers, and tried to think up your own examples to clarify the question—in short, if you have followed all the above suggestions and you are still stuck on a few questions, there are a few more things you can try before you resort to blind guessing.

7. *Sometimes you will read a multiple-choice question and draw a complete blank. Leave the question itself and read each of the answers separately and thoughtfully.* Sometimes one of them will give you a clue to the meaning of the question itself.

8. Another way to attack a difficult multiple-choice question is to *read the question repeatedly with each separate answer.* Sometimes one of the answers will appear to complete the thought of the question better than the others. This won't guarantee that the answer is the right one, but reading the question in this way will give you a slightly better chance at the correct answer than blind guessing.

9. If you can, without distorting the test writer's meaning, *paraphrase or restate a difficult question in your own words.* Then try to think of some examples that will make the meaning even clearer. Go back and reread the original question and see if it is easier to answer than it was at first.

10. *Use what you have learned from the test itself* to help you answer the tough questions you have saved for the end. Actively look for information to help you answer the questions on which you are stuck.

11. *As an absolute last resort, guess on the remaining questions.* But before you do, make sure there is no penalty for wrong answers. Some test writers subtract all the wrong answers, or at least a percentage of the wrong answers, from the right answers. If such is the case, answer only the questions you know for sure. Guessing could lower your grade by giving you more wrong answers than if you had left them blank.

12. *Proofread the entire test before you turn it in.* You may have learned new information from the test itself which makes it obvious that some of your answers are wrong. If so, change them. The old idea that your first impulse answer on an objective test is always the right one has now been proved a myth. Change any of your answers if you have good reason to do so. All last-minute changes, however, should be well thought out.

The Quantitative Exam[1]

You will encounter quantitative exams in your math, science, and other technical courses. In such exams you will be called upon to solve math problems, to read and solve word problems, and to apply math skills. Here are some *test-taking strategies* to keep in mind when you are taking exams of this type.

1. *Start with the questions you know how to do.* Carefully read and work each of them. Then go back and try the harder ones.

2. *When you go back to the unanswered questions, read each of them carefully for clues to help you answer these questions.* Here is an example:

> What is the density of an ideal gas at standard temperature and pressure in molecules per cubic centimeter?

Even if you do not know or remember what density is, this question tells you how to work the problem because it asks for the density in molecules per cubic centimeter. That means you want to divide the number of molecules by the volume they occupy, given in cubic centimeters.

3. *Use your time well.* Quite often the points allotted to each question are noted on the exam. If you are pressed for time, work on the problems that are worth most. Don't waste ten minutes of an hour exam on a five-point problem, unless it is the only one left.

4. *Never just write an answer. Always show all your work* so that your professor can see how you arrived at the answer. Don't skip steps or do them in your head because you think they are trivial. Skipping easy steps encourages careless mistakes. Here is an example of a problem given to a large group of college freshmen:

> Given the equation $PV = nRT$, solve for n.

[1] From materials supplied by Barbara Prater.

Fifteen percent of the students solved this problem in their heads and came up with the wrong answer: $n = RT/PV$. If they had written

$PV = nRT$ (To find n, divide both sides of the equation by RT)
$PV/RT = n \cdot RT/RT$
$n = PV/RT$,

then they would have avoided their mistake, because they'd have put in the necessary step.

   5. *Remember that you are explaining to the professor what you know, so do it logically and clearly.* Always explain, preferably by equation, how you got your answer. Here is an example of a question with three answers that are labeled "bad," "fair," and "good." Accompanying each answer is an explanation that tells why they are labeled as they are.

   The question: If it takes ⅟₁₆ lb. of lettuce to make one taco, how many lbs. of lettuce will be required to make 100 tacos?

   A bad answer: $\dfrac{6.2}{16\overline{)100}}$ (6.2)
                      $\dfrac{96}{40}$

This answer is bad because the professor has little idea of how the student arrived at the answer. You can often get partial credit for partially correct reasoning, if you have shown your logic. This answer, however, does not give a clear idea of the logical thought process the student used to answer this question.

   A fair answer: ⅟₁₆ · 100 = 6.2 lb.

Here the student has shown clearly the process used for finding the answer. But whether the student was thinking clearly or was just lucky is unclear.

   A good answer: ⅟₁₆ lb. lettuce/taco · 100 tacos = 6.2 lb. lettuce

Here the student has shown the entire thought process involved in calculating the correct answer.

   6. *Check when you have finished to make sure that your answers are logical.* For instance, if your answer to the above problem was less than ⅟₁₆ lb. of lettuce, you would know it was wrong; ⅟₁₆ lb. was needed for one taco and you have 100.

   Check to see if your answers are consistent with each other and if they are consistent with other information on the test. For instance, if you need 6.2 lb. of lettuce for 100 tacos, and later calculate 1 lb. will make 200 tacos, one answer is obviously wrong. Use one question to help you with another. Quite often problems are related simply because few good or easily worked problems exist.

   7. *If you think you are missing a necessary piece of information,* check to

see if you calculated it or if it was given in a previous problem or in a previous part of the question.

8. *Check to see if you used all of the data given.* Not often will a professor put extra or unnecessary information into a problem. If you are given a piece of information that you didn't use, you may not have worked the problem correctly. This rule is less applicable for upper-level courses.

9. *Proofread for careless errors.* If there is time, a good way of locating careless errors is to rework the problems rapidly to see if you come up with the same answers the second time. When you do not, locate the errors and correct them.

The Essay Exam

The essay exam answer is written in paragraphs. Each essay answer should begin with a starting sentence that comes right to the point. The remainder of the answer should address all parts of the question in relevant detail and reflect the writer's skill in topic development and composition. Here are some *test-taking strategies* to help you develop skill in writing answers for this type of exam.

Before you begin to write:

1. *Put your name on your exam booklet and read through the entire test rapidly.* Read the general instructions to determine exactly what is required. Notice point distributions for each question and make a quick estimate of how much time you should alot to answering each question. Now quickly read the questions. There may be as few as three or as many as ten. Select the easiest ones to answer first. Don't panic if there are some you don't know. Lapses of memory are normal during exams. After you have started writing, information for the other questions will often come to you. All this helps you see what you are up against before you begin to write so that later, as you write the answer to the first question, you won't be worrying about the other ones.

2. *Analyze, mark, and number the parts of each question before you begin to write the answer.* Don't let haste or nervousness cause you to misread important words in the question, such as *physiological* for *psychological,* or *environmental* for *evolutional.* Underline key terminology. Circle the words that tell you what to do, such as *compare, contrast, list, describe, enumerate, critically evaluate, explain,* and then do exactly what those words direct you to do as you think through and compose your answer. You should also number the parts of the question so that you won't neglect to answer any part of it. Finally, notice, if you are asked to reproduce material from the textbook or lectures, if you are asked to give your own opinions, evaluations, examples, or if you are asked to do a combination of these things. Make sure you do exactly what you are directed to do.

Here is an example of a question that has been marked and numbered and can now be answered:

1. (Explain the difference) between specialized and general vocabulary and (give an example) of each. (Name and describe) three methods for learning both types of vocabulary that are taught in the textbook. (Identify the method) that works best for you, (give an example) of how you have used it, and (explain why) you prefer it to other methods.

You may find it helpful to mentally rephrase or rewrite essay questions as a series of positive statements that help you understand exactly what you must accomplish in your answer:

1. I will explain the major difference between specialized and general vocabulary.
2. I will give an example of each type.
3. I will name and describe three methods from the textbook for learning both types of vocabulary.
4. I will identify the method that works best for me.
5. I will give an example of how I have used that method.
6. I will explain why I prefer it to other methods.

Such close analysis helps you understand a question and reminds you to answer all parts of it.

   3. *Understand the meaning of key direction words and then do what they ask.* Here is a list of some common ones:

a. *Compare* asks you to show similarities. It can also ask you to show differences. Read the question carefully to see if you are asked to do both.
b. *Contrast* asks you to show differences.
c. *List, outline,* or *enumerate* ask you to abandon usual paragraph format and to number and list items down the page.
d. *Explain* and *discuss* call for a complete explanation, written in paragraphs, with a topic sentence and plenty of supporting details from the course itself.
e. *Describe* asks for characteristics and even details that you can visualize.
f. *Critically evaluate, interpret, give your opinion about,* or *tell what you believe* invite you to include your own ideas again in paragraph form.
g. *Identify* means to name and to give information.
h. *Define* asks for the meaning of the item.
i. *Prove* or *show* asks you to persuade or convince the reader with explanations, quotations, statistics, facts, or even graphs or charts.

   4. *Jot ideas for each answer in the margin of the exam next to each question. Number these ideas to form an outline.* Here is a question with such an outline jotted in the margin:

1. spiral
   a. together-file
   d. inserts-mix up
4. I use: 2 looseleaf
   a. everything-inserts
   d. loose items-holes tear

3. folders
   a. separate-inserts   *d. flimsy-loose papers*

There are at least three basic ways to organize your study materials. Name them and describe at least two advantages and disadvantages of each system. Briefly describe the method you have chosen.

You might prefer to write these jottings on a piece of scratch paper or on a page from your exam booklet. Some students who know their material well write only the initials of words. If initials aren't enough, then write words. But write as little as possible and as quickly as possible.

This writing of ideas for your answers should continue throughout the exam. For instance, if you are writing the answer to one question and you suddenly think of an idea for another question, stop and jot it down immediately so that you won't forget it.

Your brief outlines will help you in several ways. They will help you write well-organized essay answers. They will give you confidence and reduce tension because you will know that you have something to say for each question when you come to it. Furthermore, if you continue to jot down ideas as you work on the exam, your confidence will increase, and the tension you usually feel at the beginning of an exam will be channeled into productive activity. Finally, these brief outlines will help you make the mental switch from one question to the next. Most people have had the experience of concentrating so hard on the first question that when they turn to the next one they feel drained and can't think of anything to say. A brief outline helps you move from one question to the next quickly.

Depending on the length of the exam, it will take you five to ten minutes to analyze the questions and preplan your answers. Don't let it take longer than this before you begin to write, and don't be bothered by the person sitting next to you who may have filled half an examination booklet before you begin. Just remind yourself that ultimately you are saving yourself time. When you begin, you will be able to concentrate on composition and move smoothly from one question to the next rather than inefficiently groping for ideas.

As you write:

1. *Manage your time.* Keep glancing at your watch so you will not go over the time you have allotted for each question. Remember that if you run out of

time and write only half of the exam perfectly, you will get 50 percent on the exam.

2. *Answer all parts of the question.* Refer back to the numbered parts of the question or to your list of positive statements about what your answer should contain. Make sure you answer every part in detail.

3. *Come right to the point in the first sentence.* You might begin an answer to the question above, about ways to organize study materials, like this:

> The three basic ways to organize study materials are in spiral notebooks, in looseleaf notebooks, or in folders with pockets. The advantages of spiral notebooks are . . .

4. *Stick to your outline.* Start a new paragraph for each new section on your outline. Give details and examples. Remember your reader who will be looking for a complete and efficient answer that is clear and easy to comprehend.

5. *Be specific by using various types of supporting material in your answer.* Quotations, statistics, examples, facts, comparisons, contrasts, even graphs and diagrams are all appropriate when they make your answer clear and show that you know what you are talking about.

6. *Use transitions for even more clarity.* Any type of transition can be appropriately used in essay answers. Preoutlining, enumeration with key phrases, transitional words and phrases, and paragraph linking are particularly appropriate.

7. *Write all that is relevant and no more.* Some exam questions seem to invite long, rambling answers that contain opinions, personal experiences, bits of information from the course, quotations from the professor, and so on. Avoid the tendency to pad your answers, digress, or make things up, hoping that they might be right. Answers of this type waste your time in the exam and your professor's reading time. Read the question in Figure 12.1. The student could have gotten off the subject in responding to this question. Instead she marked the important words in the question, numbered its parts, and then wrote a brief outline in the margin before she began to compose her answer. In her answer she used material that she learned in the course itself, came right to the point in the first sentence, and wrote a tight, efficient, and complete answer that is supported with examples. She received full credit when the professor graded it.

After you finish writing:

1. *Proofread and neatly edit your work.* Don't take time to recopy. Instead, read your answer as though you were the reader instead of the writer. Cross out words that don't make sense and add words when necessary. Use a ∧ to show where words should be inserted. If you write only on the right-hand pages of your exam booklet, you can add afterthoughts on the left-hand pages. Use a line and a ∧ to show where this material should be inserted. Make sure you have written complete sentences. Improve punctuation and spelling.

The question

phys. arous. *labeling* *ex: speech* *date*	*1.* (How) do you know what you "feel"? *2.* (Discuss.)

The answer by Sandra Sweeney

One knows what one is feeling by two methods. The first is physiological arousal. The body becomes aroused and feels different (maybe increased heart rate, sweating, respiration, stomach pain, and so on). However, since there are no really clear differences in physiological arousal between various emotions, one must also label the feeling. This is done by analyzing the situation for clues that may lead the person to identify appropriately what he or she's feeling and to recall past similar experiences for additional clues. For example, if one is about to make a speech in front of an audience, past experience labels the butterflies in the stomach as stage fright. If one experiences those same butterflies when getting ready for a date, past experience helps to label those feelings as excitement. The physiological symptoms in both situations are identical, however.

Figure 12.1   An essay question from a psychology class with a student's full-credit answer

2. *Recheck the question and your answer to make sure you have answered all the parts.*

Learn to Control Exam Anxiety

You may at times experience some exam anxiety. Research suggests that 25 – 50 percent of students experience sufficient anxiety to lower their test scores. If you are highly test-anxious, you are likely to be a somewhat nervous individual to begin with, and you may also be inclined to "negative self-talk," which can make you feel even worse. Examples of negative self-talk are, "I can't do this," "I didn't study enough," "There isn't enough time," "Everyone else is smarter and knows more," and so on. You can combat the tendency to indulge in such thoughts by reminding yourself that they are very difficult to prove and by replacing them with positive ones. "I've studied this material well, and it's fresh in my mind," "I can concentrate," "I don't know the answer to this question, but that happens all the time, I'll come back to it later," "I have already answered some questions successfully," and "I'm really doing well on this test."

Another characteristic of highly test-anxious students is that they usually have poor study skills. The emphasis in both this chapter and the last has been on careful and systematic preparation for exams. Such preparation is the best way to deal with exam anxiety.

Besides preparing well there are a few other ways to keep anxiety at a tolerable level while you are taking an exam. Get a good night's sleep the night before; exhaustion intensifies nervous feelings. Arrive at the exam a few minutes early. Do not talk to other class members who may be ventilating their own anxieties about the exam. Instead, find a place to work in the examination room where you feel comfortable, get out the materials you will need to take the exam, and spend the last few minutes glancing through your study sheets.

When you begin the exam, you should feel somewhat nervous if you are to do a good job. Your body is creating this energy to help you deal with your exam, to help you recall more, invent your own ideas, organize your responses more rapidly, and write faster.

During the test, use your energy to concentrate on the requirements of the exam and on what you know. Avoid looking at the other students in the room or wondering how they are doing. If you have a question about the test, ask it. Work first on the parts of the exam that you know best to build confidence. If you should become uncomfortably tense, stop for a few moments, and do some slow, deep breathing. It also helps to stretch and yawn a couple of times. Then go back to the test and concentrate on reading, analyzing, underlining, and numbering the parts of each question carefully before you answer it.

If, after following these suggestions, you continue to experience much anxiety during a test, visit your Counseling Office. A number of techniques to help students with this problem have been developed, and you may be able to solve your anxiety problem by spending a few hours with a counselor.

Manage the Testing Conditions

Focus on and recognize negative factors in the test environment to help minimize their negative effects on you. External distractions, for instance, can break your concentration. They include noise outside the room, people moving through the room, an uncomfortable temperature in the room, a desk that is too small, or an exam proctor who moves around excessively. Internal distractions can also interfere with concentration. They include daydreaming, worry about failure, hunger, thirst, boredom, or a blank mind. When you find yourself bothered by external or internal distractions, recognize them and then consciously refocus your attention on the test to keep them from unduly interfering with your exam performance.

A recent study has identified a number of "testing cues" that either enhance or impede students' test performance. These cues include environmental factors, the instructor's testing policy, and even the format of the test itself. Of the fifty-five cues originally identified in this research, seventeen were found to be "potent," meaning that there was 90 percent agreement among the students studied that these cues were extremely helpful or disruptive. Furthermore, it was found that the disruptive cues sent students' blood pressure up, caused their pulse rate to quicken, and kept them from working well on their tests. Here are the potent disruptive and helpful testing cues.

Disruptive Testing Cues
1. When a teacher is *not* specific about the test content.
2. When a teacher does not state in advance information about the test format.
3. When a teacher gives additional assignments before the test, such that there is no time to study.
4. When a teacher fails to give feedback on a previous test.
5. When a teacher *frequently* makes corrections during the exam concerning format or content.
6. When a teacher describes in advance the content and format of a test but you find a *surprise* during the test.
7. When there is no choice of essay questions.
8. When a desk is too small and you must continuously fold and shuffle papers.
9. When the room is too hot or cold.
10. When you have too many tests in one day.

Helpful Testing Cues
1. When a teacher allows you to drop the lowest test.
2. When a teacher provides copies of old exams.
3. When a teacher gives a list of possible questions.
4. When a teacher shows interest in students.
5. When a teacher reviews a test to show students the correct answers or allows students to keep the test when the class has a comprehensive final.

6. When the test format is multiple-choice but space is provided to work problems for partial credit.
7. When the test format is of good quality.[2]

Being aware of the items on these lists should help you minimize the negative effects of disruptive cues and use the positive cues to improve your test performance. It is usually easier to cope with negative influences when we can recognize and understand them.

Learn from Your Mistakes

Study all returned exams, analyze them for errors, and work to avoid making the same errors again. Professors often identify the errors students make by writing comments in the margins of the exam. Here are some of the comments that professors write most frequently on exams. They were found by reading through the margins of more than fifty exam booklets:

Who?	Too vague	Give other reactions
What?	Discuss	What about other points?
Where?	For instance?	What opportunities?
When?	What time?	Give an example
Why?	Be specific	Why this disjointed exposition?
How?	What kind?	What is the significance?
	Irrelevant	

Next time you write an exam, keep this list of comments in mind and write an answer that won't prompt such responses from your professor.

Another list designed to help you avoid making errors on exams contains the common mistakes that students make. It was compiled from more than a hundred student exams. Become familiar with this list of errors as well as the cause and solution for each of them. Try to avoid making them yourself when you take exams.

> *Error 1.* Answering with the wrong list or the wrong concept.
> *Cause:* Memorizing material as separate lists and ideas rather than getting an overall view of the material by organizing it on study sheets and learning it as an organized mass of material.
> *Avoid* by making study sheets with clear titles and topic headings.
>
> *Error 2.* Writing a sketchy answer.
> *Cause:* Skimpy lecture notes and skimpy study sheets.
> *Avoid* by taking complete lecture notes and making complete study sheets.
>
> *Error 3.* Answering a question in the wrong way.
> *Cause:* Careless, hasty reading of the question and the desire to write about what you have studied, whether or not the professor asks about it.

[2] See William J. Kermis, "The TCIQ: An Identification by Intensity of Potent Testing Cues in Science," *Journal of Research in Science Teaching,* Fall 1984, pp. 609–621.

Avoid by reading the question well, marking and numbering its parts, and referring back to it from time to time as you write. Ask the professor to clarify a difficult question, if this can be done without giving away the answer.

Error 4. Not knowing the key terms either as they appear in the question or as they are needed in the answer.

Cause: Neglecting to isolate and learn key terms throughout the semester.

Avoid by writing key terminology on lists or cards and learning what these terms mean before an exam.

Error 5. Not knowing how to apply the material from the course to new situations (occurs in math and science as well as in liberal arts classes).

Cause: Not thinking enough about the material being learned during the semester.

Avoid by inventing original examples, applying what you have learned to new situations, looking for fresh relationships, and writing your insights and ideas in [square brackets] in lecture notes, textbooks, and on study sheets.

Error 6. Leaving out important material such as parts of the question, supporting details, or ramifications and implications.

Cause: Not reading the question well enough and not knowing how much information to include in the answer.

Avoid by writing all you can that is relevant to the question. Use plenty of detail and examples. Reread the question when you have finished writing your answer to check whether you have answered all parts.

Error 7. Writing long, rambling answers that are inefficient, redundant, and full of irrelevant material.

Cause: Neglecting to plan and make brief outlines of answers before beginning to write.

Avoid by making brief outlines next to exam questions, adding to them as thoughts occur to you during the exam, and following them when you compose your answers.

Error 8. Failing to proofread answers before turning them in.

Cause: Running out of time because you haven't watched it carefully enough.

Avoid by leaving enough time at end of exam to edit answers. Cross out material that does not contribute to the answer. Neatly add material that does. Make sure you have written complete sentences and that your handwriting is legible.

Figure 12.2 shows a student's answer to an essay question that contains at least six of the common exam errors. Take a look at it so that you can see how these errors appear in the context of an exam answer. This, in turn, should help you avoid making these errors yourself.

Whenever you do poorly on an exam, check the common errors to see how many of them contributed to your poor grade. If you are still baffled by your failure, go to your professor and ask how you can improve on your next exam. Do not go in defensively and suggest that your exam was graded unfairly. Then little can be accomplished. Rather, approach your professors with the attitude that you want to do better next time. Then they will help you.

As you study your failure in exam taking, begin to generalize from your

Errors:

1. Failed to mark and number parts of question. Then, did not answer all parts of it (error 6).
2. Did not make a jot outline. Answer is poorly organized (error 7).
3. Did not start with a sentence that comes right to the point (error 7).
4. Confused key terminology. Wrote summarizing when meant surveying (error 4).
5. Padded the answer with irrelevant material (error 7).
6. No example included (errors 2, 5, and 6).
7. Failed to proofread and correct run-on sentence (error 8).

QUESTION

Name and describe the steps used in reading and remembering a chapter in a textbook. Give a specific example of how you have used each step in reading one of your textbooks.

ANSWER

Remembering what you have read is a difficult task. You can read something and in the next 24 hours completely forget it. This is why summarizing a chapter first, then reading it is quite a help. Go back within the next 24 hours and look over the chapter again, this way everything should be clear to you. Reciting and grouping will also help you to remember. Group words you don't know with familiar words of your own. Recite vocabulary words and anything that you feel you should remember. Underline important phrases and things that show the most importance in the chapter so when test time comes around you will have the main ideas of the chapter all right up in front of you. Summarize and then read the chapter or chapters before the exam. Remembering for most people is hard, that's why if you can develop good habits for remembering what you read, you will have less trouble and a chance of knowing quite a bit if not all of what pops up on an exam. When summarizing through a chapter read all titles, headings, and subheadings, all pictures and diagrams and the summary

Figure 12.2   An essay answer that contains some of the common errors

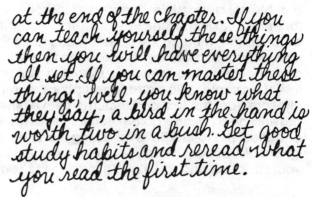

at the end of the chapter. If you can teach yourself these things then you will have everything all set. If you can master these things, well, you know what they say, a bird in the hand is worth two in a bush. Get good study habits and reread what you read the first time.

Figure 12.2 (cont.)   An essay answer that contains some of the common errors

errors. Note the mistakes that you make over and over again. Start trying to correct these errors, and improvement will come gradually. Remember that exam writing is a skill that takes time and effort to develop.

At the Very Least . . .

This chapter has presented some ideal ways of taking examinations. If you cannot follow all of these suggestions, *at the very least,* do the following:

1. *Before the test*
   a. Study and learn the material.
   b. Get enough sleep.
   c. Get to the exam with time to spare and with the materials you need.
2. *During the test*
   a. Read and analyze questions before answering them.
   b. Jot outlines for essay answers.
   c. Watch the time.
3. *After the test*
   a. Proofread your answers and edit them.
   b. Make certain you answered all parts of every question.

SUMMARY

Study well for all exams so that you begin each of them with a full and orderly mind. When you are handed the exam, read it through quickly to see what you will have to do. Then plan how to use your time so that you will complete the entire exam, not just part of it. Other general rules for exams are: (1) read each question carefully, mark the important parts, and answer it exactly; (2) do the easy questions first and the more difficult ones later; and (3) answer all parts of all questions as completely as possible. For essay questions write a brief outline for each question. When you answer the question, use good organization, write on the question and nothing else, make the answer tight and efficient by eliminating any padding or digression, and use as much supporting material as you can — lots of examples, diagrams, descriptions, quotations, and citations from the text and lectures. Leave time to proofread all answers on all exams before you turn them in. Work to keep your anxieties at a tolerable level during the exam and learn to ignore distractions. Finally, study all returned exams, identify your mistakes, and try to avoid making the same mistakes again.

Exercises

A. Chapter Questions

1. Circle all suggestions in the following list that would help you take an objective exam.
   a. Answer the easy questions first.
   b. Read all questions carefully, circling important words and underlining qualifying words.
   c. Guess blindly on true-false questions; your chances are only fifty-fifty anyway.
   d. All multiple-choice questions are "tricky," and you need to look for trick words.
   e. All the answers in a multiple-choice question may be partly true — choose the best of them.
   f. Use what you have learned from the test to help with difficult questions.
   g. Proofread the test before you turn it in.
2. What procedure should you follow when taking a quantitative exam?
   a. Compute rapidly in your head and write only the answer.
   b. Show most of your work, but skip some of the trivial steps.
   c. Always show all of your work for each question.
   d. Rewrite the question in your own words.
3. Circle the items in the following list that describe a good essay answer.
   a. It answers all parts of the question completely.
   b. It goes into detail, with examples, diagrams, quotations, and other supporting material.
   c. It is long.
   d. It comes right to the point in the first sentence.
   e. It is carefully proofread.
   f. It contains interesting and humorous digressions.
   g. It is well organized.
4. Which would *not* be a good suggestion to help you combat test anxiety?
   a. Talk to your friends about what you know and don't know just before the test.

b. Get a good night's sleep.

c. Use positive self-talk.

d. Take some slow, deep breaths when you feel tense.

5. Under what circumstances will professors clarify a question in a test?

   a. If they can without giving away the answer.

   b. If you ask them to define a major term in the question.

   c. If you ask them to do so politely and privately.

   d. All of the above.

B. Application of Skills

1. Read the following essay question, mark it, and reword it, using four positive statements that describe exactly what you must do to answer it completely:

   > Choose one of the cognitive styles discussed in class and discuss its meaning, how it is measured, and at least one "real world" behavior to which it relates.

2. You have read an example of a poor essay answer for a question on reading textbooks in Figure 12.2. If you did exercise B2 at the end of Chapter 11, you made your own study sheet on how to read textbooks. Study this sheet for ten minutes. Then put everything away, and see if you can compose a better answer to the same question:

   > Name and describe the steps used in reading and remembering a chapter in a textbook. Give a specific example of how you have used each step in reading one of your textbooks.

3. If you made a study sheet on how to take lecture notes for exercise B2, Chapter 11, study it until you think you know the material on it. Put it away and write an answer to the following essay question:

   > Name and briefly explain five ways to improve your lecture note taking in class. Describe in detail what you do with your notes after you have taken them. Give a specific example of how you use the left-hand margin.

4. If you received a poor grade on either of the essay questions printed above, check your study sheets. Are they complete? Do they contain the information you needed in order to have written complete answers? Did you make any of the common errors listed in this chapter when you wrote those answers? If you did, list your errors along with suggestions to help you avoid repeating them in the future.

5. Take thirty minutes to make a study sheet on how to prepare for and take examinations. Study it until you know the information. Write an answer to the following essay exam question. Try to avoid making the common errors.

   > Describe in detail the procedure given in this book for studying for and taking objective, quantitative, and essay exams, beginning with the first day of class

until you turn in the completed exam. Give two examples of common errors you have made in writing exams.

C. Topics for Your Learning Journal

1. Give some examples of the negative self-talk that sometimes goes through your mind when you are taking an exam. How can you turn these negative thoughts into positive ones?
2. Look back at the list of disruptive testing cues. Which do you find particularly distracting? What can you do to minimize their negative effects?
3. Make a list of suggestions that would help you personally to lower test anxiety.
4. List the internal and external distractions that you find most distracting when you are taking a test. How can you minimize their negative effects? What helps you refocus your attention on the test.

PART FIVE

Writing the Paper

13

Writing a College Paper

When you have finished reading this chapter, you will know the following:

1. How to interpret a writing assignment.
2. How to think before you write.
3. How to write, rewrite, revise, and proofread.
4. How to prepare final copy, including notes and bibliography.

Interpreting the Writing Assignment

Professors make writing assignments to see if you can initiate and complete independent, creative projects that involve reading, thinking, and writing about a subject. Sometimes professors describe in detail how to complete the assignment. At other times, you have to make most of the decisions about how to proceed. Papers assigned to you may range from two pages of your ideas about something discussed in class to a fifteen- or twenty-page term paper that requires considerable library research. Furthermore, you are likely to encounter paper assignments in any college class, including liberal arts, engineering, business, math, and the sciences. You will write more papers your junior and senior years than you will while you are a freshman or sophomore.

Assignments for written papers are often the most complicated assignments you will receive in college. In fact, getting the assignment straight and then completing all parts of it accurately can be half the battle in writing college papers. Be sure to listen and write down every detail of a writing assignment.

Once you have recorded the assignment in complete detail, you need to determine exactly what is required of you. Look up or ask about the meanings of unclear words, understand the details, and break a complicated assignment into manageable parts. Then plan deadlines for completing each part. It is taken for granted that you will spend several hours more on a college writing assignment than you would on a comparable high school assignment.

Follow a Process in Writing Papers

Allow time in your plan for doing a writing assignment to follow a process in writing. A process has some built-in features that will help you write a good paper. The remainder of this chapter describes a writing process that progresses in stages: from *prewriting*, to *writing* and *rewriting*, and, finally, to *revision* and *proofreading*. At every stage you will be writing, but not all of this writing will be turned in. A good paper requires a lot of thought and decision making and these can be accomplished best by writing lists, outlines, ideas, and, finally, the paper.

Be forewarned that the writing process is a creative act that is, by its nature, often spontaneous, inspired, and difficult to see as clearly defined in stages. In actual practice the various stages of the process will at times overlap, backtrack, repeat themselves. Understanding the process will help you get started and prod you to continue until your work is finished. You should avoid trying mechanically to follow steps in a process without thinking. Creative powers interacting with the discipline and motivation that the writing process provides will help you write a paper that will ultimately satisfy both you and your instructor.

Prewriting Activities

1. Decide What to Write About

Paper topics are sometimes assigned by professors. More often, however, the professor expects you to select a topic that has been generated by the lectures and discussion in the course itself, or, you might be given a completely free choice of topic. Free choice is most likely to occur in writing classes. The assignment will also usually specify what sort of purpose you are to fulfill in the paper: explaining, arguing, persuading, or describing.

When you are expected to participate in the topic selection, you should at the outset think about several things at once. You will want to write about a *subject* that is appropriate for the *audience* who will read your paper. This *audience* may be the professor and other similarly informed professionals. Or, the audience might include your classmates, particularly if you will be presenting the paper orally in class. You should also select a topic that is appropriate to the *occasion*. An informal, superficial, and trite topic is far less appropriate to the college classroom than a scholarly, formal topic that can be treated with thought and in detail. Finally, you should think about the *purpose* of the paper and select a topic that will help you meet it. Are you expected to give information only? Then select a topic that you can find enough information about. Are you expected to argue? Then you will need a topic that you can argue both for and against before you reach a conclusion. If the purpose is to be persuasive, you will need to select a topic that you believe in if you are to persuade others to accept your point of view. Or, if you are assigned to describe, you must search for a topic that lends itself to extended description and explanation.

When you are assigned to select a topic that is generated by the course itself, examine your lecture notes, reading notes, and notes on class discussions for ideas. While you were taking these notes, you may have already identified possible paper topics by writing *P*'s by paper topics in the margins. List these topics along with the various issues and questions that have been raised in the course. Such questions might include, "Does collective bargaining have a future?" in a management course, "What is an effective type of consumer research?" in a marketing course, "Can the dangers of nuclear power plants be resolved?" in a physics course, or "What does the narrator reveal about his own personality?" in a literature course.

If you are in a skill-building class, such as a writing class, it won't have its own subject matter like history, sociology, or psychology. Consequently, you may be given free choice of topic. In this case, begin by making a list of your hobbies, interests, future educational or professional plans, and interesting ideas and information from your other classes. Consider what you have read lately in a magazine, newspaper, or book, or what you have heard in conversations that has caught your interest. Think about experiences you have had that might interest others.

When you look back at your lists, whether generated by the course or by free choice, select one item that is appropriate to your audience and the occasion, and that will help you fulfill the purpose of the assignment. Select, also, a topic that you can get information about. If you want to read original newspaper and magazine commentary on the building of the Panama Canal, check to see if your library can make such material available to you. If you can't find the material you need, you should modify or change your topic. You should also choose a topic that you have sufficient background to handle. If you are a freshman in biology, do not choose a difficult topic from microbiology. If you do, you may find yourself tangled in complicated terminology and difficult concepts that you have insufficient education to understand. When you have studied more, you will be able to tackle such material. For the time being stick with material you have the background and education to read and write about with ease.

2. Focus Your Topic

The topic of your paper may quickly emerge as narrow and well defined, but this is unlikely. In most cases you will need to choose one aspect of a broad subject on which to write. You cannot write a good five-page paper on "Collective Bargaining"; "Should Collective Bargaining Be Adversarial: Advantages and Disadvantages" might be a better possibility.

One way to narrow and focus your topic is to choose a broad subject that interests you, like computers or solar energy or Indians. Write it on a piece of paper. Then brainstorm this topic by making a quick list of everything you know *about* the subject that is interesting to you. For instance, suppose that you want to write a three- to five-page research paper about Indians. Figure 13.1 shows the results of some brainstorming about Indians.

Take a look at this list. Some of the items on it are still too broad or too general to be good subjects—for example, "religion" or "language." You could write chapters on each of these subjects, and you only have to write five pages. Some are more specific and would be easier to work with, such as "The Indians' Theories Concerning the Origin of Life." Broad or narrow, however, at

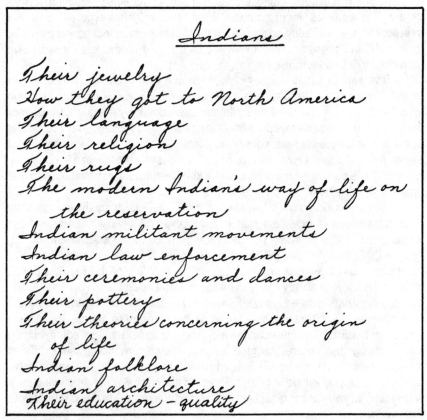

Figure 13.1   Results of brainstorming

this point you have a list of topics that interests you. Now choose the item on your list that most appeals to you as a paper topic. Let's say you decide you like "The Quality of Indian Education" best.

At this point in the paper-writing process this topic looks narrow enough to handle in the allotted space. It is something about the general subject of Indians, and your present knowledge makes you think that you could deal with it adequately in five pages. You remind yourself, however, as your work with this topic progresses, that it may need to be narrowed further. Indeed, you may find that you can handle only one aspect of it.

3. Ask Some Questions

Determine now what you already know about your topic and what additional information you will need to know to write about it. This activity will save you hours of inefficient, misdirected research in the library and will also help to establish you as the author of your paper. By writing down ideas that will later be incorporated into your paper, you will not, as so many students do, go to the library, copy material out of books, string it all together, and turn in a dull hodgepodge of other people's accounts and opinions.

There are several specific questions you can ask to start thinking creatively and independently about your topic. As you consider these questions, actually write out answers to them.

a. *What ideas do I already have about this subject?* What opinions do I hold? What facts do I know? How do these facts and opinions relate to the subject and to each other?

b. *What sources can I consult?* Has the professor mentioned any books or articles during the semester that might get me started? Who can I ask for help in finding good sources?

c. *What must I read to get some general background information so that when I begin to do research, the subject will make sense?* Will it be adequate to consult an encyclopedia, or should I skim through a couple of background books?

d. *How will my audience influence my writing?* If I am writing for my professor, I need to consider his background and knowledge. On the other hand, if this paper will be presented to other students, I will probably need to give more background information.

e. *What examples and other forms of supporting material might I use?* Do I know of any examples from my own experience that I might include in my paper? Brainstorm for examples and other support.

4. Use Other Ways to Invent Ideas

You now know several ways to invent ideas for your paper. You know how to evaluate and draw on your past knowledge and experience, you know how to brainstorm and list ideas, and you know how to ask questions to help you generate subject matter. There are other techniques to help you develop ideas.

You might use any or all of them during these early or even the later stages of the paper-writing process. They include reflecting and thinking about your topic, discussing your ideas with others, reading on your topic, listening to a speaker on your topic, observing, or interviewing.

If your college has a writing center that is equipped with writing tutors, use them to help you think through your paper. They will be able to ask the kinds of questions that will help you invent ideas. Another source of information is the library. The next chapter explains how to do the library research required for a research paper assignment.

5. Learn to Listen to Your Subconscious Mind

Inventing and thinking about the ideas in a paper you are writing is partly a conscious and partly an unconscious process. When you have spent time working intensively on ideas for a paper, you should then set them aside for awhile. When you return to your ideas later, you will often discover new insights and see connections that eluded you before. Your subconscious mind has been at work while your conscious mind was busy with something else. Learn to take advantage of the work done by your subconscious mind. Your best ideas, for example, may come to you when you first wake up. Be prepared to jot them down and add them to the other ideas you have generated during prewriting stages of paper writing.

6. Shape Your Paper by Outlining

Think of an outline as a *tool* to help you organize all the material you have accumulated up to that point and as a *guide* to help you write. With an outline in front of you, you will not be puzzled about what to write next because your outline will tell you. By the time you have an outline, you will have thought through your paper from beginning to end. When your outline is done, very often the hardest part — the original thinking — of your paper is done.

Outlining can be done in several stages during prewriting, and each revised outline will be more complete than the last. Your first outline can be written early during prewriting activities and can be no more than a list of three or four main heads that you might use in your paper. You might also at this time write out a thesis or purpose sentence, such as the following: "The purpose of this paper is to examine the current status of the education of modern American Indians and then to evaluate it." You realise that, as your paper grows, you may want to change this sentence. It may, on the other hand, become the final thesis sentence for your paper. If you get an idea for the introduction, make a note of this also on the early outline.

At this time you can also begin to think about an organizational plan for your paper. If your material seems to fit into topics or categories, you can use a topical pattern. If it more naturally can be discussed step by step or as it occurred over a period of time, use a chronological pattern. Or, if you are writing a persuasive paper, you may prefer to use a problem-solution or cause-

and-effect pattern. Argumentative papers are often organized by stating the issue, giving the arguments for and against, and, finally, stating your position and supporting it.

You should not attempt library research without some sort of brief tentative outline to guide your research. Without such a guide, you may find yourself reading everything in the library on your topic — and wasting a lot of time. A tentative outline focuses and directs your reading so that you read to support your thesis and fill in the information gaps. Your research outline, a somewhat extended version of your first brief outline, should have a tentative thesis written at the top along with the possible main heads, some subideas and examples if you have thought of them, and a brief description of how you plan to go about your research. As you do research, continue to add to and revise this outline, including your thesis, if necessary.

When you have finished all prewriting activities, including library research, you should make a final outline. It can be elaborate and detailed and contain cross-references to every note card you have made. Or, at the other extreme, it can be a few notes jotted on the back of an envelope. You will have to learn to make the kind of outline that works best for you.

For a research paper, one way of doing a final outline that is quick and does the job, is to write the headings and subheadings on lined notebook paper, section by section. Leave plenty of space between each section so that you can paper-clip the research cards that you intend to use in that section to the side of the outline.

In some classes you will be told to turn in a particular type of outline, such as a sentence outline, along with your final paper. When this is the case, follow your professor's instructions for the form of such an outline exactly.

As you go through the prewriting activities, it is essential that you *write everything down*. When you first begin to think about a subject, you are often more creative than at any other time. If you do not make a record of your initial creative thoughts, you will forget them, or, worse, as you pursue your research, other people's ideas will intrude on your own until eventually you will forget that you ever had any original ideas about your subject. With all of your notes, lists, ideas, and your outline spread out in front of you to refer to, you can now write your paper.

Writing and Rewriting Activities

Your object, at this next stage, is to get a first draft of your paper. It does not have to be perfect. It only has to be good enough to work with later.

There are two ways of drafting a paper. Use the one that works best for you. The first way is to write rapidly and keep writing. You will be working to capture the flow of ideas represented by your outline. To do this you will have to get them down on paper as quickly as you can. You will be thinking fast as you move through your outline this time, and you should write fast enough to keep up with your thoughts. Do not stop to reread. Do not worry about sentence structure, word choice, punctuation, or misspellings at this point. You will take care of these things later.

If getting the first sentence on the page seems to be difficult, write a phrase. After you put down a few phrases, you will usually begin to write in sentences. If you are writing smoothly and then suddenly get blocked, unable to figure out how to express an idea, write phrases again. Leave blank spots if you cannot immediately think of the right word. Later you can complete sentences and add and change words.

A second way of composing a first draft is to do a considerable amount of rereading and rewriting as you write. Rewriting while writing is an excellent skill to learn because your paper will require less revision later. Writing and rewriting involves constantly going back to read what you have just written and making improvements at once. For instance, as soon as you write a word, you may think of a better one. Go ahead and substitute the better word. Or, you may start a sentence that becomes confused and refuses to end as you had hoped. If you can think of a better way to write it, do so immediately. At the end of each paragraph, reread the entire paragraph and make additional changes and im-

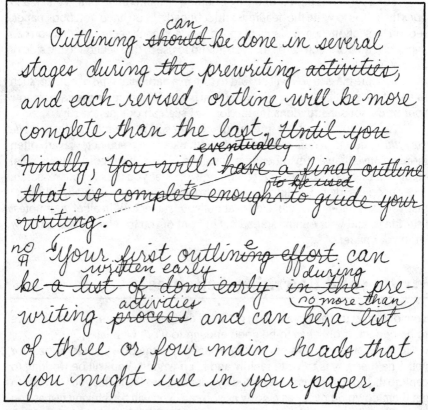

Figure 13.2 An example of writing and rewriting done as simultaneous activities

provements. Your draft, when you finish writing it, will look like the material in Figure 13.2.

Writing requires making one decision after another: about what to say next, what word to select, how to start a sentence, how much to write. Follow this second method of writing the first draft only if you can do so without belaboring these decisions. Your object is to get your thoughts on paper as soon as possible. If rewriting decisions are slowing your writing down so much that you lose your train of thought, then revert to the first method of writing quickly without rereading and rewriting. You can always go back and rework material when it is finally down on paper.

Using Source Material

As you write, remember that *you* are the author of this paper. Your ideas will shape and structure the paper. If you are writing a research paper, use the research materials you have taken from other sources to expain, clarify, or lend more weight to what you are saying.

You will learn how to take research notes in the next chapter. Basically, however, your notes will be of two sorts: the direct quote, which is copied word for word, and the paraphrase, which is a rephrasing in your own words of someone else's ideas. When you use either of these types of material to support your ideas and observations, you must let your reader know where they came from originally. There are two ways to give credit to the original author: by using footnotes and bibliography or by using in-text citations and a list of works cited.

1. Footnotes and bibliography You may footnote borrowed material at the bottom of the page or on a final sheet at the end of the paper where all endnotes can be listed together in consecutive order. Figure 13.3 shows the footnote method. Notice also how a direct quotation can be interwoven with one's own statements. The quoted material is acknowledged with a footnote at the bottom of the page. When you use this method of acknowledgment, attach a bibliography at the end of your paper. A bibliography lists by author and in alphabetical order the works you have quoted or paraphrased in your paper. Use the format illustrated in Figure 13.6 to prepare a bibliography.

2. In-text citations and a list of works cited A simpler way of acknowledging sources is to place brief notes in parentheses in the text itself and cross-reference them to an alphabetical list of works cited at the end of the paper. This method is now preferred to the older footnote and bibliography method.

All that is required is that you place in parentheses the author's last name and the page number on which the material appeared at the end of the quote or paraphrased material. Figure 13.4 illustrates this method of citation and also shows how paraphrased material can be interwoven into the context of one's paper. The reader who wants to know more about the source will consult the

```
        In 1972 the Indian Educational Act was passed by Congress       ⎫
    and the next year the National Advisory Council on Indian Edu-      ⎬  you explaining
                                                                          factual
    cation was appointed by the President.  The purpose of both           information
    government acts was to improve the quality of Indian education.       that is general
                                                                          knowledge and
    In the Council's third annual report to Congress, there is evi-       does not need
    dence that some progress toward improvement has been made, but        to be quoted
    the Council also admits that severe problems still remain:        ⎭

    "Dropout rate among Indian youth is the highest in the country.   ⎫
                                                                          National
    Delinquency among Indian youth is the worst among all other          Advisory
    youth groups.  Suicide rate is among the highest of any group     ⎬  Council
                                                                          supporting
    in our society.  Poverty is rampant on Indian Reservations as         what you
    is alcoholism, mental illness, and a general state of hopeless-       have said
    ness."¹                                                          ⎭

    ────────────────────

        ¹National Advisory Council on Indian Education, The Third    ⎫  footnote
    Annual Report to the Congress of the United States (Washington,   ⎬  telling reader
    D.C.: U.S. Government Printing Office, March 1976), p. 23.            where you
                                                                      ⎭  found quoted
                                                                          information
```

Figure 13.3   The footnote method of acknowledging a source

"List of Works Cited" attached to the end of the paper where the full biblio-graphical reference is listed. Figure 13.6 is an example of list of works cited. It contains a full reference for the book by Dippie that is only briefly cited in the text.

To help you prepare your in-text notes and also to put together your final list of works cited, buy yourself a good handbook for doing research papers. Your bookstore will have several of them. The form used in this chapter is that provided by *The MLA Handbook for Writers of Research Papers*, 2d ed., 1984, published by the Modern Language Association. Another widely used hand-

```
The basic purpose of education for Indians has not   ⎫
always been clear and consistent. For many years     ⎬  you talking
government-run Indian schools pressured Indians to
abandon their native culture and to assimilate with  ⎭
the dominant American culture. John Collier, a re-   ⎫
former who agitated in favor of Indians and their    ⎬  paraphrased support for
culture from the early 1920s until his death in 1968,    what you have said
had a different idea. He believed that instead of ef- ⎭
facing native culture, Indian schools should encour-  ⎫  in-text citation telling
age and revitalize it. (Dippie 276, 325).            ⎬  reader where you
                                                         learned about Collier's
                                                      ⎭  ideas
```

Figure 13.4   The in-text method of acknowledging a source

book for preparing papers is the *Publication Manual of the American Psychological Association,* 3d ed., 1983. This handbook also teaches an in-text citation format that includes the author's last name and the date of publication: (Jones, 1981). The important thing is to choose one form to acknowledge your research sources and then use it consistently throughout your paper. Your instructor may insist on a specific form or style of citations.

Revision and Proofreading Activities

As soon as you have a complete draft of your paper, put it aside for a few hours or overnight before you begin revision. The few hours delay will give you the insight necessary to create a polished final product. You rarely have such insight right after you have finished writing the first draft.

As part of the revision and final proofreading activities, be sure to include the following:

1. Check the organization Read through fairly rapidly to see if your ideas are presented in an order that makes sense. You may want to move an entire section or a part of a section to another place in your paper. Cut out any material that is off the subject or that does not contribute to the development of your topic.

2. Make sure that each main section of the paper contains a clear topic sentence This will help make your main ideas stand out. Support main ideas with subideas and/or supporting material.

3. See if you have enough transitions Use transitions to make the organization of the main ideas clear to your reader. Refer back to Chapter 8 if you need to review types of transitions. Make certain, also, that your paragraphs are linked together so that your reader can follow your thought processes from one paragraph to the next. You can link paragraphs by putting in the first sentence of each paragraph words or phrases that refer back to the idea in the preceding paragraph. Then your reader can see how each paragraph relates to the one that precedes it. Paragraph linking is also illustrated in Chapter 8.

4. Read your introduction to make sure that it introduces what you have written When you have made sure that the organization of the body of your paper is straight and is made clear to your readers through the use of topic sentences and transitional material, go back and read your introduction to make sure that it introduces what you have written. It will help your readers to understand your paper if you provide them with an initial mental focus by writing a purpose or thesis sentence toward the end of your introduction. It does not need to be elaborate, but it should clearly state what they can expect as they read your paper. The sample first page of a paper in Figure 13.5 has a thesis sentence at the end of the first paragraph.

5. Take a look at your summary or conclusion If your paper is short, you will not need a detailed summary, or restatement, of your ideas, but you will want to write a concluding point that will provide a note of finality for your paper. Choose your concluding point with care.

6. Work to improve your sentences Make sure you have used complete sentences. If a sentence does not make sense to you, it won't to your reader either. Rewrite it to state exactly what you want to say.

Work for variety in sentence structure. If all of your sentences start with a subject, change some of them so that they begin with clauses. Vary their length. Your style will then be less monotonous. Remember also at this point that good writing is efficient writing. Whenever you can say the same thing in fewer words, do so.

7. Locate and correct all remaining errors, including spelling, punctuation, and incorrect words Punctuate each sentence correctly. Look up every word that looks like it might be incorrectly spelled. Save time by using a spelling dictionary that gives no meanings but simply lists words alphabetically. If you do not like a word you have used, consult a dictionary or thesaurus and read through some synonyms to see if you can find a more appropriate word.

8. As a final check, read your paper out loud Pretend now that you are the reader instead of the writer. Locate and change all remaining errors. Many mistakes that your eye has missed will offend your ear.

Preparation of the Final Copy

When you have completed revision and proofreading activities, you can type your paper and turn it in. Use standard 8½-by-11-inch paper. Leave one-inch margins at the top, bottom, and sides of each page. One inch from the top of the first page, by the left margin, type the following items with double spacing between each of them: your name, your instructor's name, the course number, and the date. Double-space again and center the title. Quadruple-space, indent five spaces, and begin typing your paper. There is no need to number the first page. From page 2 on, however, type page numbers in the upper right-hand corner one-half inch from the top. Type your last name before the page number on all pages. Keep a carbon or Xerox copy of the entire paper for yourself. Professors do not mean to lose papers, but they sometimes do. When they do, they expect you to be able to provide a second copy.

Figure 13.5 shows the completed first page of the paper on Indian education that has been used as an example in this chapter. All source material has been acknowledged with in-text citations. Notice that only the page numbers are required in the first citation since the author's name is included in the text.

Missy Spresser
Professor Shaw
Engl. 3101
April 15, 1986

The Education of the American Indian:
A Current Evaluation

All Americans are at least vaguely familiar with the
plight of the American Indian. Cutbacks in federal programs for Indians have made their problems even more
severe in recent years. Josephy reports, ''By the end of
1981 it was estimated that cutbacks in federal programs
for Indians totaled about $500 million'' or more than ten
times the cuts affecting their non-Indian fellow Americans. Additional cuts seem to be threatened in the future.
This reduced funding is affecting almost all aspects of
reservation life, including education (257-258). If the
Indians could solve their educational problems, solutions
to many of their other problems might not be far behind. In
this paper the current status of Indian education will be
described and evaluated and some ways of improving this
education will be proposed.

Whether to assimilate with the dominant American
culture or to preserve Indian culture has been a long-
standing issue in Indian education. After the Civil War
full responsibility for Indian education was turned over
by the government to churches and missionary groups. The
next fifty years became a period of enforced assimilation
in all areas of Indian culture, but especially in religion
and eduction (Jacoby 83-84).

John Collier, a reformer who agitated in favor of
Indians and their culture from the early 1920s until his
death in 1968, had a different idea. He believed that
instead of effacing native culture, Indian schools should
encourage and revitalize it (Dippie 276, 325).

Pressure to assimilate remains a potent force today,
however. More and more Indians are graduating from high
school and college and becoming eligible for jobs in the
non-Indian society. ''When Indians obtain the requisite
skills many of them enter the broader American society and
succeed.'' At present approximately 90 percent of all
Indian children are educated in state public school systems (Taylor 136, 155).

How well these children compete with the members of
the dominant society, however, is another matter.

Figure 13.5 An example of the first page of a research paper

List of Works Cited

Dippie, Brian W. The Vanishing American. Middletown:
Wesleyan UP, 1982.
''In the Wake of the Siege at Wounded Knee.'' U.S. News and
World Report. 21 May 1973: 112-113.
Jacoby, Alvin M., Jr. Now That the Buffalo's Gone: A Study
of Today's American Indians. New York: Knopf, 1982.
LaFarge, Oliver. ''The Enduring Indian.'' Scientific
American. February 1960: 37-44.
National Advisory Council on Indian Education. The Third
Annual Report to the Congress of the United States.
Washington, D.C.: Government Printing Office, March,
1976.
Taylor, Theodore W. The Bureau of Indian Affairs. Boulder:
Westview Press, 1984.

Figure 13.6 Sample list of works cited

Figure 13.6 is an example of a list of works cited that should be the last page of your paper. Included on this list are books, an unsigned article, a signed article, and a government document with a corporate author (The National Advisory Council). In-text citations for these various types of references would be as follows:

Books: author and page number (Jacoby 72).
Unsigned article: a short version of the title and page number ("In the Wake" 112).
Signed article: author and page number (LaFarge 43).
Corporate author: name and page number (National Advisory Council on Indian Education, 12).

A better way to cite this last source would be to include the name of the council in the text: "According to the National Advisory Council on Indian Education . . . (12)."

At the Very Least . . .

This chapter has described the ideal way of writing a paper. If you can't follow all of these suggestions, *at the very least:*

1. Write down your topic and brainstorm for ideas.
2. Make some sort of an outline that shows your ideas and the order in which you will treat them.

3. Write, revise, and proofread the paper. Make certain it is *absolutely free of errors.*

SUMMARY

You can make paper writing easier and more successful if you follow a process. Analyze the assignment first and divide your work into manageable steps. Use prewriting activities to help you select a topic, generate ideas, and organize your paper. Write your paper rapidly, capturing the flow of ideas on your outline. Do as much rewriting as you can while you write. In writing research papers, acknowledge all materials from outside sources with footnotes or, preferably, with in-text citations. List sources in a bibliography or in a list of works cited at the end of your paper. Revise and proofread your paper, type it, and turn it in.

Exercises

A. Chapter Questions

1. True or false: Writing assignments are often the most complicated and detailed assignments you will get in college.
2. Which is the recommended procedure for writing a paper?
   a. Follow a process that includes prewriting, writing and rewriting, revision, and proofreading.
   b. Outline the paper and write it over a period of several days.
   c. Outline the paper and write it in one sitting to capture the flow of ideas.
   d. Write the paper and then outline it to check on its organization.
3. Which was not listed as a prewriting activity?
   a. Interviewing
   b. Brainstorming
   c. Persuading
   d. Outlining
4. How would you distinguish rewriting and revision?
   a. They are not distinguishable since they mean the same thing.
   b. Rewriting is done in conjunction with writing and revision is done later.
   c. Revision is done as you write, whereas rewriting is done just before you turn in your paper.
   d. Rewriting, another name for revision, is done after you have finished the first draft.
5. Which is the preferred way to document your sources?
   a. Footnotes and bibliography
   b. Endnotes and bibliography
   c. In-text citations and list of works cited
   d. Footnotes or endnotes and bibliography

B. Application of Skills

1. Select a topic from the following list and brainstorm by quickly listing ideas and examples that you could include in a two-page paper.

    1. How to organize study materials.
    2. How to survey a textbook.
    3. How to survey a chapter.
    4. How to take notes on a college textbook.
    5. How to take lecture notes.
    6. How to study lecture notes.
    7. How to discover the student's responsibilities in a college class.
    8. How to remember more.
    9. How to concentrate when you don't want to study.
    10. Some places to study.
    11. How to solve your time problems.
    12. How to study for an exam.
    13. How to analyze your personal learning style.
    14. How to analyze a professor's teaching style.
    15. Support services at your university.
    16. How to choose a topic for a paper or oral report.
    17. How to keep track of assignments.
    18. Why and how to acknowledge material in a paper.
    19. How to outline a paper or oral report.
    20. How to "map" a section of material.
    21. How to use the dictionary.
    22. How to improve your vocabulary.
    23. How to revise a paper.
    24. How to read and take notes on a math text.
    25. How to take lecture notes in math.
    26. How to take part in class discussion.
    27. Why it is important to read the introduction or preface to a book.
    28. How to find the main idea in a section of material.
    29. How to brainstorm a topic.
    30. How to improve the quantity and quality of your own creative thinking.
    31. How to take essay exams.
    32. How to take objective exams.
    33. How to take quantitative exams.
    34. Common exam errors and how to avoid them.
    35. How to proofread and correct an exam or paper.

    Briefly outline the paper and write a rough draft. Do as much rewriting as you can and still keep your train of thought. Revise, proofread, and type your paper and turn it in.

2. If you have to write a paper in one of your other classes, follow all of the suggestions for prewriting that are made in this chapter. Remember to write everything down as you practice these activities.

C. Topics for Your Learning Journal

1. Write out one topic, issue, or major question that has been dealt with in each of the classes you are taking this semester. Put stars by the ones that would make good paper topics.
2. Write and rewrite a paragraph on the following topic: "Writing a paper is (fun, easy, difficult, terrifying, impossible) for me." Supply your own adjective. Reread and improve each sentence as you write it. Then reread and rewrite the entire paragraph until you are satisfied with it.

14

Doing
Library Research

When you have finished reading this
chapter, you will know how to:

1. Get organized for research.
2. Build a bibliography.
3. Find research materials in a university
   library.
4. Take research notes.

Get Organized for Research

Begin library research by getting organized to do research. Buy a package of
four-by-six-inch cards (since you will take all of your notes on them), get
together three or four pens or pencils, and buy an appropriate file to use to
organize your note cards. Cardboard expanding files used for canceled checks
are good for keeping note cards organized because you can label the tabs on
the pockets with your main heads, as shown in Figure 14.1. Then it is easy to file
your note cards where they belong as soon as you write them. Buy a roll of
self-sticking labels, which you can peel off and use if you want to change the
headings on these tabs. Whatever filing system you use, make sure that it is easy
to carry around, that it is big enough to hold all of your note cards plus some

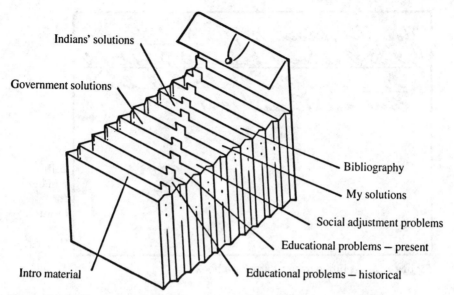

Indians' solutions

Government solutions

Bibliography

My solutions

Social adjustment problems

Educational problems — present

Intro material

Educational problems — historical

Figure 14.1   How a canceled check file can be used to organize research materials

blank cards, and that it can be secured with a rubber band or fastener of some kind when you are ready to close up for the day.

Start with the Bibliography

Your first job when you go to the library to begin research is to accumulate a list of sources, or bibliography. If you remember that *biblio* means "book" in Greek, it will be easier to remember that a bibliography is a group of books and articles about your subject. Use the ideas you jotted down while prewriting to help you start locating materials. Consult the card catalog and various indexes in the library to help you find material. (There is information later in this chapter on how to use these devices.)

Make a record of bibliographical items before you locate the items themselves in the library or start taking any notes on their contents. For the paper on Indian education, for example, you would need a record of all the books and parts of books on this subject that are available in the library. You would also need a record of magazine and journal articles written on your subject. You might also see if some newspaper articles are available. Finally, you might get the names of some government publications that would describe official government action concerning Indian problems. Do not worry if your bibliography seems long. When you actually look for these materials in the library, you will not find all of them. Some will be checked out; others will not be in your library's holdings.

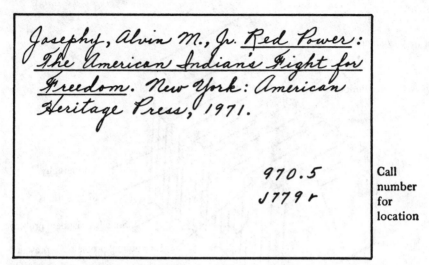

Josephy, Alvin M., Jr. <u>Red Power:</u>
<u>The American Indian's Fight for</u>
<u>Freedom</u>. New York: American
Heritage Press, 1971.

970.5
J779 r

Call
number
for
location

Figure 14.2   A bibliography card for a book

As you accumulate sources, keep your "tentative outline to guide research" handy, and find materials that are relevant to that outline. Do not record books and articles that are not about some part of your subject. Library research takes a lot of time. Every source you record should be one you might use.

Write each bibliographical item on a separate card. A bibliography card for a book should include author, title, place of publication, publisher, date of publication, and call number so that you can later locate it in the library. Figure 14.2 provides an example. A bibliography card for an article should include author (if one is listed), title of article, name of publication, volume (unless it is a weekly publication, in which case the date of publication is sufficient), page numbers, and location in library. Figure 14.3 provides an example. Here are two additional examples of how to write complete bibliographical information for an article in a magazine or journal in which you would include the volume number:

Gosling, J. T., and A. J. Hundhausen. "Waves in the Solar Wind." *Scientific American* 236 (1977): 36–43.

and, for an article in a newspaper in which the date of publication is sufficient:

Cowen, Edward. "World Oil Shortage Is Called Inevitable." *New York Times* 17 May 1977: 1.

You make bibliography cards as suggested above for several reasons. They serve as a guide to the next step in your research process, which is to find the sources listed on your cards and then to read and take notes on these sources. Whenever you take notes on one of these sources, you will *not* need

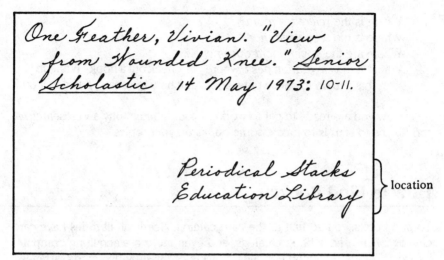

One Feather, Vivian. "View from Wounded Knee." Senior Scholastic 14 May 1973: 10-11.

Periodical Stacks Education Library } location

Figure 14.3 A bibliography card for an article

to write out more than a short title on your note card to identify the book, since the complete information will be on your bibliography card. As an alternative to short titles, some people number their bibliography cards and write the corresponding number on their note cards to identify the source of the note. Later, you will use the information on your bibliography cards when you write your in-text citations or footnotes. Finally, with all your sources on cards, it is easy to alphabetize them and type a list of works cited or bibliographical listing to append to your paper. Until you are ready to write acknowledgments and to assemble and type the list of works cited, however, keep all these cards in the back bibliography section of your note card file, where you can easily find them during the research process.

In order to accumulate a complete bibliography, you will need to use various parts of the library. Take fifteen minutes in a new library to find out how it is laid out. Begin by locating an information desk, a reader's advisor, or someone at the circulation desk who can answer questions. Tell this person that you are new to the library and ask if a map or directory is available. If you get one, use it, look around, and ask questions of your resource person until you have answers to the following basic questions.

Where is the *card catalog?* Or, if the catalog is on the computer: Where are the *terminals?*
Where are the *books* themselves?
Where are the *indexes to periodicals?*
Where are the *periodicals* (magazines and journals) themselves?
Are the periodical and book stacks "open" so that you can go into them, or are they "closed" so that you will have to send a library employee for the material you need?
Where are the *microforms?*

Where is the *reference room?*
Where is the *reserve section?*
Where are the *government documents?*
Where is the *circulation desk,* where you check out a book? What do you
    have to do to check out a book, and how long can you keep it out?

Now you are ready to get to work on your bibliography and research. A
good place to start is to locate some books on your topics.

How to Find Books

To find books, you go first to the card catalog. Nearly all libraries have card
catalogs. A few have book catalogs, and even more are acquiring computer
indexes. The card catalog contains drawers of three-by-five cards, arranged
alphabetically, which give you information about the books in the library and
tell you where to find them. Most books are represented in the card catalog by
at least three cards. One card lists the book under the last name of the author,
one under the title of the book, and one, or sometimes several, under various
broad subjects. Books of fiction often do not have subject cards. Figure 14.4
shows examples of the author, title, and subject cards for one book.

Learn to read and understand the cards in the card catalog. Notice how
the author is written on one line and the title below, with only the first word in
capitals. The call number enables you to locate the book in the library. When
you find one book on your topic, look at the bottom of the catalog card for other
subject headings under which your book is listed. Then look under those
headings to find other books that might be related to your subject.

The computer index has all the information you would find in the card
catalog stored in the computer. You read the information about your book on
the screen of a computer terminal rather than on a card. Terminals may be
located throughout the library. Computer indexes are "user friendly" and tell
you, usually on the screen itself, exactly what you must do to use them. Special
advantages of computer indexes are: (1) their terminals may be placed
throughout the campus as well as in the library; (2) they not only give the usual
information about a book but also its current status, such as whether it is
checked out, on reserve, or on order; and (3) they enable you to search by
author, title, subject, or by combinations of these. Usually you will need to copy
the information about your book off the screen. Some libraries, however, are
able to provide a printed copy of all the books they own on a particular subject.
You have to ask for this service, and there will usually be a fee to pay.

If you have trouble figuring out broad subject headings related to your
topic, go to the reference room and ask for the Library of Congress *List of
Subject Headings* (it may also be available near the public catalog). This is the
list librarians use to catalog books by subject. Write down those subject headings that might lead you to books on your topic.

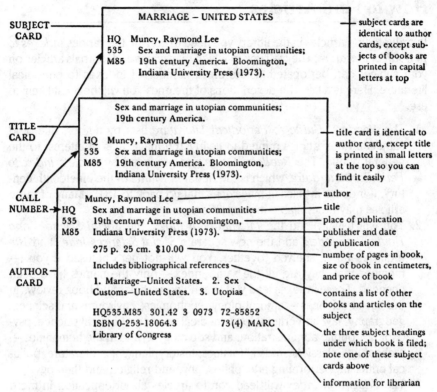

SUBJECT CARD ———

MARRIAGE – UNITED STATES

HQ   Muncy, Raymond Lee
535   Sex and marriage in utopian communities;
M85   19th century America. Bloomington,
                Indiana University Press (1973).

subject cards are identical to author cards, except subjects of books are printed in capital letters at top

TITLE CARD ———

Sex and marriage in utopian communities;
19th century America.

HQ   Muncy, Raymond Lee
535   Sex and marriage in utopian communities;
M85   19th century America. Bloomington,
                Indiana University Press (1973).

title card is identical to author card, except title is printed in small letters at the top so you can find it easily

CALL NUMBER →

AUTHOR CARD ———

Muncy, Raymond Lee ——— author
HQ   Sex and marriage in utopian communities ——— title
535   19th century America. Bloomington, ——— place of publication
M85   Indiana University Press (1973). ——— publisher and date of publication

275 p. 25 cm. $10.00 ——— number of pages in book, size of book in centimeters, and price of book

Includes bibliographical references ———

1. Marriage—United States.   2. Sex
Customs—United States.   3. Utopias

contains a list of other books and articles on the subject

HQ535.M85   301.42 3 0973   72-85852
ISBN 0-253-18064.3   73(4) MARC
Library of Congress

the three subject headings under which book is filed; note one of these subject cards above

information for librarian

Figure 14.4 Author, title, and subject cards for one book

For those books that look useful, write out bibliography cards as described above. When you write down the call number, write down all of it, to the last decimal point, or you will have trouble locating your book. When you have made your bibliography cards, the next step is to discover how to get the books. A directory is usually in plain sight in the lobby. It tells you on what floor and in what general area on that floor you will find a book with a specific call number. On each floor of the library you will find other directories to help you locate material there.

If you cannot find a book in the stacks, there are a number of things you can do. First, look around a bit on the shelves — above, below, and from side to side — to see if someone put it back in the wrong spot. If you still cannot find it, look at the other books in the area. They will be on or near your topic also, and one or more might serve as well as the one you were trying to find. You can also go to the circulation desk and ask if your book has been checked out, placed on reserve, or lost. If it's on reserve, you can read it in the *reserve section*. If it is lost, the library can trace it and try to find it for you. If it is checked out, you can find out when it is to be returned and then ask that it be held for you. The library will notify you when it comes in, and you can pick it up at the circulation desk.

How to Find Articles

In order to find articles in the library you need to consult the various *indexes to periodical literature*. They tell you in which magazines and journals articles on your subject can be located. There are a number of indexes to periodical literature. Here is a list with descriptions of the ones you will be most likely to use.

1. The *Readers' Guide to Periodical Literature* lists by author, title, and subject all the articles printed in nearly 160 magazines of interest to the general public. The *Readers' Guide* was preceded by *Poole's Index to Periodical Literature*, which is the *Readers' Guide* of the nineteenth century. It indexes articles in magazines that go back to 1815. Many of these articles may be available in your library on microfilm.

2. You will usually find the *International Index*, the *Social Sciences and Humanities Index*, and the new separate *Social Sciences Index* and *Humanities Index* shelved together. You will not get confused if you remember that they are all the same index — only the names have been changed. These indexes lead you to scholarly articles and book reviews in the social sciences — anthropology, economics, environmental science, geography, law and criminology, medical sciences, political science, psychology, public administration, and sociology — and in the humanities — archeology, classical studies, folklore, history, language, literature, political criticism, performing arts, philosophy, and religion and theology.

3. The *Education Index* will lead you to articles about education in more than two hundred different periodicals.

4. The *Engineering Index, Art Index, Applied Science and Technology Index,* and *Industrial Arts Index* are other specialized indexes that lead you to magazine and journal articles in the fields indicated by their titles.

5. *Abstracts*, like periodical indexes, list articles on particular subjects. They also list the books on these subjects. They give short summaries of both books and articles. Abstract periodicals are available in psychology, biology, philosophy, folklore, geography, history, anthropology, sociology, and other subjects.

6. The *Biological and Agricultural Index* is useful to biology and agriculture students.

The first time you look into a periodical index you will probably need some help in reading it. But once you learn to read one index, you can read the others, since most of them are similar in format. Here is an entry from the *Readers' Guide to Periodical Literature.* Under the general heading "Women" and the specific subheading "History" the following article is listed:

> What ought to be and what was: women's sexuality in the nineteenth century. C. N. Degler, bibli f Am Hist R 79:1467–90 D'74.

The title of the article and its author are listed first. "Bibli f" means that there are bibliographical footnotes in this article that will lead you to other sources of material on this subject. The article appears in the magazine abbreviated as "Am Hist R." You will have to consult the Abbreviations of Periodicals Indexed at the front of the book to find out that this abbreviation stands for the *American Historical Review.* You will need the full name of the magazine before you attempt to find it in the periodical stacks. After the name of the magazine, some numbers are listed. The first number, 79, is the volume number. All issues of the *American Historical Review* published in the year this article was printed were bound together at the end of that year as volume 79. After the volume number is a colon, followed by the page numbers 1467–1490. Finally, the date is listed. Only one month begins with D, and the year is 1974.

Here are three other bits of advice to help you use periodical indexes efficiently. First, take five minutes to read the title page and preface to find out how the index is arranged, how often it comes out, what sort of material is indexed, whether or not it includes summaries of each item indexed, what abbreviations are used, and if there are any other pointers to help you use it. Second, remember that all periodical indexes come out periodically themselves, like the magazines and journals they index. In choosing the particular volume of an index to use, look in indexes printed at the time that the subject was of the greatest current interest. Finally, consider the point of view of the index you are consulting. If your subject is air pollution and you want popular articles of general interest, look in the *Readers' Guide.* If you want an engineering or scientific point of view, look in the *Engineering Index* or the *Applied Science and Technology Index.*

When you have completed your bibliography cards for the articles you wish to consult, you then need to find where the journals themselves are located. Some libraries catalog their periodicals and shelve them with the book collection. Others place them in periodical stacks, which may be "open," so that you can walk through and search for your own periodicals, or "closed," so that you will have to send a library employee for what you want. Before you enter these stacks, find the directory to them. It may be a Linedex, which is a revolving, upright card file, or a Serial Holdings List, which is a list of all periodicals, as well as their locations, owned by the library. Look up the stack number of the periodical you want, find the magazine, then the volume, then the month, and finally the pages where the article appears, in that order.

How to Find Material in Microform

You now know how to find books and articles when they are in volume form. More and more materials, including rare or old books, magazines (*Time* and *Newsweek,* for example), journals, and newspapers are now being put in microform because they take up less space than they did in their original form. You will know that *books* are in microform when the card catalog call number includes one of the microform abbreviations: *mic, mf, mc,* or *mfc.* Similarly, if you see one of these abbreviations next to the name of a *periodical* in the Linedex, the Holding List, or the card catalog, you will need to look for the periodical in microform.

You read microform material on machines that enlarge the tiny photographed images of pages so that you can see them easily. The first time you use one of these machines you will have to ask the microform librarian for help. But after the first time, you will probably be able to manage the machine yourself. If you find a page you need to copy, copy machines for microforms are available in most libraries.

With the aid of the card catalog and Linedex, you will have no trouble finding out about and reading *books* and *magazines* on microfilm. The Linedex and card catalog will not help you, however, in locating material in *newspapers*. There are special indexes to help you find material in microformed newspapers. Here are the most important and most useful of them:

1. *Newsbank* will lead you to newspaper materials published after 1970 on almost any contemporary subject you can think of (drug abuse, student protests, abortion, birth control, air and water pollution, and so on). *Newsbank* articles are drawn from 150 newspapers representing 103 major cities in the United States. To locate several newspaper articles on your subject, consult the *Newsbank* index first. It will lead you to a microfiche card that may contain fifteen to twenty different articles on your subject.

2. *The New York Times Index* differs from *Newsbank* in that it goes back further in time (to 1851), it indexes only one newspaper, and that entire newspaper is microfilmed each day. For each year there is a separate volume. To use *The New York Times Index,* look up your topic at the time it was in the news. Articles are arranged under the topic in chronological order.

The New York Times Index not only lists the titles of the articles, it also gives summaries or abstracts of them. Thus, from the *Index* itself you can get a capsule of a story or series of stories. If you want more detail, the *Index* tells you which issue of the *Times* you need to find on microfilm in order to read the entire story.

3. Indexes for the *Wall Street Journal* and for the *Christian Science Monitor* are also available. Usually you can find your local newspapers on microfilm in the library too. These will go way back if you live in an old town or city. Ask your librarian what sort of index is available to help you locate stories in these newspapers.

4. For a different point of view you can look up your topic in the *Index to the Times (London)*. From 1962 on this index is available in bound volumes. Prior to 1962, and going back to 1790, the index is on microfilm. The newspaper itself, also on microfilm, goes back to 1785.

How to Use Other Sources of Information in the Library

In doing research you will not always limit yourself to information from books, magazines, journals, and newspapers. You may also want to find out *biographical information* about someone, locate information in *governmental publications,* get help with your own *bibliography* building, find an *essay, play, short story,* or a *poem,* or even check on the *history of a word.* There are volumes to help you do all these things, and they are usually located in the reference room.

1. *Biographical information* can be obtained from a variety of volumes, including the *Biography Index,* the *Dictionary of American Biography,* the *Dictionary of National Biography, Current Biography,* and the various *Who's Whos* (in America, the South and the Southwest, International, and so on).

2. If you are interested in locating information in *government publications,* there are two main indexes you can consult — the *Public Affairs Information Service Bulletin* and the *Monthly Catalog.* The relatively new *Index to U.S. Government Periodicals* is also a useful guide. See if your library also owns the periodicals it indexes, called *U.S. Government Periodicals,* which are on microfiche and are arranged by subject like *Newsbank.*

3. If you have been through the card catalog and some of the indexes to periodicals and still want to expand your bibliography, use the *Bibliographic Index.* It will tell you where to find bibliographies on your topic that have been published either as parts of books, pamphlets, in periodicals, or as separate books.

4. Sometimes you want to locate an *essay, short story, play,* or *poem* that you know is published in some anthology, but you do not know which one. To find an essay, look in the *Essay and General Literature Index;* to find a play, look in the *Play Index;* to find a short story, use the *Short Story Index;* and to find a poem, look under the author, title, or first line in *Granger's Index to Poetry.* If you want the original source of a familiar saying or quotation, look it up in *Bartlett's Familiar Quotations.* These are only examples; other sources for such materials are also available.

5. Finally, you should know about the biggest and most complete *dictionary* of them all, the *Oxford English Dictionary.* You would use the *O.E.D.* if you wanted to study the history of a word: to learn its origin and see how it has changed in spelling and meaning over the years.

There are many other sources of specialized information in the reference room. Your best guide is the reference librarian, who can usually tell you where to look to find literally any type of information about anything.

How to Do a Computer Search

Most libraries now offer a computer search service that permits you to search the world's literature, in addition to that possessed by your library, for information on your topic. In doing computer searches, your library works through a vendor, such as Dialogue, or Bibliographic Retrieval Service (BRS), to access large data bases that can provide you with lists of sources on your topic within seconds. To use them effectively, you will need to make a tentative outline with a research question or tentative thesis and a list of main ideas. Use this to come up with some key words that describe the information you are seeking. There are some special advantages of computer searches: (1) the information is the most current available; (2) the search can be done much faster than by hand

and more thoroughly since combinations of subjects and/or authors can be used at once; (3) you can specify that the search be done in scholarly or popular literature, that it cover a particular time period, and even that it be confined to a particular language; (4) you will end up with a printed bibliography. In fact, when the data base includes abstracts, you will be provided with an annotated bibliography. Expect to help the library to pay for your search since computer time is expensive. Since you are searching the world's literature, you cannot expect your library to have all of the sources on the computer list. Use the interlibrary loan service to order missing material from another library. Expect such an order to take two to three weeks' time.

Whenever in Doubt in a Library, Ask Questions

Librarians do not mind being asked questions. Here are some examples of the types of questions you might ask the readers' adviser or the reference librarian while you are doing research, and some examples of the answers you might receive. As you read the questions, cover up the answers, which are in the right-hand column, and see how well you can provide answers of your own. There are often several places to search for information. See if, on the basis of this chapter, you can anticipate some of the answers provided or even add additional sources of your own. Note also that some additional indexes and other sources are mentioned beyond those discussed thus far in this chapter.

Questions	*Answers*
I am interested in divorce laws in various states. Where could I find a sampling of current legislation?	In *Newsbank*. Look under the broad category of "Social Relations," and the subcategory "Divorce and Divorce Laws." You will find articles from newspapers from various states which you can then read on microfiche.
I am doing a paper on the "open classroom." Where can I find information on it?	Look up "open classroom" in the *Education Index*. It will lead you to articles on the subject. The ERIC (Educational Resources Information Center) microfiche collection would also have information on the subject.
I want to know the latest scientific research about DNA. Where do I find it?	Look up DNA in the subject index in the back of the most recent volume of *Biological Abstracts*. There will be a list of articles

Questions

How can I find out the current
    birth and death statistics?

I am interested in memory, and I
    want to find the latest articles
    about it.

Where can I find the latest
    information on the world food
    crisis?

I want to do a paper on
    Hemingway. Where do I look
    for critical articles and books
    about his work?

I am doing a paper on Wordsworth
    for my English class. I do not
    want to read a whole book
    about his life. Where can I get
    some quick biographical
    information?

Answers

with the abstract number beside
them. Look up the abstracts by
their numbers in the volume and
read the summary of the
research. Also take a look at
Microbiology Abstracts.

Look in the *Public Affairs
Information Service Bulletin* for
census statistics put out by the
government. *The American
Statistics Index, The Statistical
Abstracts of the United States,*
and the *World Almanac* are
useful sources for locating
statistical information also.

If you want scholarly articles,
consult the *Social Sciences
Index* or *Psychological
Abstracts.* If you want popular
articles, consult the *Readers'
Guide to Periodical Literature.*

The *Public Affairs Information
Service Bulletin* will lead you to
government and other
publications not always listed in
the *Readers' Guide.* The
Readers' Guide is another good
source. For more scholarly
information consult the *Social
Sciences Index.*

Look in the *Humanities Index* and
the *Social Sciences and
Humanities Index.* Look also in
the card catalog. Books *by him*
will be cataloged *first.* The
books *about him and his work,*
which are what you are looking
for, will be cataloged *second.*

Look in the *Dictionary of National
Biography.* It will not only give
you the pertinent facts of his
life, but it will also provide you
with a bibliography to help you
get started on your research.

Questions	*Answers*
	Any general encyclopedia will also provide information about Wordsworth.
How can I find out how people felt about the Panama Canal when it was first being built?	Look in *Poole's Index to Periodical Literature* for the years during which and just after it was built.

Evaluate the Research Material You Have Selected

One of your concerns in doing research is to select the books and articles that will give you the most informed, detailed, up-to-date, reliable, and intelligent information available. Here are some suggestions to help you pick the best sources. When you first pick up a book or article, check introductory material and/or headnotes to get some idea of its quality and the author's general competency. Notice also *when* the material was published. Sometimes you will need the most recent material available, or you may want material published at the time your topic was of greatest concern to the most people.

You can find out still more about a book and its author by reading some book reviews in the *Book Review Index,* the *Book Review Digest,* or the *Technical Book Review Index* in the library. Reviews will give you some idea about how the book was originally received by experts in the field. You might also consult a biographical dictionary to get additional information about the author.

Your professors can also tell you about the reputation, quality, and general worth of books and articles written in their own fields. In fact, asking your professors for the titles of some of the best books and articles on their subjects is often one of the best ways to start research.

Finally, you can compare passages on the same subject in several different books to judge which seem better than the others. If one or two of the books seem to be more accurate and to contain fuller explanations and more documentation than the others, you would probably be safe in choosing those books as the best of the several available.

How to Take Research Notes

When you have gathered together a variety of the best research sources your library has to offer on your subject, you are then ready to begin reading and taking notes. Keep your tentative outline handy so that you will not read off your subject. Furthermore, as you read, make any necessary changes in your tentative outline. You may find that one item on the outline interests you more than the others. Early in your research, then, recast your paper. Revise your outline, relabel some of the tabs in your file, and then read for material to fill in the new, revised outline.

Don't try to read each book and article you have selected all the way through. You will find the material you need more rapidly and accurately if you survey all books and articles you use before you take any notes from them and then consult the index. Use the methods for surveying described in Chapter 7. Look especially for the chapter or chapters that are relevant to your research. During this process you may also spot one or two chapters that set forth the author's major theories in the book. By reading or surveying these chapters, you can often gain almost as much information as you would by reading the entire book.

The skimming methods that you will develop if you work through the ten labs in the appendix to this book will also help you do library research more efficiently. Use all of these methods to speed up the process of looking for information that is relevant to your topic.

As you read and take notes, think about the final outline for your paper and solve as many organizational problems as possible as you go along. One student made a fifteen-page final outline for a paper intended to advocate certain legislation *before* he began his research. When he began to read, he found the legislation had already been passed. His fifteen-page outline was useless. He had to shift his focus to ways in which the new legislation could be made generally known to the public, and redid his outline. His mistake was making an elaborate outline before he began to read. A brief, tentative outline would have saved him time. You cannot know how your subject may shift and change until you get into your reading. Then you need to be alert enough to shift and change with it.

Every once in a while you should take the cards from behind a heading, read through them, and put them in a sequence that seems logical to you. Move some of them to other sections if it seems appropriate to do so, or create new sections. As you move your cards into sequential order, you are continuing to shape your paper while you do research. You will not make the mistake, so commonly made by students, of accumulating a pile of dozens or even hundreds of note cards, all loosely related to your subject, with no idea of how to use them in your paper.

In addition to jotting the subject of each card at the top, it is also important to indicate briefly, below the subject, the source of information on that card. The author's last name is usually enough; if you have two or more sources by the same author, write the title of the source in brief form. You may have numbered your bibliography cards. Then all you need write on the note card is the corresponding number. You can be brief because the complete information about the source is on the bibliography card.

The note cards you make will be of three types. First, there is material that you want to quote exactly as the author wrote it. Write it on your card exactly as it appears in your source. Put quotation marks around it so that you can later incorporate this material in your paper as a direct quote. It's a good idea to double-check for accuracy all direct quotes you record. Figure 14.5 shows a

Introduction – problems

Natl. Advisory Council, <u>Third Annual Report</u>.

"Dropout rate among Indian youth is the highest in the country. Delinquency among Indian youth is the worst among all other youth groups. Suicide rate is among the highest of any group in our society. Poverty is rampant on Indian Reservations as is alcoholism, mental illness, and a general state of hopelessness ...." p. 23 quote

Figure 14.5 First type of note card: Direct quote from a book

card that contains a direct quote from a book. Notice that the numbers of the pages on which the material originally appeared are written at the end of the quote. Note, also, that only one side of a card is used. Never take notes on both sides of a note card. You need to be able to lay cards out on your desk to see patterns of ideas. If a quote is too long to fit on one card, use two. Write a brief title with the abbreviation *cont.* on the second card, and number the cards.

You will not always want to quote directly from the sources you are researching. You should quote exactly when the material is particularly well expressed or when the author is well known and you prefer to use his or her exact words. More often, however, you will paraphrase, or put into your own words, what the author has said. The paraphrased note is the second type of research note you will take. Figure 14.6 provides an example from a magazine article. In paraphrasing it is important to read and rephrase the material carefully so that you will not change the author's meaning and thus misrepresent the material. Indicate paraphrasing on your note card by omitting the quotation marks and by writing *paraphrase* on the card. You must clearly state on the card the source and page number of the paraphrased material. Even though you have changed the wording, you must let your reader know its origin.

A third type of note you will make as you do your research will have *mine* or *me* written at the top. On these cards record ideas that occur to you as you read and work with your subject. Usually the more of these you have, the better. For some papers it is essential that you have ideas of your own. For others that are more purely research papers, the notes on sources will be more important. Figure 14.7 provides an example of this third type of note card.

Continue to read or skim through the material in your bibliography, continue to take notes, to label and file them, and your paper will take shape. Check occasionally to see if one area of your paper is sketchy and another too

Introduction - statistics

U. S. News - Wounded Knee Siege
1970 U. S. Census statistics for Indian
families on reservations:
Ave. family income: $1500 (less than half
present poverty level)
Unemployment: 40-80%
Life Expectancy: 44 years (compare 64 for
other Americans)
Infant mortality 3 times greater than
for other Americans
p. 113 paraphrase

Figure 14.6 Second type of note card: Paraphrased note from an article

detailed. At any one point during your research you may decide to delete a
meager section and divide a large section into subsections. Or you may decide
to do more research on the meager section.

When you have finished your research, read through all your cards. Make
sure they are all labeled. Put them in the sequence that you will follow in writing
your paper. After you have finished your paper, reorder them alphabetically and
use them to compile the final bibliography or list of works cited.

Solutions - preservation of culture prob.

Mine:
Indian history and culture can be
preserved through education. Yet educated
Indians leave the reservation and
enter the public sector. 90% of Indians
now attend public schools. Public
schools may have to help preserve
native culture if it is to survive.

Figure 14.7 Third type of note card: Your original idea

At the Very Least . . .

This chapter has described some complete and thorough ways of doing library research. If you do not use all of these ways, *at the very least* do the following:

1. Learn to use the card catalogue and find a book.
2. Learn to use periodical indexes and find an article. Start with the *Reader's Guide.*
3. Learn to read material on the microform reader. Start with *Time* and *Newsweek.*
4. Take some notes on cards, writing one idea or piece of information per card. Include the sources and page numbers.

SUMMARY

Use your tentative outline to guide your research. Look for bibliographical items relevant to headings on this outline. Each source in your bibliography should be recorded on a separate card. A complete bibliography usually includes the names of books, magazine and journal articles, and materials from other sources, some of which might be in microform. Once you have found that your library owns the sources in your bibliography, you then need to find them, evaluate their relative worth, and take research notes on them. Notes should be taken on cards, with one item of information per card. Notes are of three types — direct quotes, paraphrases, or your own ideas. As you accumulate research materials, label and organize them as you go along. Then it will be relatively easy to make your final outline and write your paper.

EXERCISES

A. Chapter Questions

1. Match the items in the two lists below

    _____ **a.** card catalog   _____ **f.** call number
    _____ **b.** stacks   _____ **g.** microforms
    _____ **c.** periodicals   _____ **h.** bibliography
    _____ **d.** periodical indexes   _____ **i.** circulation desk
    _____ **e.** abstracts   _____ **j.** subject, author, and title cards

    (1) There is at least one of these for each book in the library, with the exception of some novels.
    (2) Books that help you locate magazine and journal articles on a given subject.

(3) The place to check out books.

(4) A card file for the books in the library.

(5) Where the books in the library are found.

(6) Material published at regular intervals, such as magazines and journals.

(7) Give short summaries of books and articles in a subject area.

(8) List of books on a subject.

(9) Used to locate a book in a particular place on a particular shelf.

(10) Material filmed so small that it must be read on a special reading machine.

2. What is the difference between bibliography cards and note cards?

3. How many ideas or pieces of information should you write on each note card? _____ Why?

4. You will make three sorts of note cards, each recording a different type of information. What are these types of information?

5. What is a paraphrase?

B. Application of Skills

1. *Finding books.* Select a topic that interests you or that you have to research anyway. Go to the card catalog and find the names of three books on the topic. Make a bibliography card (Figure 14.2) for each of these books. Check the directory to find where these books are located. Then go to that area and find *one* of them. Survey the book as you were taught to do in Chapter 7. Then locate a chapter that has a useful treatment of your topic. Survey it as you were taught to do in Chapter 7. Make two note cards. One of these note cards should contain a direct quote (Figure 14.5). The other should contain a paraphrase (Figure 14.6).

2. *Finding articles.* Use the periodical indexes to look up three articles about your topic. Make a bibliography card (Figure 14.3) for each article. Use the Serial Holdings List, or whatever other system your library uses, to help you locate the periodicals in which these articles appear. Find *one* of the articles, survey it for five minutes, and write two note cards, one a quote and one a paraphrase. You should now have an idea of your own about your topic. Record this idea on a third note card (see Figure 14.7).

3. *Using microforms.* Look up your topic in one of the newspaper indexes. Find three newspaper articles about your topic and write a bibliography card for each of them (Figure 14.3). Find a copy of *one* paper in which one of these articles appears and read it on the microform reader. Write *one* note card, either a quote or a paraphrase. Write another note card that contains an observation or idea of your own.

C. Topics for Your Learning Journal

1. Go to the reference section of the library, select any reference book, and write a short essay about it. Include the book's title and information about its purpose, organization, and how it might be useful to you. Add one interesting bit of information from the book.

2. Look up *The New York Times* on the microform reader for the day you were born. Write a paragraph about what else was going on in the world that day.

3. Browse through any section of the library and write the authors and titles of five books that look like they might be interesting to read. Describe why you think they might be interesting to read.

15

Adapting the Paper for Oral Presentation

When you have finished reading this chapter, you will know the following:

1. How an oral report is different from a written report.
2. How to give an interesting oral report.

The Difference Between Oral and Written Reports

To make an oral presentation of a written paper interesting to the class, you will need to make a few changes in it. Your changes can be written in the margins of the paper itself, or you can make a speaking outline. To make these changes, you will need to know the main differences between oral and written style. Here they are.

1. Oral reports have **fewer main ideas** *than written reports*
Listeners, unlike readers who can go back and reread, have only one chance to get the main ideas. If too many of them are presented in a short time, the listener tunes out and misses most of them. Therefore, in adapting a paper for oral presentation, your first step is to go through your paper and underline and number the most important ideas. Cross out the less important ones. It is better

for your audience to understand a few ideas well than not to understand anything you say.

2. *Oral reports contain* more supporting material *than do written reports* The reason, again, is that the listener has only one chance at the ideas being presented. If these ideas are accompanied by multiple examples and perhaps a diagram on the blackboard or some other type of illustration, the listener will be more likely to understand and remember the main ideas. When you adapt a paper for oral presentation, think up more examples and other bits of supporting material, jot them in the margin, and include them when you give your oral report.

3. *Oral reports have* more transitional material *than written reports* Transitions, you will remember (and if you don't, review Chapter 8), are used to show when a speaker or writer is leaving one idea and introducing the next. Furthermore, transitions emphasize ideas and sometimes state how one idea relates to another. One uses more of them in oral reports than in papers because they make the main points more obvious for the listener. When you are getting your paper ready for oral presentation, write in some obvious transitions so that your main ideas won't be lost on your listeners. A preoutline in the introduction will help your listeners identify your main ideas. Enumeration plus the use of a key phrase is one of the bluntest and most obvious ways to make your main ideas stand out. It is particularly effective for the listeners who, remember, get the main ideas when they hear them the first time or miss them altogether. You can also write internal summaries into your paper before you give it orally. Ideas stand out when you stop occasionally to restate what you have said so far, and then introduce your next topic. Finally, although your written paper may have ended with a conclusion, your oral report will be more effective if you end with a summary, or a repetition of your main ideas.

The transitions described here might seem rather blunt and obvious if they were used in quantity on the printed page. Listeners will not find them so. Instead, with the added transitional material, they will be much more likely to grasp the main ideas of your report. And when listeners are getting the ideas, they are almost always attentive and interested.

4. *Oral reports are* more repetitious *than written reports* Speakers not only repeat ideas in preoutlines, internal summaries, and final summaries, they also repeat key phrases ("these differences," "these changes and adaptations"), whenever necessary, so that the listeners will know at all times exactly what is being talked about. It is not uncommon for speakers to repeat a complicated main idea right after they have said it the first time, in slightly different language, so that the audience will get two chances at it.

5. *Oral reports contain* more personal pronouns *(I, you, us, we) than do written reports* The speaker directly addresses the listening audience because it is there, immediately present. Write a few personal pronouns into your report to establish a less formal, more personal rapport with your audience.

6. *Oral reports contain* more direct questions to the audience *than do written reports* The purpose of such questioning is to create greater audience involvement. Questions invite the members of your audience to think through their own experience and to begin to anticipate what you might say. They become more involved and interested.

7. *Oral reports sometimes have* less perfect sentence structure *than do written reports* You can use your voice, rather than syntax or punctuation, to emphasize an important idea. A dangling participle, for instance, may dangle to the eye but not to the ear. "Having wasted time all day, there was no time left for either study or play," looks bad on the printed page. It makes sense, however, when said aloud, and would not stand out in an oral report as a particularly gross error. In speech you can also get away with a whole string of short sentences that would make a written report appear choppy and abrupt.

8. *Finally, oral reports are* much less formal and are more conversational *than written papers* The reason for this difference is, again, that the audience is present. Consequently, in an oral report, it is better to say, "Let's not forget" rather than "It should be noted that," and "I think" rather than "According to this writer." In fact, your report will go better if you look away from your manuscript as frequently as possible to speak to your audience as though you were in a conversation with them.

The Speech Outline

One way to adapt your written report for oral presentation is to write your changes on the original manuscript. You may find, however, that you have written in so many changes that it is almost impossible to speak from this marked-up, confusing paper. Solve the problem by using your notes on the paper to guide you in writing a speech outline. You would also make a speech outline for any oral report that was not based on a previous written assignment.

A speech outline is somewhat different from other outlines in the following ways:

1. The introduction should be written out in complete sentences exactly as you intend to give it. Underline the purpose sentence so that you won't forget to emphasize it when you give your report.
2. Write out all the main ideas and the major transitions in complete sentences. These are important parts of the report, and you don't want to muff them in delivery.
3. Write out the summary in complete sentences just as you intend to say it. It is another important part of your report.

4. All subideas and supporting material may be listed as phrases on the outline.

When you have finished making your outline, read it out loud rapidly in order to make sure that there are no awkward or unclear parts and that you can speak from it fluently.

Visual Aids

Any oral presentation will be more interesting and memorable if you use some visual aids. Blackboards and actual specimen examples are good, as are prepared charts, diagrams, graphs, or a list of main points on poster board. Opaque or overhead projectors, videotapes, films, and cassette tapes can also enliven an oral presentation. In order to use visual aids successfully, there are two important rules to remember:

1. Make them BIG enough so that everyone in the room can see them easily.
2. Pull them out only when you are actually going to refer to them. If they are out during your entire speech, they will distract your audience.

The Importance of Practice

When you have finished planning and writing the outline for your oral report, *practice* the report silently to yourself at least two times and out loud to the wall at least once. A half hour spent in this way will ensure fluent delivery, which is important if you are to keep your audience's attention. It will also keep you from getting excessively nervous while you are giving your report. Time your report so that you will not go overtime. Speak loudly so that your audience can hear you, and look them in the eye. Work to develop a genuine sense of communication with your audience.

At the Very Least . . .

This chapter has presented some ideal ways of doing an oral report. If you cannot follow all of the suggestions, *at the very least* do the following:

1. Plan and make a brief outline of your report.
2. Rehearse it until you can give it fluently.
3. Don't go overtime.
4. Use eye contact and work to communicate with your audience.

SUMMARY

Since listeners cannot go back and reread, they must get the ideas in an oral report when they hear them the first time. Make it easier for your listeners to understand your points by limiting the number of main ideas in your oral reports, by adding supporting material and transitions, and by repeating important phrases and ideas. Make your oral reports more interesting by using personal pronouns, by asking questions of your audience, by speaking as though you were conversing with them, and by using visual aids. Adapt a written report for oral presentation by writing the changes to oral style in the margins or by rewriting the entire report in speech outline form. Finally, practice oral reports so that you will be fluent and not excessively nervous when you give them.

Exercises

A. Chapter Questions

1. Why do oral reports have fewer main ideas than written reports?
   a. The audience has only once chance to get the ideas and can't grasp more than a few.
   b. An oral report is shorter than a written report.
   c. An oral report must be developed in outline form.
   d. Main ideas are more important in an oral report than they are in a written report.
2. Which of the following is the *most* effective type of supporting material in oral reports?
   a. quotations   c. comparisons and contrasts
   b. statistics   d. visual aids
3. What is the *most* important reason for using more transitional material in an oral report than in a written report?
   a. To make the main ideas stand out so that the listeners will be sure to get them
   b. To move from one idea to another
   c. To state relationships between ideas
   d. To summarize ideas
4. What are some particularly blunt transitions that are useful in the oral report?
   a. A preoutline in the introduction
   b. An internal summary
   c. The words *however* or *moreover*
   d. Enumeration plus a key phrase
   e. The words *if . . . then*
   f. The phrase *at the other extreme*
5. How should you practice your speech or oral report?
   a. Say it silently a few times and out loud at least once.
   b. Read it over to yourself.
   c. Get an audience together and rehearse it in front of them.
   d. Say it out loud until you have memorized it word for word.

B. Application of Skills

Look back at page 186 and choose a topic from the list in Exercise B1. Write a brief speech outline for a five-minute oral report. Practice and deliver the report to your class. Use a visual aid during your report.

C. Topics for Your Learning Journal

1. Either as a class project or individually, consider the problem of stage fright. Are you bothered by it? How do you feel when you are suffering from it? What can you do to cope with it? Write a brief plan for yourself that includes all of the ways that will help you handle stage fright.
2. Either by yourself or as a class project, describe the qualities that you admire in an excellent speaker. Describe the qualities that irritate and distract you in a poor speaker. Which excellent qualities could you incorporate into your own speaking style?

PART SIX
Summary

16

Evaluating Your Skills

When you have finished reading this chapter, you will know the following:

1. The major skills and qualities that you need for college success.
2. How developing these skills and qualities will improve your chances of finding employment after college.
3. Which skills you should review and continue to develop.

The Skills and Qualities Essential for Academic Success

Not long ago the faculty members at a large university were asked, "Are there skills that you wish your students had but that you yourself have neither the time nor the desire to teach?" They were also asked, "Which skills do you consider essential to earn an A in your class?" The faculty listed the following qualities and skills, all of which can be developed while you are a university student.

1. Develop your writing skills All of your professors, whether they teach math, English, history, or physical education, expect you to be able to write clearly and legibly. Everything you write should be well organized and written in complete sentences. Type papers if possible. Double-space and write in ink when you can't. Your handwriting need not be pretty, but it is essential that your professors be able to read it.

2. Improve your reading skills Your professors expect you to be able and willing to read difficult material. You will have to read for all of your classes. In some you will read greater volumes of material than in others. You probably should not take more than one or two heavy reading classes each semester. Then you will have time to read for every class as closely and thoroughly as possible. Reading skills considered especially important by university professors are as follows: reading the textbook regularly; reading and interpreting graphs; thinking about what you have read and evaluating it critically; reading and interpreting test questions.

3. Improve your speaking and listening skills Your professors will assume that you can listen, take notes, and remember the material from long, complicated lectures. Furthermore, they will expect you to be able to participate in discussion and give oral reports in the smaller classes you take. If you are not satisfied with your present skills, take a speech course while you are in college.

4. Develop some degree of computer literacy Even if you never work directly with computers, your life will still be affected by them both while you are in college and after you graduate. You should plan to learn some uses of computers, develop a minimal computer vocabulary, and learn the rudiments of operating a personal computer.

5. Develop an adequate math background Your professors will assume that you have an adequate math background for those courses that require it. A basic background in math, algebra, and trigonometry is important for most university science classes and for virtually all engineering and math classes. If you don't have a good math background, and intend to take classes that demand math, you will have to develop it. See if your university has facilities to help you remedy a weak math background. If it does not, you may have to take some math classes at a nearby high school or take individual instruction from a math tutor.

6. Plan to think while you are in college Your professors all want you to think. Of the more than 100 professors polled, 86 percent said that an ability to reflect on and understand the concepts taught in their classes was essential to success. They expect you to try to apply what you are learning to everyday examples, to make what you are learning useful. Furthermore, your professors hope that you will not be intellectually timid. Most professors will be far more interested in your ability to think about their subject than in your ability to parrot back what they have said.

7. Take time to memorize The ability to memorize is important, however, and should not be slighted. If you are to think and reflect, you must have something to think about. So, first, you must memorize material as a prelude to, and sometimes as a companion to, reflective thought.

The ability to memorize is essential in languages, chemistry, biology, and math classes. In such classes you must memorize material daily in order to keep up. Even though most college history professors do not usually demand that you know the exact date for every historical event, they do expect you to know approximately when things happened. You will find it useful to plot and memorize a time line that encompasses major historical events. Such a time line will serve you over and over again in many other courses besides history, such as English literature and the history of art or science.

8. Develop self-discipline, a certain degree of self-confidence, and a willingness to take responsibility In other words, your professors want to be able to count on you. They expect you to come to class. Furthermore, they expect you to get the assignments straight and to finish them on time without much supervision. They expect you to keep the quality of your assignments consistently high. If you miss a class, they expect you to take the initiative to find out what you missed and to do something about it. They expect you to be willing to work both in class and outside of class. In cumulative subjects, such as math, science, and foreign languages, in which the material of the class builds on all that has gone before, your professors expect you to learn material daily and to review and relearn it regularly so that new material will make sense to you.

9. Learn patience and determination You should not, your professors say, expect instant answers to everything. Reading and listening in college are more time-consuming and much more difficult that in high school. You may be able to comprehend ideas quickly, but to master and remember them takes time. You should resign yourself from the outset to putting in one, two, and sometimes three hours of study time outside of class for every hour you spend in class. This much is expected of you, and you will experience greater success if you accept and meet these demands.

10. Foster a mature attitude toward your college professors and the classes they teach There are no "discipline problems," as there may have been in your high school. Your professor is on your side and wants to work for you and with you. Don't be shy about seeking your professor's help. One third of the professors polled said they would like to have more contact with students. They cannot seek you out, however. You must go to them, and the best time is during their posted office hours.

11. Finally, make an effort to look like a student in class It doesn't matter what you wear to class so long as you come with notebooks, pens, and the textbook if it is to be discussed. Then, work to overcome your shyness. Participate in class. Establish eye contact with the professor. Don't be afraid to ask questions, even if you are afraid they may be dumb ones. Three out of four of the professors polled indicated that students had to be able to learn during class time in order to get an A grade.

The Skills and Qualities Essential for the World of Work

Now, look back over this list of eleven skills and qualities your university professors expect you to have. They are exactly those qualities your future employers will also be seeking. The College Board recently sponsored some dialogues with 200 business leaders and educators, and the general conclusion reached by these individuals was that both professors and employers expect you to have the same skills, qualities, and special competencies to succeed in college *and* in the workplace. Both expect you to be proficient in the basic communication skills and in mathematics and both expect you to be able to study, think, and know something about computers. The reason for this conclusion is obvious. The most successful people in the workplace are those who have learned how to learn and who then continue learning throughout their lifetimes. Those are the individuals who get ahead.

You have three main tasks to accomplish in college: getting an education; getting an idea of what you want to do when you leave school; and developing the skills and abilities described in this chapter. If you accomplish these three tasks, you will be both educated and employable when you leave college. And those are accomplishments that almost every college student would admit are worth the time necessary to obtain them.

Evaluate Your Skills

Use the following scale to evaluate your use of the skills and abilities taught in this book. When you have read through the list and have checked the appropriate columns, analyze your responses. The checkmarks in columns 4 and 5 indicate that you are successfully developing good learning skills and habits in those areas. The checkmarks in columns 1, 2, and 3 remind you of those areas where you need more work. If you have forgotten a technique and want to review it, turn to the chapter listed in the review column 6.

Column 1. **DIDN'T TRY** because don't understand or unconvinced it will work. Column 2. **UNDERSTAND AND INTEND TO USE** but haven't yet. Column 3. **USED ONCE OR TWICE** but haven't used since. Column 4. **USE OFF AND ON** when I need to. Column 5. **ALWAYS USE** either since learning in this book or from past habit. Column 6. **CHAPTER FOR REVIEW**	DIDN'T TRY	INTEND TO USE	USED ONCE OR TWICE	USE OFF AND ON	ALWAYS USE	CHAPTER FOR REVIEW
ADAPTING TO CLASSES						
1. Analyze the organization of each class						3
2. Analyze your responsibilities in each class						3
3. Take advantage of outside help						3
ASSIGNMENTS						
1. Understand and record assignments accurately on assignment sheets						2
2. Write due date for each assignment						2
3. Divide long assignments into short steps						2,13
4. Do assignments regularly and on time						2
CONCENTRATION						
1. Have a regular place to study						2
2. Recite and write while studying						10,11
3. Reward yourself for starting and finishing a job						1,2
4. Solve problems instead of worrying about them						1
5. Set priorities for jobs						2
6. Work to finish a job rather than to put in time						2
7. Avoid distractions while taking notes or studying						1

	1. DIDN'T TRY	2. INTEND TO USE	3. USED ONCE OR TWICE	4. USE OFF AND ON	5. ALWAYS USE	6. CHAPTER FOR REVIEW
Column 1. **DIDN'T TRY** because don't understand or unconvinced it will work. Column 2. **UNDERSTAND AND INTEND TO USE** but haven't yet. Column 3. **USED ONCE OR TWICE** but haven't used since. Column 4. **USE OFF AND ON** when I need to. Column 5. **ALWAYS USE** either since learning in this book or from past habit. Column 6. **CHAPTER FOR REVIEW**						
8. Read summary of previous class just before next class						4
9. Label lecture notes in left-hand margin to force concentration						4
10. Take marginal notes while reading						9
DISCUSSION IN CLASS 1. Prepare for discussion						6
2. Take some notes on discussion						4,6
3. Listen well, and when you contribute, keep on the subject						6
EXAMS, PREPARING FOR AND TAKING 1. Allow yourself plenty of time to prepare for an exam						11
2. Make table of contents sheets to organize your exam studying						11
3. Make study sheets by topic when studying for exams						11
4. Read all exam questions thoroughly, noting important words						12
5. Answer the questions you know first						12
6. Proofread exams carefully						12
7. Show all your work on quantitative exams						12
8. Use what you have learned from the test itself to help answer difficult questions						12

Column 1. **DIDN'T TRY** because don't understand or unconvinced it will work. Column 2. **UNDERSTAND AND INTEND TO USE** but haven't yet. Column 3. **USED ONCE OR TWICE** but haven't used since. Column 4. **USE OFF AND ON** when I need to. Column 5. **ALWAYS USE** either since learning in this book or from past habit. Column 6. **CHAPTER FOR REVIEW**	1. DIDN'T TRY	2. INTEND TO USE	3. USED ONCE OR TWICE	4. USE OFF AND ON	5. ALWAYS USE	6. CHAPTER FOR REVIEW
9. Write brief outlines for essay questions						12
10. Manage your time during an exam						12
11. Come right to the point in essay answers; don't pad or digress, but do support your answer						12
12. Work to ignore distractions						12
13. Work to control exam anxiety						12
14. Learn from your errors on exams						12
LEARNING STYLES 1. Understand your preferred learning style						3
2. Adapt your style of learning to your different classes						3
LECTURE NOTE TAKING 1. Make notes into chapters with title at top						4
2. Outline lecture notes as much as possible						4
3. Be an active, aggressive note taker						4
4. Always attend lectures						4
5. Take complete lecture notes						4
6. Develop abbreviations and symbols for note taking						4
7. Put your own ideas into your lecture notes						4
8. Write in ink and on one side of paper						4
9. Revise notes within 24 hours						4

	1. DIDN'T TRY	2. INTEND TO USE	3. USED ONCE OR TWICE	4. USE OFF AND ON	5. ALWAYS USE	6. CHAPTER FOR REVIEW
Column 1. **DIDN'T TRY** because don't understand or unconvinced it will work. Column 2. **UNDERSTAND AND INTEND TO USE** but haven't yet. Column 3. **USED ONCE OR TWICE** but haven't used since. Column 4. **USE OFF AND ON** when I need to. Column 5. **ALWAYS USE** either since learning in this book or from past habit. Column 6. **CHAPTER FOR REVIEW**						
10. Label notes in margin, cover notes, then learn, using labels as cues						4
11. Write brief summaries of your notes						4
LIBRARY RESEARCH 1. Know how to find books, articles, and other materials in the library						14
2. Ask questions whenever you get confused or can't find something in the library						14
3. Survey a book or article before taking research materials from it						14
4. Evaluate how competently written your research sources are						14
MATH AND PROBLEM-SOLVING COURSES 1. Write in lecture notes both problems on blackboard and verbal explanations given by professor						4
2. Make math strategy cards						9
3. Make math fact cards						9
4. Write definitions of math symbols and specialized vocabulary on definition sheets						9
MEMORY 1. Look for a logical pattern of ideas in material you wish to remember						10
2. Associate the unfamiliar with the familiar						10

Column 1. **DIDN'T TRY** because don't understand or un- convinced it will work. Column 2. **UNDERSTAND AND INTEND TO USE** but haven't yet. Column 3. **USED ONCE OR TWICE** but haven't used since. Column 4. **USE OFF AND ON** when I need to. Column 5. **ALWAYS USE** either since learning in this book or from past habit. Column 6. **CHAPTER FOR REVIEW**	1. DIDN'T TRY	2. INTEND TO USE	3. USED ONCE OR TWICE	4. USE OFF AND ON	5. ALWAYS USE	6. CHAPTER FOR REVIEW
3. Make lists, diagrams, or "maps" of materials to be learned						9,10
4. Write and recite when you study more than you read and listen						10
5. Visualize and draw diagrams and pictures						10
6. Think up your own examples						10
7. Memorize facts for some classes						10
8. Make up sentences, rhymes, or words to help you remember						10
9. Memorize just before you go to sleep						10
10. Review every week or two						10
11. Elaborate on material you are learning						10
12. Use your internal monitoring system to tell you when you have learned something						10
MOTIVATION 1. Have a reason for going to college						1
2. Set short-term and long-term goals and work to achieve them						1
3. Use positive self-talk when doing difficult tasks						1
4. Find something interesting in boring classes						1
5. Work yourself out of dead ends						1

Column 1. **DIDN'T TRY**
because don't understand or unconvinced it will work.
Column 2. **UNDERSTAND AND INTEND TO USE**
but haven't yet.
Column 3. **USED ONCE OR TWICE**
but haven't used since.
Column 4. **USE OFF AND ON**
when I need to.
Column 5. **ALWAYS USE**
either since learning in this book or from past habit.
Column 6. **CHAPTER FOR REVIEW**

	1. DIDN'T TRY	2. INTEND TO USE	3. USED ONCE OR TWICE	4. USE OFF AND ON	5. ALWAYS USE	6. CHAPTER FOR REVIEW
ORAL REPORTS						
1. Give all oral reports in oral style						15
2. Speak from a speech outline when giving an oral report						15
3. Rehearse all oral presentations						15
4. Enliven oral reports with visual aids						15
ORGANIZING IDEAS						
1. Perceive the organization of a course						3
2. Perceive the organization of a lecture						4
3. Perceive the organization of a book						7
4. Perceive the organization of a chapter						7
5. Organize your own ideas in writing a paper						13
6. Organize your own ideas in doing a speech or oral report						15
7. Organize material by topics on study sheets for exam preparation						11
8. Organize essay exam answers before you begin to write						12
ORGANIZING STUDY MATERIALS						
1. Organize lecture notes, class materials, and reading materials so you can find them						2
ORIGINAL THINKING						
1. Put own ideas in [square brackets] in lecture notes						4

	1. DIDN'T TRY	2. INTEND TO USE	3. USED ONCE OR TWICE	4. USE OFF AND ON	5. ALWAYS USE	6. CHAPTER FOR REVIEW
Column 1. **DIDN'T TRY** because don't understand or un-convinced it will work. Column 2. **UNDERSTAND AND INTEND TO USE** but haven't yet. Column 3. **USED ONCE OR TWICE** but haven't used since. Column 4. **USE OFF AND ON** when I need to. Column 5. **ALWAYS USE** either since learning in this book or from past habit. Column 6. **CHAPTER FOR REVIEW**						
2. Write own ideas in margins and on fly-leaves of textbooks						9
3. Write own ideas before doing research for a paper						13
4. Write own ideas on study sheets						11
5. Present original material in exam answers						12
6. Think about what you are learning both inside and outside of class						4,10
READING 1. Survey a book before you read it						7
2. Survey a chapter before you read it						7
3. Identify the main idea in paragraph or section of material and note how it is developed						8
4. Jot down main ideas in margin						1,9
5. Note how ideas in a chapter are organized						8
6. Write summaries at end of each section of textbook material						9
7. Map the main ideas						9
8. Recite main points in a chapter as soon as you've read it						10
9. Isolate and define unfamiliar concepts in your textbooks						5,9
10. Take summary notes on library reading						9

	1. DIDN'T TRY	2. INTEND TO USE	3. USED ONCE OR TWICE	4. USE OFF AND ON	5. ALWAYS USE	6. CHAPTER FOR REVIEW
Column 1. **DIDN'T TRY** because don't understand or unconvinced it will work. Column 2. **UNDERSTAND AND INTEND TO USE** but haven't yet. Column 3. **USED ONCE OR TWICE** but haven't used since. Column 4. **USE OFF AND ON** when I need to. Column 5. **ALWAYS USE** either since learning in this book or from past habit. Column 6. **CHAPTER FOR REVIEW**						
11. Develop a range of reading and skimming speeds						Labs Appendix
TIME MANAGEMENT 1. Make a Time Analysis Worksheet						2
2. Make Time Management Worksheets						2
3. Learn during class time						2
4. Study when you're most alert and get off to a fast start						2
5. Use small amounts of time such as hours between classes						2
6. Find enough time to put in one, two, or three hours outside of class for every hour in class						2
VOCABULARY 1. Isolate, write on vocabulary sheets, and learn the specialized and general vocabulary for each course						5
2. Know and use vocabulary terms when taking exams						5
3. Use a dictionary or glossary regularly						5
4. Consult a thesaurus for synonyms						5
WRITING PAPERS 1. Select, narrow down to manageable size, and focus a subject for the paper						13

	DIDN'T TRY	INTEND TO USE	USED ONCE OR TWICE	USE OFF AND ON	ALWAYS USE	CHAPTER FOR REVIEW
Column 1. **DIDN'T TRY** because don't understand or un-convinced it will work. Column 2. **UNDERSTAND AND INTEND TO USE** but haven't yet. Column 3. **USED ONCE OR TWICE** but haven't used since. Column 4. **USE OFF AND ON** when I need to. Column 5. **ALWAYS USE** either since learning in this book or from past habit. Column 6. **CHAPTER FOR REVIEW**	1.	2.	3.	4.	5.	6.
2. Invent ideas for your paper with prewriting activities						13
3. Make a tentative outline to guide research						13
4. Take all research notes on cards						14
5. Make note cards with direct quotes, para-phrases, and your own ideas						14
6. Make an outline to guide your writing						13
7. Compose rapidly when writing a paper; do some rewriting as you write						13
8. Revise for organization, sentence struc-ture, words, and punctuation						13
9. Read paper aloud when revising						13
10. Eliminate all writing errors before submit-ting paper						13

APPENDIX

Ten Labs to Improve Your Reading Speed and Skimming Skills

Introduction

The purpose of this section of the book is to provide you with higher speeds than you presently possess for those occasions when it is appropriate to use them. You will use your highest reading speeds when you are reading novels and light nonfiction, newspapers, news magazines, skimming research materials in the library, and surveying or reviewing textbook assignments. YOU SHOULD NOT EXPECT TO SPEED READ YOUR TEXTBOOKS. Any material, like a textbook, that is new and complicated and that must be learned will have to be read slowly and carefully.

How to Work with the Reading Labs

The ten labs in this part of the book are all organized in the same way. Each begins with some *instruction* on improving reading speed. The instruction is followed by a *procedure* to help you improve your speed. Next you will make a *lab sheet* for each of the ten labs. Keep your lab sheets in a folder. Finally, you will chart your progress both in speed and comprehension on the *graphs* on page 251.

You may do the ten reading labs every day for ten consecutive days or once a week for ten consecutive weeks. Either way, these labs will be effective in improving both your reading speed and your comprehension.

You may work through these ten labs by yourself. All you need is a watch or, preferably, a kitchen timer and a book that interests you. If you do the labs by yourself, you will have to check your own comprehension. There will be suggestions made later for how you can best do this.

As an alternative, you may work through the ten labs along with a friend. You can then check each other's comprehension. Finally, you may find yourself doing all ten labs in a classroom where this book is used as the text. There the teacher may time your reading and check your comprehension for you. The labs will be effective whichever way you choose to work through them — by yourself, with another individual, or in a group.

Select a Book to Read during Labs

Go to the library or bookstore and select a book that interests you. It should be a novel or light nonfiction, and it should be a book you are willing to continue to read during all ten reading labs. Open it up and sample it before you begin. Does it catch your attention? Is the vocabulary easy enough so that you understand almost all of the words? Read at least two paragraphs to make certain that you can understand the author without difficulty. If the book is too hard to read, select an easier one. You will develop higher reading speeds more easily if you practice with a book that is both interesting and easy for you to read.

Select a book that has uniform printed pages. Rule out books that have large amounts of blank space on most of the pages or that are printed in several sizes of type. Plays, poetry, and collections of short stories or essays are not good for speed practice. The books in the following list, on the other hand, are good, and they are books that most college students like to read. The books in the left column are somewhat easier than those in the right. All of the books are marked as fiction or nonfiction.

1. *The Catcher in the Rye* by J. D. Salinger (fiction)
2. *Marathon Man* or *The Color of Light*, both by William Goldman (fiction)
3. *Pieces of the Game: The Human Drama of Americans Held Hostage in Iran* by Col. Charles W. Scott (nonfiction)
4. *Gifford on Courage* by Frank Gifford (nonfiction)

1. *God Bless You, Mr. Rosewater; Slaughterhouse-Five; Cat's Cradle;* or *The Sirens of Titan;* all by Kurt Vonnegut, Jr. (fiction)
2. *Hanna and Walter: A Love Story* by Hanna and Walter Kohner with Frederick Kohner (nonfiction)
3. *Megatrends* by John Naisbitt (nonfiction)

5. *Of Mice and Men* by John Steinbeck (fiction)
6. *The Old Man and the Sea* or *The Sun Also Rises*, both by Ernest Hemingway (fiction)
7. *The One-Minute Manager* by Kenneth H. Blanchard (nonfiction)
8. *Mary* by Mary E. Mebane (autobiography)
9. *Animal Farm* by George Orwell (fiction)
10. *Airport* and *Hotel*, both by Arthur Hailey (fiction)
11. *Captains and the Kings; Ceremony of the Innocent;* and *Testimony of Two Men;* all by Taylor Caldwell (fiction)
12. *Carrie; The Shining; The Dead Zone; The Stand; The Firestarter;* all by Stephen King (fiction)
13. *The Danger* or *Banker,* both by Dick Francis (fiction)
14. *The Matarese Circle; The Holcraft Covenant; The Gemini Contenders; The Chancellor Manuscript;* and *The Aquitaine Progression;* all by Robert Ludlum (fiction)
15. *Motherhood: The Second Oldest Profession* by Erma Bombeck (nonfiction)
16. *Murder on the Orient Express* by Agatha Christie (fiction)
17. *Changes* by Danielle Steele (fiction)
18. *Blood and Money* (nonfiction) and *Serpentine* (fiction), both by Thomas Thompson
19. *Ordinary People* by Judith Guest (fiction)
20. *The Call of the Wild* by Jack London (fiction)

4. *Grapes of Wrath; Tortilla Flat;* or *East of Eden;* all by John Steinbeck (fiction)
5. *On the Road* or *The Dharma Bums,* both by Jack Kerouac (fiction)
6. *Brave New World* by Aldous Huxley (fiction)
7. *One Flew Over the Cuckoo's Nest* by Ken Kesey (fiction)
8. *Marie: A True Story* by Peter Maas (nonfiction)
9. *Stranger in a Strange Land* by Robert Heinlein (science fiction)
10. *Without Feathers* and *Getting Even,* both by Woody Allen (fiction)
11. *The Color Purple* by Alice Walker (fiction)
12. *Heartburn* by Nora Ephron (fiction)
13. *The Women's Room* by Marilyn French (fiction)
14. *Behind the Camera* by Dan Rather (nonfiction)
15. *The Hobbit* by J. R. R. Tolkein (fiction)
16. *A Separate Peace* by John Knowles (fiction)
17. *Jane Eyre* by Charlotte Brontë (fiction)
18. *Ghost Story* by Peter Straub (fiction)
19. *The Electric Kool-Aid Acid Test* by Tom Wolfe (fictionalized biography)
20. *All Creatures Great and Small; All Things Bright and Beautiful;* and *All Things Wise and Wonderful;* all by James Herriott (nonfiction)

How Fast Do You Read Now?

Check how fast you are able to read in the book you have selected. In order to do so, you will have to first *calculate the words per page.* Most books have between 250 and 500 words per page, with 320 to 350 the average for paperback books. If you decide to estimate the words per page, go on to the next step: *how to count the pages you have read.* If you want to make an exact calculation of the words per page, use the following procedure.

How to Calculate Words Per Page
1. *Find a full page that is covered with print.* Don't choose the first or last page of a chapter, which might only be partially filled with print.
2. *Count all the letters in one full-length line* on the page. Don't use the first line of a paragraph or any other short line. Do count commas and periods (example: 51 letters).
3. *Divide this number of letters by 5 for the average number of words per line* ($51 \div 5 = 10$ words per line).
4. *Count all the lines down the page,* including the short lines (example: 44 lines).
5. *Subtract 2* from the number of lines to accommodate for short lines ($44 - 2 = 42$ lines per page).
6. Multiply the number of *lines per page* by the number of *words per line* ($10 \times 42 = 420$ words per page). Write this number down in the first blank on the sample lab sheet on page 232.

Now you are ready to test your reading speed. You will need to time your reading for fifteen minutes. A kitchen timer works best because you can set it and forget it until it goes off. If you have to use a watch, set the minute hand at twelve and put it right above your book so that you can glance at it quickly without interrupting your reading. If you use a timer, set it for fifteen minutes. If you use a watch, remember that you will stop when the minute hand registers fifteen minutes past the hour.

As soon as the timer or watch is set, start immediately to read. Read at your normal rate. Don't try to rush at this point. When the time is up, stop and mark where you finished reading in the book. Now count the number of pages you have read.

How to Count the Pages You Have Read
1. Count all the full pages first and jot down that number.
2. Go back and count the short pages such as the pages at the beginning and end of chapters and the page you were reading when you ran out of time. Total these as pages and a fraction of a page (example: 2⅓).
3. Add this number to the number of full pages you jotted down.
4. Mark this total number of pages read in the second blank on the sample lab sheet.

Now you are ready to calculate how many words per minute you have read.

How to Calculate Words Per Minute

1. Multiply the numbers you have written in the first two blanks on the sample lab sheet below (the words per page times the total pages read) to find the *total words read*. Mark this number in the third blank on the lab sheet.

SAMPLE LAB SHEET

Copy this lab sheet on notebook paper for each of the ten labs.

Student's Name _____

Lab#____

Words per page ____ × total pages read ____ = total words read ____

divided by total minutes spent reading ____ = words per minute ____

Name of book _____ Stopped reading, page ____.

Summary:

Lab Instructor's or Student Reader's Comments:

Grade on summary: ____

---

2. Divide the total words read by the total minutes spent reading (record 15 in first blank in second line) to arrive at the *number of words per minute* you have read (record in last blank in second line).

Finish filling in the sample lab sheet by writing your name at the top and writing the name of the book you have read on the third line. Finally, spend five minutes writing a short summary of what you have read in the space provided. Write from memory without looking back at the book.

How to Interpret and Record Your Results on the Graphs

Now look at the words per minute at which you read. The average beginning college student reads such material somewhere in the range of

140–240 words per minute (abbreviated w.p.m. from now on). If your rate falls somewhere in or around this range, you can expect to improve your rate to 400–600 w.p.m., or even more, by working through the ten labs.

At this point read through your summary. Is it complete and detailed? Does it help you remember what you read? Or is it skimpy and general ("this book is about a boy and a dog") so that it doesn't help you remember anything? Judge for yourself how well your summary reflects your understanding and memory of the material. Give yourself a grade on your summary—superior, excellent, very good, adequate, fair, or poor—and mark it on the bottom of the sample lab sheet. If you are working with a friend or a member of a class, have your friend, instructor, or a fellow student read your summary and evaluate it according to the above scale. Your readers should grade your comprehension superior or excellent if reading your summary gives them a sense of having read that part of the book themselves. If it tells them quite a bit about what you have read but leaves gaps, it should be scored adequate or very good. It should be scored fair or poor if you've only written three or four fragments that tell little or nothing about your reading comprehension.

Now, turn to the graphs on page 251 and record the results of both your beginning reading speed and comprehension for this sample lab. If you read at 165 w.p.m., record this fact on the speed graph, to the left of the page, as in Figure A.1. If you or your reader scored your comprehension as excellent, record this fact on the comprehension graph to the right of the page, as in Figure A.2.

This is the base speed and comprehension from which you will work during the next ten lab sessions. Your goal is to improve your speed while maintaining adequate or better comprehension.

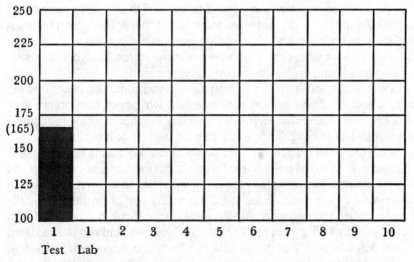

Figure A.1 The speed graph

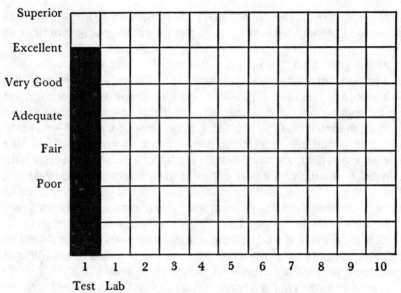

Figure A.2   The comprehension graph (Now record your own beginning speed and comprehension on the graph on page 251.)

Reading Lab 1

Instruction

If your beginning speed was less than 240 w.p.m., you may be wondering why you read so slowly and how fast you should read. The purpose of the instruction in this first lab is to answer both of these questions.

Most people who have never tried to improve their reading speed read everything in the same way and at the same rate of speed. The reason for this is not difficult to discover. Your first reading teachers had you read aloud so that they could hear whether or not you were making progress. You got in the habit of seeing and saying each individual word as you read.

Later, when you were told to read silently, you continued to see and say words to yourself. Some people, in fact, audibly whisper or visibly move their lips as they read. Others may not move their lips, but they mentally pronounce each word while reading. Whispering, moving the lips, or mentally pronouncing *each* word while reading is called *vocalization*. Vocalizing difficult words or passages, even to the point of reading them out loud, at times can help you understand them. The spoken word is always easier to understand than the written word. Thus, even the fastest readers vocalize part of the time, especially when the material is condensed and the vocabulary difficult to understand. Fast readers do not vocalize all or most of the time, however, and you want to learn to avoid doing so also. You do not have to silently pronounce words like *boy, girl, dog, when* each time you see them in order to understand them. You can glance at such words and comprehend them in a fraction of a second — in much less time than it would take you to audibly or mentally pronounce them.

From long habit, however, you may still be mentally pronouncing every or nearly every word you see. It is not difficult to discover whether or not you are. Your beginning reading rate will tell you. If you were to start reading aloud right now, you would read comfortably at about 120–150 w.p.m. Reading aloud rapidly, you might reach 220–240 w.p.m. No one can read aloud much faster than that. Neither can anyone who, reading silently, mentally pronounces each word. If your reading rate did not exceed 240 w.p.m., you are mentally pronouncing most, if not all, of the words you read. You can develop a silent reading rate that is four or five times faster than your oral reading rate. The know-how and practice provided in these ten labs will help you do so. You can start right now to develop a silent reading rate that cuts down considerably on your present habitual amount of vocalization.

Procedure

If possible, use the book you read for the sample lab. You will make better progress if you stick with the same book through all ten labs. If you read a different book each time you practice, you will waste time getting used to a new style, level of language, plot, characters, and train of thought. Every time you start a new book, you slow down. As you get into it, your speed picks up. So pick one book and plan to finish it.

Prepare to time yourself as you read. You will read for fifteen minutes during each reading lab. A kitchen timer will work best, but you may also use a watch or have a friend or instructor time you.

During this first fifteen minute reading lab your goal is to begin to push yourself above your present beginning reading level. If you are vocalizing most of the time, you will need a way to begin to cut down on vocalization and thus increase speed. Use a four-by-six index card (or any other small square object that will slide down the page, like a ruler, a folded piece of paper, or another paperback book). Open your book to the page where you last finished reading. Place the card just above the first line of print. As you read, move the card down the page so that it is constantly pushing you to read a little faster than you have ever read before. Practice doing this for a page or two before you begin to time yourself, so that you get used to the card. If you are doing it right, you will be uncomfortable. You will, in fact, make yourself read uncomfortably fast during each of the ten labs. As you do so, your "comfortable speed," the speed you drop back to for pleasure reading, will increase with each reading lab.

Sliding the card down the page as you read serves two functions: (1) It *pushes* you along so that you automatically begin to read faster. This is all that the most expensive "reading machines," which are designed to improve speed, are able to do. (2) It *covers up* what you have just read so that you are forced to concentrate and understand the first time. Thus you avoid compulsively *regressing* or going back to reread over and over again material that you should have comprehended and can teach yourself to comprehend the first time.

Read now and time yourself for fifteen minutes, using the card as described. Now make a lab sheet like the sample on page 232. Count the pages you read, compute your speed in w.p.m., and record it. Write the name of your book and the page you were on when you stopped reading. Then you will know where to start when it is time to do Lab 2.

Now close your book and, from memory, write a summary of what you have read. Go into as much detail as possible. Don't write for more than fifteen minutes. If you are working alone, read over what you have written and give yourself a score on your comprehension (as described on page 233). Then mark both your speed and comprehension on the graph on page 251. If you are working with a friend, or as a member of a class, mark only your speed on the graph and wait until your comprehension has been scored to record it. Either your instructor or another class member will read your summary and give you a comprehension score. When you are finished, put your lab sheet in a folder. You will need to check it before you do Lab 2 to see on which page you left off reading.

Reading Lab 2

Instruction

The instructional section of Reading Labs 2, 3, 4, and 5 will deal with some of the differences in the eye movements of fast readers and slow readers. When you understand how fast readers read as rapidly as they do, it will be easier for you to pick up speed also.

The first difference in the eye movements of a fast reader and a slow reader is the number of words taken in with each eye fixation. As your eyes move across a line of print, they actually make small, jerking motions from one point of focus, or eye fixation, to another. Only when the eyes stop and fixate do you actually see. When they are moving, you see only a blur. Movement of your head rapidly from ɪeʀt to right with eyes staring straight ahead produces only a blur. In the next paragraph each x indicates an eye fixation and demonstrates how their relative frequency either slows you down or speeds you up.

```
   x      x     x     x    x     x        x       x     x      x       x     x
(slow) (read) (ers) (fix) (ate) (many) (times) (as) (their) (eyes) (trav) (el)

    x       x     x       x     x     x    x     x     x       x      x     x
(across) (the) (page.) (They) (may) (fix) (ate) (on) (every) (word) (or) (they)

   x      x     x      x       x      x        x        x          x            x
(may) (fix) (ate) (twice) (on) (some) (words.) (The) (average be) (ginning col)

    x          x        x          x            x          x        x
(lege reader) (takes in) (slightly) (more than) (one word) (per eye) (fixation.)

       x              x           x            x            x
(On the other hand,) (the fastest) (college readers) (take in) (2½ to 3 words)
```

x   x   x   x
(per eye fixation.) (Fast readers' eyes, thus,) (stop to fixate) (fewer times as)

x   x   x   x   x
(they move across) (the page,) (and these readers) (are able to) (read a line)

x   x   x   x   x
(of print) (two or three) (times faster) (than the average) (college reader.)

Two and a half or three words, by the way, seems to be about the most that you can expect your peripheral vision to pick up in each eye fixation. There is no point in trying to stretch your eye fixations beyond that. Eye movement photography has demonstrated that it cannot be done.

Notice, however, that you can read the following passage, which is printed in a column with no more than two or three words per line, by fixing your eyes in the middle of the column and moving them straight down the page. Avoid the tendency, from long habit, to allow your eyes to move from left to right.

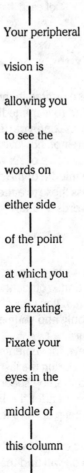

|
Your peripheral
|
vision is
|
allowing you
|
to see the
|
words on
|
either side
|
of the point
|
at which you
|
are fixating.
|
Fixate your
|
eyes in the
|
middle of
|
this column
|

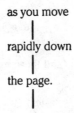

as you move

rapidly down

the page.

Now, try reading the following "clumps" of words by fixating once in the middle of each of them.

Notice	vision	side to
that·your	extends not	side but
peripheral	only from	also up
and down	able to	in the
so that	fixate	middle
you are	only once	of each
of these	and	
groups	still read	
of words	them.	

If books and magazines were printed in the columns or clumps like those you just read, your speed would improve immediately. You would be using your maximum peripheral vision and making your eye movements as efficient as possible. Books and magazines are not, however, printed this way. The average newspaper column, in fact, contains five or six words per line. If you try to read it by moving your eyes down the middle of the column, you will see the two or three words in the middle and miss those to either side. You have to fixate twice per line in order to see all the words in a newspaper article.

Procedure

As soon as your speed begins to go up, your eyes automatically begin to take in more words per eye fixation. You cannot feel this happening. Neither can you decide to make it happen. If you consciously try to take in two or three words per eye fixation, you will only find yourself concentrating on eye movements instead of on your reading.

So the way to make your eye movements more efficient is to use some means to speed up your reading. During the last lab period you used a four-by-six card to push from above and thereby speed you up. Use the card for this exercise, too, but this time place it under the line you are reading and pull it down the page. You will read to keep up with it. Again, make sure that you are reading uncomfortably fast.

During the first seven lab periods you will be experimenting with different ways to speed up your reading. You will find that you prefer one of them to the others. You will use the way that is best for you during the last three labs. At this point notice whether you prefer the card pushing from above or pulling from below as a device to speed you up.

Now proceed with Lab 2 exactly as you did with Lab 1: Start where you left off in your book and time your reading for fifteen minutes. Use the card as just described. Then make out a lab sheet as you did for Lab 1, calculate your speed and comprehension scores, and mark the graphs on page 251. Put lab sheet 2 in your folder.

Reading Lab 3

Instruction

In the last lab you learned that fast readers take in more words per eye fixation than do slow readers. Fast readers also spend less time on each eye fixation than do slow readers. Photography of people's eye movements while they are reading reveals that 92 – 94 percent of the time you spend reading you are pausing, or fixating, on various points along the line of print. The other 6 – 8 percent of your reading time is spent jumping from one eye fixation to the next or moving from the end of one line to the beginning of the next.

Eye movement photography also shows that with the fastest reactions possible, or with eyes working at top efficiency, it is physically possible to *see* 1,451 w.p.m. At this rate, however, you have no time to comprehend what you have read. If you want both to see and to comprehend all the words you are reading, 800 w.p.m. is about the top speed you can expect to achieve. When you go above 800 w.p.m., you are skimming rather than reading. You will find, as you practice to improve your speed, that 500 – 550 w.p.m. will seem very fast to you — indeed, it is a fast rate.

The results of eye movement photography are included here to suggest how fast you can expect to learn to read as you move through the ten labs. They are also meant to warn you against speed reading programs that claim to be able to teach you to read at 1,500 – 3,000 w.p.m. It is physically impossible to *read* this fast and comprehend all of the words. On the other hand, one can learn to skim this fast and get many of the ideas, especially if the subject is familiar and the material is easy. Skimming is a useful skill. But it should neither be substituted for nor confused with reading.

Your goal during these ten lab periods is, then, to improve your present reading speed to 500 – 800 w.p.m. During the final two labs you will be given a technique for skimming that may raise your rate above 800 w.p.m.

It has been suggested so far that as you achieve faster rates, your eyes will automatically begin to take in two or three words per eye fixation. They will also pause for shorter durations of time on each eye fixation. Rather than reading "a/red/apple" in three long, ponderous eye fixations, during which time you perceive each of the three words separately, you will read " a red apple" with one or two fast eye fixations and perceive the three words as one thought, or one object. As your speed increases, you will regularly begin to read phrases rather than words.

Again, there is no point in consciously trying to make your eye movements faster. It is well to understand how your eyes operate but not to think about them or try to control them while you read. Doing so will only interfere with comprehension. Rather, concentrate on understanding what you read and your eye movements will automatically become more efficient. You will become a better and faster reader only with practice, which is exactly what you are doing during each of these ten reading labs.

Procedure

Today try another means of mechanically speeding up your reading. Instead of a card, use your index finger to underline rapidly each line you read. The moving finger moves on, and you try to keep up with it. Some reading experts think that using your index finger in this way may be the best and fastest way to improve speed. Many students find it works very well.

If you don't want to use your finger, use a pencil. Don't let it touch the page, however, and make marks which would be distracting. Remember to keep either your finger or pencil moving uncomfortably fast across the page.

Proceed now with Lab 3. Time your reading for fifteen minutes, make out a lab sheet, and mark the graphs on page 251. File lab sheet 3 in your folder.

Reading Lab 4

Instruction

We have been identifying some of the differences between fast readers and slow readers. Besides taking in more words per eye fixation and spending less time on each eye fixation, fast readers also skip some words that they know from long habit are there, but that don't carry much meaning. In this way they eliminate some eye fixations altogether. Examples of words they might skip are *a, an, the, is, are,* some pronouns *(we, you, they),* some adjectives *(high, low, every),* some prepositions *(to, of, for).* People who read novels in one sitting may skip entire passages of description or exposition in order to get on with the story and find out what happens at the end.

Look at the following two passages. Read them both rapidly. In which of them do you find yourself easily and automatically skipping a few words and still getting the sense?

Passage 1

Thelma Green shook her plump face vigorously. "It's a dirty shame the way they treat people who are a trifle overweight," she said. "They don't consider our problems at all, and we've got lots."

Annette Holmes smiled and nodded encouragingly. Thelma Green certainly did have "lots" — about 280 pounds of "lots," and the woman couldn't be more than 5 feet 2 inches tall. But Annette liked the woman and, in her capacity as therapist at the Weight Control Clinic, wanted to help Thelma shed some of those pounds if she could. So Annette just nodded and smiled and waited to see what Thelma had in mind.

"Take, for instance, clothes." Thelma Green picked at the blouse she was wearing. "Who makes good-looking clothes for somebody as fat as me? Potato sacks is what they sell us, and we have to buy them because there's nothing else available."

Annette looked carefully at Thelma's clothes. They didn't look all that bad. The woman was neat in her appearance despite her size. But Annette continued to nod her head.

"And anyhow, what kind of wardrobe can you have when you shoot up or down 30 pounds every six months?" Thelma continued. "I've got a wardrobe full of clothes that are either too big for me, or too small for me. I'm like a yo-yo. I gain a little, so I don't fit most of the things I have. And then I go on a crash diet, and I lose 40 pounds, and I *still* don't fit my clothes because now they're too big for me."[1]

Passage 2

Three new functions are introduced here: the inverse sine, the inverse cosine, and the inverse tangent functions. As their names imply, they are closely related to the sine, cosine, and tangent functions. The definition and basic properties of these inverse trigonometric functions are special cases of a more general concept of inverse function. We shall consider this general situation in order to obtain an easy method of graphing the inverse trigonometric functions, as well as other inverse functions. Additional facts about inverse functions in the general situation are discussed in the DO IT YOURSELF! segment at the end of this section.[2]

The first passage is from a short story in the psychology textbook *Understanding Human Behavior*. The vocabulary is simple; the sentences are short; there is conversation; the subject is interesting. The second passage is from a math textbook. Notice that the material is densely written, that there are few words that can be skipped if you are to make any sense of it at all. Reread these two passages again, using your index finger to move through them as rapidly as possible. In the first passage it is possible to skip some of the words and still understand what is said.

You should not at this point consciously try to skip words. You might skip the wrong ones and your comprehension would suffer. Rather, use the procedures for improving speed described for each of the reading labs. As your speed improves, your eyes and mind will, by themselves, focus on and comprehend the words that carry most of the meaning in the passage. Your eyes will either not see at all or they will fixate very briefly on the less important words.

[1] James V. McConnell, *Understanding Human Behavior,* 3d ed. (New York: Holt, Rinehart and Winston, 1980), pp. 287–88.

[2] Thomas W. Hungerford, Richard Mercer, Sybil R. Barrier, *Precalculus Mathematics* (Philadelphia: Saunders College Publishing, 1980), p. 458.

Procedure

Today repeat the procedure for improving speed that you tried yesterday. Use your index finger to underline each line rapidly as you read. Only today move your finger faster than you did yesterday in quick, sweeping movements across the page. Proceed now with Lab 4. Make out a lab sheet, calculate speed and comprehension, and mark the graphs on page 251. Finally, file your lab sheet with the others.

Reading Lab 5

Instruction

In Lab 3 you learned that fast readers spend less time pausing on each eye fixation than do slow readers. Many times they are able to read a familiar phrase, particularly, in one quick fixation that lasts only a fraction of a second. In this small fraction of time the fast readers cannot see all of the letters in a phrase. They can, however, see the overall shape of the phrase and recognize it by its shape. Here are some familiar phrases that you have seen since you first started reading. One third to one half of the letters have been omitted from them. Yet you are so used to seeing them on the printed page that you can read these phrases by shape alone:

> Th_ Un_t_d St_t_s
> H_me Sw__t H_m_
> Moth__ a_d F_th__³

By contrast, here are some phrases that you do not frequently see. It is more difficult to omit letters from them and still recognize them by their shape:

> e__s__n h__ms l__ds_apes
> th_ pr_c__bri_n p__i_d
> eth__c id__t_ty
> i_t_rv_n_ng v_r_abl_s

The phrases in this second group are "erosion harms landscapes," "the precambrian period," "ethnic identity," and "intervening variables." These are phrases you might encounter in textbooks. They are not so familiar as those in the first group. A fast reader would read the first group of phrases rapidly with quick comprehension. Those in the second group, particularly if they were not familiar, would be read much more slowly. The mind needs time to comprehend or to realize it hasn't sufficient knowledge to comprehend.

It helps to improve your speed if you are able to recognize many familiar words and phrases by their shape alone. And there is only one way to become

---

³ The phrases are "United States," "Home Sweet Home," "Mother and Father."

skillful at doing so: The more you read, the more familiar frequently used words and phrases become to you. Lots of reading practice builds phrase familiarity and consequent increases in both speed and comprehension.

By the time you have finished this lab you will have completed half of the ten labs. Today you should add some additional practice reading outside of lab. Start today to read a book for fun. Read at least fifteen to thirty minutes per day. Do so from now on. It doesn't matter what it is. Anything you read will contain the commonly used words and phrases of the English language. The more you see them, the faster you will learn to recognize them. You will then continue to read them quickly when you find them interspersed with difficult concepts and words in your textbooks. Your textbook reading will still not be quick and easy. Daily reading practice will, however, make your most difficult textbook reading quick*er* and easi*er*.

Procedure

Place your open hand on the page and drag it down the page as you read. Read to keep up with your hand as it moves. Move it fast enough to force uncomfortably fast reading. Read and time yourself for fifteen minutes. Then make out lab sheet 5, mark the graphs on page 251, and file your lab sheet with the others.

Reading Lab 6

Instruction

By this time you know basically how some people are able to read faster than others. You have also probably figured out that there are some times when even the fastest reader has to slow down considerably in order to comprehend well

As you work through these reading labs, you are working mainly to improve your *flexibility* as a reader. Remember when you first tested your reading speed? Check to see how fast you read that first time by looking at the first column on your speed graph. If you read then at a speed of less than 240 w.p.m., and that was as fast as you could read, you were an inflexible reader. By this time you should be reading 100–300 w.p.m. faster than you did then.

The speed at which you read any material will always be influenced by four factors, the first of which is the *type of material* you are reading. If the material is written in relatively short sentences and paragraphs and contains familiar vocabulary and ideas, it will be easier to read than dense and difficult material that contains complex ideas and unfamiliar vocabulary. You will, for example, read *The Catcher in the Rye* by J. D. Salinger faster than you will read Aristotle's *Rhetoric*. A philosophy professor friend once remarked, "Please don't teach our students to read Plato fast."

Another factor that will influence your reading speed is your purpose or reason for reading a particular selection. You read much more slowly when you are reading to comprehend thoroughly and remember what you read. You read faster when you want quick information, when you are reading for pleasure, when you are reviewing something you have read before, or when you are panicked and have to know *something* before you take a test or participate in a discussion.

Your reading speed will also be influenced by the amount of interest you have for whatever you are reading. For example. you may be a freshman biology major right now with plans to go to medical school. You are not yet particularly interested in your biology textbooks, however. By the time you get to medical school you will have read a great deal of biology, and you will have generated a strong interest in it. Books that you read slowly and ponderously now will take much less time and generate much greater interest then. It is always easier to read any material rapidly if you already know something about it and if you are interested in it.

The last factor that influences your reading speed is the degree of general alertness and intensity of concentration that you can generate each time you read. Most students, knowing that they have to write summaries, become alert, concentrate, and read rapidly during reading labs. Whenever you find yourself slowing way down or even dozing off over material that you know you should read more rapidly, try writing brief summaries in the margins, at the bottom of the page, or at the end of the chapters. Such activity will almost always improve your concentration and, consequently, your speed.

Procedure

Try speeding up your reading during the lab period by placing your index finger in the middle of the page and moving it in a straight line down the middle of the page while you read. Keep your finger just within the range of your peripheral vision so that as your finger moves down the page your eyes will move faster to keep up with it. Move your finger fast enough to push your reading rate above a comfortable speed. Time your reading for fifteen minutes. Then make out lab sheet 6, mark the graphs on page 251, and file your lab sheet with the others.

Reading Lab 7

Instruction

In these ten lab periods you are not developing higher reading speeds in order to read everything fast. In the last lab you learned that you need high speeds for certain types of material and purposes, while you need lower speeds for others.

The purpose of the reading lab practice is to help you develop a *wider range* of reading speeds than you had when you started. Most people, before they have worked to improve their speed, have a range of 100 to 200 or 250 w.p.m. They can't read faster than that top speed. With practice, almost everyone who knows how to read to begin with can extend the top range, when necessary, to 500–800 w.p.m.

By now you have begun to widen your range of speeds. Notice that after you have practiced at high and uncomfortable speeds in the lab sessions, you can now drop back to lower comfortable speeds. However, these lower speeds are never quite so low as they were when you started. For example, if you started with a range of 100–250 w.p.m., and you are now able to reach 500 w.p.m. under lab conditions, you will probably find that you read easy materials comfortably at 350–400 w.p.m. and difficult materials easily at 125–150 w.p.m.

Developing a range of reading speeds is a useful skill for college students. Imagine a semester during which you enrolled in philosphy, physics, and the British novel. Your reading assignments for one week might include 15 pages of philosophy, 25 pages of physics, and the first 300 pages of a Victorian novel. If you tried to read all of this material at 100–150 w.p.m., you would never finish. With a well-developed range of speeds, however, you could read the novel at 350–500 w.p.m., or even faster, and you would still have time to read your philosophy and physics at the much slower speeds necessary to master them.

Procedure

Use your index finger to improve your speed just as you did in the last lab. Instead of moving it straight down the page, however, move it down the page in a zigzag motion. Don't watch your finger—concentrate on what you are reading. Try to keep your finger in your peripheral vision, however, and read to keep up with it.

Proceed now as usual with Lab 7. Make out a lab sheet, calculate speed and comprehension scores, mark the graphs on page 251, and file lab sheet 7 with the others.

Reading Lab 8

Instruction

You have marked your speed graph seven times now, and you should be able to look at it and see a pattern developing. The typical speed graph will have some downward dips in it, but if you were to draw a straight line connecting the tops of the highest bars on the graph, you would find that the general movement is upward. Figure A.3 shows an example of a typical graph at this point.

Almost no one improves at a consistently uniform rate of speed during each lab period. The occasional drops in speed are usually caused by lack of concentration.

There are a couple of things you can try today to improve your concentration. First, read the summary that you wrote on your last lab sheet 7. Concen-

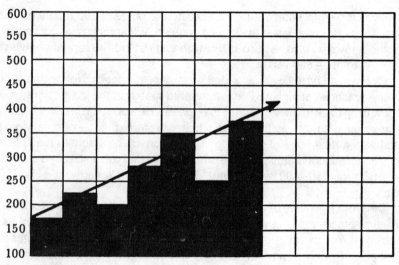

Figure A.3 A typical speed graph after seven labs

trate exclusively on the material in the summary. As you read, think ahead about what might happen in the material you are about to read today. For example, if you wrote in your summary that the heroine stole a gun and put it in her handbag, you should ask yourself when and how she will use it. Then read to find the answers. When your mind is focused exclusively on what you are reading, you are thinking ahead to anticipate what the author will say next, and finally, when you are reading too fast to allow your mind to entertain other thoughts, your concentration will improve.

Procedure

You have now tried six different ways to improve your reading speed: (1) you have pushed a four-by-six card down the page while you read below it; (2) you have pulled a four-by-six card down the page, underlining your reading; (3) you have underlined each line rapidly with your index finger as you read; (4) you have moved your open hand down the page; (5) you have pulled your index finger down the page in a straight line; finally, (6) you have moved your index finger down the page in a zigzag motion. One of these methods will have worked best for you.

Select the best of the above six methods and use it today to increase your speed. Get off to a flying start by reading and concentrating on the summary you wrote last time and by thinking ahead to what you might encounter in today's reading.

Read and time yourself, make out lab sheet 8, mark your graph on page 251, and file your lab sheet.

Reading Lab 9

Instruction

You have been reading the same book for eight lab periods, so you should be quite familiar with it by now. In this reading lab and in Lab 10 you will practice a *skimming* technique designed to move your speed up to 1,000 w.p.m. or more. At this speed you will not see every word. Your present familiarity with your book will, however, make it possible for you to grasp enough material to write a fairly complete and competent summary even after reading at such a rapid rate.

The skimming technique you will use today involves skipping through the

Buildings Without Furnaces

Outside   −40° .   inside   building
   70° . Why   unusual?   building has no heating system.
      new   complex,   gets all
heat from people, lights,   equipment. uses superinsulation   solar-heat
gain.   dramatic example
         not alone. Stung by   costs,   people
designing buildings   little or no conventional heat.
         structures use   solar energy: heating   rocks, water-
filled drums,   materials by   sun.
      materials store   warmth   radiate it indoors
         machinery   absent,   fans   used   blow   air   one
part   another. Some buildings   partly underground. Others
have solar collectors   wood stoves. All   insulation.
interiors,   don't look different
      Cape Cod,   homeowner $9.63 for heat dur-
ing   winter: cost   electricity   to run   fans.
   New Mexico house   heat storing adobe walls.
               homes tested
   show   residents   live comfortably   paying   10 percent
today's typical heating bills.
   Many   buildings air-condition   sunny side
   heat   shady side.   moves   heat from
   sunny to   shaded
Body heat   100 people   as much warmth each
hour   small furnace

Figure A.4 Skimming Exercise*

* By Stuart Diamond in *Omni*, 3 (October 1980): 41.

Buildings Without Furnaces

Outside it's −40°F. But inside a 20-story office building in Calgary, Canada, it's 70°F. Why is this so unusual? The building has no heating system.

The new Gulf Canada Square complex in downtown Calgary gets all its heat from people, lights, and equipment. It uses superinsulation and solar-heat gain. Though it may be the most dramatic example of new technology to save energy, it is not alone. Stung by ever-higher energy costs, many people are designing buildings that need little or no conventional heat.

All these structures use passive solar energy: the heating of rocks, water-filled drums, or other materials by the sun.

The materials store the sun's warmth and radiate it indoors as needed. Complex machinery is absent, but fans may be used to blow warm air from one part of the building to another. Some buildings are partly underground. Others have solar collectors and wood stoves. All have extraordinary insulation. The interiors, however, don't look different from conventional rooms.

On Cape Cod, Massachusetts, one homeowner spent $9.63 for heat during a recent winter: That was the cost of the electricity he used to run some fans. A New Mexico house is warmed by 10-inch thick, heat storing adobe walls. Rhode Island and Long Island homes tested by Brookhaven National Laboratory show that residents can live comfortably while paying only 10 percent of today's typical heating bills.

Many big commercial buildings air-condition the sunny side in the winter and heat the shady side. The complex in Calgary moves the natural heat from the sunny to the shaded side, eliminating both air conditioners and furnace. Body heat enters into the calculations: 100 people emit as much warmth each hour as a small furnace does.

Figure A.5 Skimming Exercise*

material, reading only the major nouns and verbs that carry most of the meaning. Your eyes will slide over articles, prepositions, adverbs, and adjectives. Your concentration will have to be exceptionally keen for you to get the gist of the material this way, since you will be reading only 50 percent or less of the words. Figure A.4 provides a simple example of an article from *Omni* magazine in which only enough words remain to allow you to get the point of the article. Almost exactly 50 percent of the article is omitted. Read through this piece quickly. Do not think about what is left out; rather, try to understand the article from what is there. Figure A.5 provides the entire text of this article so that you can see what you missed. Read rapidly through Figure A.4 twice. Then immediately turn to your book and use the identical technique there. Your speed should increase considerably.

Continue with additional speed practice outside of lab periods. Whenever you read any book, time yourself for fifteen minutes to see roughly how many

* By Stuart Diamond in *Omni*, 3 (October 1980): 41.

pages you read in that time. You may find that you read three pages of history in fifteen minutes. For the next fifteen-minute interval, count off three and a half or four pages and push yourself a little to see if you can complete it in that time span. Usually such mild pressure not only increases your speed somewhat but also improves your concentration. If your comprehension seems to suffer, however, drop back to a lower speed.

When you practice with easier books, such as novels or light nonfiction, count the pages you read in fifteen minutes. Then add a page or two during each fifteen-minute practice period thereafter until you are reading a page a minute. A page a minute is not an unreasonably high speed for novel reading. When you achieve this rate, you will be able to read a 240-page book in only four hours.

Procedure

When you have read Figure A.4 through twice, use the method you adopted as best for you and do your lab reading for today. Move twice as fast as you have so far. Then close the book and write what you can remember. If you remember almost nothing, you went too fast. You will probably be surprised to find that you remember a considerable amount.

Make out lab sheet 9 as usual, mark the graphs on page 251, and file your lab sheet.

Reading Lab 10

Instruction

In order to maintain the speeds you have now attained, you should plan to practice reading rapidly whenever it is appropriate to do so. Always use whatever mechanical device you have settled on as the best for you to help you maintain your speed. Move your finger down the page, use your finger to underline as you read, use a card, or use whatever other method has proved most effective for you. Employ this method to ensure a top speed whenever you read a news magazine or the newspaper. You will soon find that you can cover *Time* or *Newsweek* adequately in a couple of hours. Use your top speeds also to review chapters you have read before, to preview chapters you later intend to read more thoroughly, and to read novels. Get in the habit now of always having a book that you are currently reading by your bed or on your desk. It may be one you have seen in a bookstore or one that someone has recommended to you. As soon as you finish one book, start another. Reading at the rate of 30 pages in thirty minutes each day, you will finish a 300-page book in 10 days. It will take you twenty days if you have only fifteen minutes each day to read. Whether you read a book in ten days or twenty, if you do so regularly, you can read many books in one year. Whenever you finish a book that you would like to remember, write a page of notes on it. Put these notes in a file labeled, "Books Read." The briefest set of notes will trigger your memory a week or even years later so that you will remember much of what was in a particular book.

The more you read, the better you will become at reading. Remember that there is only one way to learn to read, whether fast or slow, and that is by reading. Furthermore, if you read regularly from now on, books that seem extremely difficult to understand today will seem comparatively easy two years from now.

Procedure

Begin today by looking back at the number of pages you read during the last lab. Then count off the same number of pages today and add three more. During the regular fifteen-minute period try to read as much as you read last time plus the three additional pages. Use the skimming method you used last time. Read only the words that carry most of the meaning. By the time you finish today's lab, you should have finished or have nearly finished the book you have been reading. If you're close, go ahead and finish it today.

Use your favorite method for speeding up your reading. Make out sheet 10 and mark your graphs on page 251. If you read longer than fifteen minutes to finish your book, be sure to divide the total words read by the correct number of minutes in order to calculate the correct number of w.p.m.

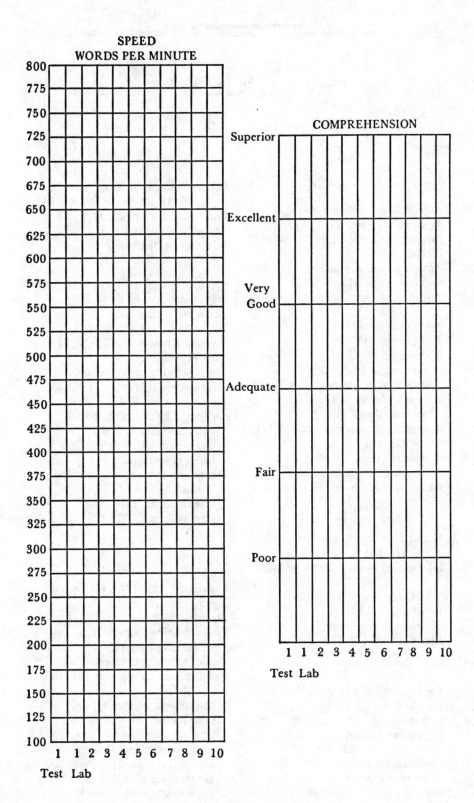

SPEED
WORDS PER MINUTE

COMPREHENSION

Index

Student Questionnaire

Usually only instructors are asked about the quality of a text; their opinion alone is considered as revisions are planned or as new books are developed. Now, we would like to ask you about *College Reading and Study Skills*, Third Edition. Your suggestions will definitely affect the next edition. Please return this questionnaire to the English Editor, College Department, Holt, Rinehart and Winston, 383 Madison Avenue, New York, NY 10017.

Name _____ Date _____

School _____ Course title _____

Instructor _____

1. Did you find this book too easy? _____ too difficult? _____

   about right? _____

2. Which chapters did you find most helpful? Why? _____

   _____

3. Which chapters did you find least helpful? Why? _____

   _____

	Helpful	Not Helpful
Getting Started		
Improving Your Concentration and Motivation	____	____
Organizing Your Study Materials, Study Place, and Time	____	____
Going to Class		
Analyzing and Adapting to Your Classes	____	____
Taking Lecture Notes	____	____
Learning Specialized and General Vocabulary	____	____
Participating in Class Discussion	____	____
Reading the Textbook		
Surveying Books and Chapters	____	____
Reading the Chapter	____	____
Taking Reading Notes	____	____
Thinking about and Remembering What You Have Read	____	____

Taking Exams

Preparing for an Exam   ____   ____

Taking an Exam   ____   ____

Writing the Paper

Writing a College Paper   ____   ____

Doing Library Research   ____   ____

Adapting the Paper for Oral Presentation   ____   ____

Summary

Evaluating Your Skills   ____   ____

4. Do you intend to keep this book for your personal library?

Yes ____   No ____

5. Any other comments or suggestions: